To: Father
    Metro Sereda

Christmas 1991

David Joan Leslie

The Ukrainian Religious Experience:
Tradition and the Canadian Cultural Context

The Ukrainian Religious Experience

Tradition and the Canadian Cultural Context

edited by David J. Goa

Canadian Institute of Ukrainian Studies
University of Alberta
Edmonton   1989

Copyright © 1989 Canadian Institute of Ukrainian Studies
University of Alberta
Edmonton, Alberta, Canada

Canadian Cataloguing in Publication Data
Main entry under title:
The Ukrainian religious experience

Based on a conference held March, 1986
at the University of Alberta.
Includes index.
ISBN 0-920862–63–2

1. Ukrainian Canadians - Religion - Congresses.*
2. Ukraïns'ka pravoslavna tserkva v Kanadi -
Congresses.   3. Catholic Church - Byzantine
rite, Ukrainian - Canada - Congresses.   I.
Goa, David J.   II. Canadian Institute of
Ukrainian Studies.
BX4711.74.U47 1989   281.9'71   C89-091162-2

**Publication of this volume is made possible in part by a grant from the
Michael and Daria Kowalsky Endowment Fund.**

Cover design: Steve Tate

Printed and bound in Canada
Distributed by University of Toronto Press
                 5201 Dufferin St.
                 Downsview, Ontario
                 Canada M3H 5T8

CONTENTS

Contributors

Bohdan R. Bociurkiw is Professor of Political Science, Carleton University, Ottawa. He has published "Institutional Religion and Nationality in the Soviet Union," in S. Enders Wimbush (ed.), *Soviet Nationalities in Strategic Perspective* (1985) and edited *Religion and Atheism in the USSR and Eastern Europe* (1975) and *Ukrainian Churches under Soviet Rule: Two Case Studies* (1984).

Dennis J. Dunn is Professor in the Department of History, Southwest Texas State University, San Marcos, Texas. He has published *The Catholic Church and the Soviet Government 1939–1949* (1977), *Detente and Papal-Communist Relations 1962–1978* (1979) and edited *Religion in Communist Society* (1983).

David J. Goa is Curator of Folk Life at the Provincial Museum of Alberta, Research Fellow of the Calgary Institute for the Humanities and a lecturer in Religious Studies, University of Alberta. He has published *Seasons of Celebration: Ritual in Eastern Christian Culture* (1986), edited *Tradition in Transition: The World Religions in the Context of Western Canada* (1982) and is currently working on a book titled *Ritual and Modernity: The Case of Eastern Christianity*.

Stephan Jarmus is Associate Professor of Theology at St. Andrew's College, Winnipeg and Chairman of the Presidium of the Ukrainian Orthodox Church of Canada. He has published *Religion, Culture and Christian Orthodoxy* (1981), *Issues, Methods and Perspectives in Pastoral Education* (1982), and *Spirituality of the Ukrainian People* (1983 in Ukrainian).

Serge Regis Keleher is Archpriest of the Eparchy of Toronto and Eastern Canada and a Fellow of the Chair of Ukrainian Studies, University of Toronto. He has published *The Paschal Vigil* (1970) and translated Cyril Korolevsky's definitive biography, *Metropolitan Andrew (Sheptytsky), 1865–1944* (forthcoming).

Andrii Krawchuk is currently completing his Ph.D. in the Department of Theology, University of Ottawa. His published articles include "Protesting against the Famine: The Statement of the Ukrainian Catholic Bishops in 1933" (1983) and "Metropolitan Andrei Sheptytsky and the Ethics of Christian Social Action" (forthcoming).

Casimir Kucharek is Archpriest of the Ukrainian Catholic Parish of St. Basil the Great in Regina, Saskatchewan. His publications include *The Byzantine-Slav Liturgy of St. John Chrysostom* (1971) and *The Sacramental Mysteries* (1976).

Evan Lowig is currently priest of Holy Resurrection Russian Orthodox Church (OCA), Vancouver. He has published occasional articles on church life in Subcarpathian Rus' communities and taught Church History, Patristics and Russian at St. Herman's Seminary, Kodiak, Alaska.

Vasyl Markus is Professor of Political Science, Loyola University of Chicago. His publications include *L'Incorporation de l'Ukraine subcarpathique à l'Ukraine soviétique* (1956) and *Religion and Nationalism in Soviet Ukraine after 1945* (1985).

Sophia Matiasz is currently completing a Ph.D. in the Department of Anthropology, University of Alberta. She is also doing a needs analysis of the non-English speaking elderly in the metropolitan area of Adelaide. She recently published an article on "Ukrainians and Welfare in Australia."

Vivian Olender is a fellow of the Chair of Ukrainian Studies, University of Toronto. Until 1986 she was a lecturer at the Centre for Ukrainian Studies, University of Manitoba. Her published articles include "The Canadian Methodist Church and the Gospel of Assimilation, 1900–1925" (1982) and "Save Them for the Nation: Methodist Rural Home Missions as Agencies of Assimilation" (1983).

Jaroslav Pelikan is Sterling Professor of History, Yale University. His publications include a five-volume work under the general title *The Christian Tradition* (1971–88), *The Vindication of Tradition* (1984), and *Bach Among the Theologians* (1986). His book on His Beatitude Iosyf Cardinal Slipy entitled *Between East and West* will be published in 1989.

Omeljan Pritsak is Mykhailo Hrushevsky Professor of Ukrainian History and Director of the Ukrainian Research Institute, Harvard University. He is author of *The Origin of Rus': Old Scandinavian Sources other than the Sagas* (1981).

Sophia Senyk is Professor of Church History at the Pontifical Oriental Institute, Rome. She has published "Rutskyj's Reform and Orthodox Monasticism: A Comparison" (1982) and *Women's Monasteries in Ukraine and Belorussia to the Period of Suppressions* (1983).

Oleh Wolowyna is Research Demographer at the Center for Development Policy, Research Triangle Institute, North Carolina. His published articles include "The Effects of Intermarriage on Bilingual Education among Ukrainians in Canada" (1985) and "Trends in Socio-Economic Status of Ukrainians in Canada, 1921–1971" (1979).

Roman Yereniuk is Assistant Professor at St. Andrew's College, Winnipeg. He has published a *Bibliography of the University of Manitoba Holdings in Eastern Christianity* (1983) and "Building the New Jerusalem on the Prairies: the Ukrainian Experience" (1983).

Paul Yuzyk was a Member of the Senate of Canada and Professor Emeritus at the University of Ottawa at the time of his death. His books include *The Ukrainian Greek Orthodox Church of Canada, 1918–1951* (1981) and *The Ukrainians in Manitoba: A Social History* (1977).

Radoslav Zuk is Professor in the School of Architecture at McGill University, Montreal. He has won numerous awards for his architectural work and his published articles include "Endurance, Disappearance and Adaptation: Ukrainian Material Culture in Canada" (1984) and "Ukrainian Church Architecture in Canada" (1968).

Preface

This volume is based on the proceedings of a conference on the Ukrainian religious experience in Canada held 13–16 March 1986 at the University of Alberta and the Provincial Museum of Alberta, in Edmonton. It was the result of a growing disquiet at how little attention scholars had given to the religious dimension of Ukrainian life in Canada. There are good studies of the Byzantine liturgical tradition and a growing stream of fine historical studies spanning the ancient patriarchates and modern conditions in Eastern Europe and the Near East. We even have solid scholarship on the Thomas Christians in Kerala, India. But despite the fact that Canada has more than 1 million people who claim the Eastern Christian tradition, of whom over 500,000 are Ukrainian, the only substantial consideration of any aspect of Ukrainian religious life is Paul Yuzyk's *The Ukrainian Greek Orthodox Church of Canada, 1918–1951* (Ottawa: The University of Ottawa Press, 1981).

As my own field research on liturgical life in Eastern Christian communities throughout Canada developed, I became concerned about this serious oversight on the part of scholars interested in all aspects of the religious life of Ukrainians and this uncharted chapter in the cultural life of Canada. In a number of discussions with colleagues in Religious Studies and Ukrainian Studies I began to distill the idea of a conference, and gradually the idea took shape. Roman Petryshyn, Executive Director of the Office of Multiculturalism and Native Programming, Grant MacEwan Community College, was especially encouraging and introduced me to Manoly Lupul, then director of the Canadian Institute of Ukrainian Studies, with whom I discussed the proposal. We enlisted the service of several colleagues during the planning stage. Bohdan R. Bociurkiw, Professor of Political Science, Carleton University, was particularly helpful. Dad Prithipaul, Professor of Religious Studies, University of Alberta, Roman Petryshyn and Manoly Lupul assisted in planning various aspects of the conference.

Our primary concern was to use the interdisciplinary group of scholars who had done some work in the area and to encourage them to turn their attention to the themes laid out for this book. The conference was an opportunity to discuss current work, to submit it to the scrutiny of colleagues and to prepare manuscripts for publication. From the beginning, the plan was to produce a coherent book on the religious experience of the Ukrainian community in the Canadian context.

The cooperation of all who participated in the conference, in their research and in discussions, has strengthened the publication. The critical work of a number of colleagues in commenting on the papers was invaluable: Harold G. Coward, Director, Calgary Institute for the Humanities; Ihor Kutsak, McGill University; John Berthrong, Interfaith Dialogue Secretary, United Church of Canada, Toronto; Oleh Krawchenko, St. Andrew's College, Winnipeg; Bohdan Krawchenko, Director, Canadian Institute of Ukrainian Studies; Charles W. Hobart, University of Alberta; and Roger Hutchinson, University of Toronto.

I would also like to acknowledge the financial assistance of the Multiculturalism Directorate of the Secretary of State, the University of Alberta, the University of Alberta Chaplaincy Association, and the Alberta Ukrainian Canadian Commemorative Society, which hosted several evenings during the conference. I acknowledge with thanks the editorial work of David Marples and Myroslav Yurkevich on this volume.

Such occasions often bring surprises. One of the most pleasant was that the participating scholars, who also happen to be members of the clergy in the Ukrainian Orthodox and Catholic churches, were able to sit around a common table and discuss many of the historical disputes that have festered between these two jurisdictions. They formed working collegial relationships and all had their appreciation of the historical dilemmas deepened. Through a conference which marked the millennium of the Christianization of Kievan Rus', a short stride was taken toward deepening our understanding of several serious concerns which have divided the Ukrainian people.

D.J.G.

Paul Yuzyk

A Personal Reflection

My interest in Ukrainian religious life in Canada originated in my family background. My father and mother, who came from Western Ukraine, then known as Galicia, before World War I, married in Winnipeg and settled as pioneers in Saskatchewan. The fierce struggles of the Ukrainian Catholic Church (then known as the Ruthenian Greek Catholic Church), its close ties with the Roman Catholic Church of Canada under French bishops, the proselytizing activities of the priests of the Russian Orthodox Church who came in large numbers from the United States as well as of the preachers of the Presbyterian Church of Canada, and the political activities of socialist radicals left my parents and other Ukrainian settlers bewildered and confused. Hence I was discouraged by them from choosing the priesthood as a career and encouraged instead to become a teacher. During the great depression I was engaged as a public school teacher in a Ukrainian-populated area near Hafford, Saskatchewan. Later, I received a promotion to high school principal in a two-room rural school in a neighbouring district. There the last hour of the school day was used to teach Ukrainian, which was not on the curriculum. In addition, in the local hall I promoted Ukrainian cultural activities in the wider community.

This was a rich experience, which made me realize that a church, of whatever denomination, was an important force in people's lives. However, I deplored the disruptive religious strife between Ukrainian Catholics and Orthodox, which often broke up families, caused violence throughout the settlements, and stood in the way of national unity at a time when communism was a powerful force in Ukrainian Canadian society.

When the Ukrainian National Federation (UNF) was founded in 1932 in Edmonton, with its prime aim the unity of the Ukrainian people, I decided to give it my full support. As first president of the Ukrainian National Youth

1

Federation, an affiliate of the UNF, I agreed to be the dominion organizer. In 1936-7, I took a year off from teaching and established twenty branches across Canada, with members of various religious persuasions.

As a veteran of World War II, I enrolled at the University of Saskatchewan. Professor George W. Simpson, Head of the Department of History and author of several articles and brochures on Ukraine and a historical atlas of Ukraine, persuaded me to leave science and to pursue an M.A. in history. Professor Simpson became my advisor and mentor. He argued that Canadians would never appreciate the manifold contributions of Ukrainian citizens to Canada until they had a knowledge of their historical background, their culture and their history in their adopted country. Since the Ukrainian people, he thought, could not be properly understood without knowledge of the role and influence of the church, I accepted his suggestion that I write my M.A. thesis on the topic, "A History of the Ukrainian Greek Catholic Church of Canada." I had only eight months to work and access to primary sources in the Archives of the Basilian Fathers was closed to me since I was a layman. Despite these difficulties I made progress and Professor Simpson was satisfied that it was a good beginning. With this encouragement, I agreed to pursue a doctorate on "The Ukrainian Greek Orthodox Church in Canada."

I was distracted from this, however, when I received a fellowship from the Manitoba Historical Society to write a study on the Ukrainians in Manitoba. In the fall of 1948 I moved to Winnipeg, the pulsating centre of Ukrainian life. My research was productive and I completed my manuscript in ten months. It was published in 1952 by the University of Toronto Press as *The Ukrainians in Manitoba: A Social History*. It dealt with all aspects of Ukrainian life, including religious events and developments.

When I began my doctoral work at the University of Minnesota in 1949 I was also heavily involved in the establishment of the new Department of Slavic Studies at the University of Manitoba. In 1951 I became an assistant professor there, teaching Ukrainian, Russian, Ukrainian literature, Slavic literature, Slavic history, and the history of Russia and the Soviet Union. I was also teaching Ukrainian history at the summer school of the Ukrainian Cultural and Educational Centre, as well as helping establish the Ukrainian Canadian University Students' Union and the Canadian Association of Slavists, a scholarly society.

In the meantime, I carried out intensive and extensive research in secondary and primary sources on the Ukrainian Greek Orthodox Church of Canada (UGOCC). Because of rules and custom, the Consistory of the UGOCC would not allow me access to its archival materials, but the president, Rev. Semen W. Sawchuk, the Secretary and editor of *Visnyk* (The Herald), Rev. Wasyl Kudryk, and Judge John R. Solomon were helpful in many ways. The most helpful and knowledgeable person, to whom I am most profoundly indebted, was Peter Svarich (Zvarych), a founder of the church. He gave me a large bound volume of primary documents, including all the official and private correspondence between Archbishop Theodorovich, Rev. Sawchuk, Rev. Kudryk, himself, and other consistory members, covering the period from 1924 to 1940. This was indeed a treasure chest. Additional valuable material I extracted from the many thousands of pages of Ukrainian weeklies. A grant from the Canadian Social Sciences Research Council enabled me to interview prominent church and lay leaders in Western Canada. I submitted the completed manuscript to the History Department of the University of Minnesota in 1958. I had no difficulty defending the thesis and thus I attained my Ph.D. degree.

With a busy life in the Senate, teaching at the University of Ottawa, and engaging in various political, cultural and community activities, I gave no thought to publishing the thesis, as it required revision. Professor Manoly Lupul not only encouraged me but agreed to make the necessary revisions. It was published by the University of Ottawa Press in 1981 under the title, *The Ukrainian Greek Orthodox Church of Canada, 1917-1951*.

My years in this field have made it clear that Ukrainian religious life in Canada is a wide-open and challenging field for students, historians and sociologists. Many events have transpired in the church and many important changes have taken place in the last thirty-five years. A new history, with new interpretations, should be written. The church with the larger following, the Ukrainian Catholic Church of Canada, still awaits its historians and scholars. Also, to my knowledge, no authentic scholarly studies have appeared on the Protestant churches among Ukrainians.

The need for scholarly study is strengthened because in more than 90 years of existence in Canada, Ukrainian society has been transformed from a preponderantly rural type before World War I to a preponderantly urban type. I endeavoured to explain the factors which have been instrumental in this transformation in "Religious Life" in *A Heritage in Transition: Essays in the History of Ukrainians in Canada*. These matters should be of paramount concern to church leaders as well as to lay leaders. The minds of leading scholars should be engaged in producing in-depth studies of the phenomena and problems facing Ukrainian Canadians. Their analysis and synthesis could provide guidance to the leaders of Ukrainian Canadian society and to Canadian leaders.

Some broad topics in the religious field that need work are the church's influence in Canadian and Ukrainian politics; the church's involvement in cultural and community affairs; the development and the work of the religious communities of the church; the Canadianization of Ukrainian churches; Ukrainian youth in church life; the declining power of the church in Ukrainian life; and the church as the backbone of Ukrainian culture.

Omeljan Pritsak

What Really Happened in 988?

I

The old Kievan chronicle presents the event of Volodimer's baptism as the turning point in the history of Rus' and devoted over thirty (printed) pages to a description of it. I will include only pertinent excerpts but I will try not to omit any essential element of the story.[1]

> Volodimer[2] began to reign alone in Kiev, and he set up idols on the hill outside the castle with the hall: one of Perun, made of wood with a head of silver and a mouth of gold, and others of Khors, Dazhboh, Striboh, Simargl, and Mokosh. The people sacrificed to them, calling them gods, and brought their sons and their daughters to sacrifice them to these devils. They desecrated the earth with their offerings, and the land of Rus' and this hill were defiled with blood. (p. 180)
>
> Now Volodimer was overcome by lust for women. His lawful wife was Rogned, whom he settled on the Lybed, where the village of Predslavyno now stands. By her he had four sons: Iziaslav, Mstyslav, Iaroslav, and Vsevolod, and two daughters. The Greek woman bore him Sviatopolk; by one Czech he had a son Vysheslav; by another, Sviatoslav and Mstyslav; and by a Bulgarian woman, Borys and Hlib. He had three hundred concubines at Vyshhorod, three hundred at Bilhorod, and two hundred at Berestovo in a village still called Berestove. He was insatiable in vice. He even seduced married women and violated young girls, for he was a libertine like Solomon. For it is said that Solomon had seven hundred wives and three hundred concubines. He was wise, yet in the end he came

5

to ruin, but Volodimer, though at first deluded, eventually found salvation.(p. 181)

This prelude is reported under the year 980. Six years later, in 986, an examination of all four monotheistic religions is supposed to have taken place in Kiev:

Volodimer was visited by [Volga] Bulgarians of Muslim faith, who said, "Though you are a wise and prudent prince, you have no religion. Adopt our faith, and revere Muḥammad." Volodimer inquired what was the nature of their religion. They replied that they believed in God, and that Muḥammad instructed them to practice circumcision, to eat no pork, to drink no wine, and, after death, promised them complete fulfillment of their carnal desires. "Muḥammad," they asserted, "will give each man seventy fair women. He may choose one fair one, and upon that woman will Muḥammad confer the charms of them all, and she shall be his wife. Muḥammad promises that one may then satisfy every desire, but whoever is poor in this world will be no different in the next." They also spoke other false things which out of modesty may not be written down. Volodimer listened to them, for he was fond of women and indulgence, regarding which he heard with pleasure. But circumcision and abstinence from pork and wine were disagreeable to him. "Drinking," said he, "is the joy of the Rus'. We cannot exist without that pleasure."
Then came the West Europeans (Nemtsi), asserting that they were come as emissaries of the Pope. They added, "Thus says the Pope: 'Your country is like our country, but your faith is not as ours. For our faith is the light. We worship God, who has made heaven and earth, the stars, the moon, and every creature, while your gods are only wood.'" Volodimer inquired what their teaching was. They replied, "Fasting according to one's strength. But whatever one eats or drinks is all to the glory of God, as our teacher Paul has said." Then Volodimer answered, "Depart hence; our fathers accepted no such principle."
The Jewish Khazars heard of these missions, and came themselves saying, "We have learned that [Volga] Bulgarians and Christians came hither to instruct you in their faiths. The Christians believe in him whom we crucified, but we believe in the one God of Abraham, Isaac, and Jacob." Then Volodimer inquired what their religion was. They replied that its tenets included circumcision, not eating pork or hare, and observing the Sabbath. The King then asked where their native land was, and they replied that it was in Jerusalem. When Volodimer inquired where that was, they made answer, "God was angry at our forefathers, and scattered us among the gentiles on account of our sins. Our land was then given to the Christians." The King then demanded, "How can you hope to teach others

6

while you yourselves are cast out and scattered abroad by the hand of God? If God loved you and your faith, you would not be thus dispersed in foreign lands. Do you expect us to accept that fate also?''

"Then the Greeks sent to Volodimer a philosopher" (pp. 183–4) who expressed brutal criticism of the three religions whose representatives attempted to convert Volodimer. Impressed by the philosopher's gift as a communicator, Volodimer asked him to present his version of the biblical story, which the philosopher gladly did, in a narrative which comprises half the conversion tale. This is known in scholarly literature as the "Discourse of the Philosopher" (rech filosofa):[3]

As the philosopher spoke thus, he exhibited to Volodimer a canvas on which was depicted the Judgment Day of the Lord, and showed him, on the right, the righteous going to their bliss in Paradise, and on the left, the sinners on their way to torment. Then Volodimer sighed and said, "Happy are they upon the right, but woe to those upon the left!" The scholar replied, "If you desire to take your place upon the right with the just, then accept baptism." Volodimer took this counsel to heart, saying, "I shall wait yet a little longer," for he wished to inquire about all the faiths.

In the year 987 Volodimer dispatched his emissaries to the Volga Bulgarians, the West Europeans, and the Byzantines, but not to the Jews, since they were living in Christian-held Jerusalem, to inquire about each religion's ritual and manner of worshipping. The envoys reported:

"When we journeyed among the [Volga] Bulgarians, we beheld how they worship in their temple, called a mosque (ropat), while they stand ungift. The Bulgarian bows, sits down, looks hither and thither like one possessed, and there is no happiness among them, but instead only sorrow and a dreadful stench. Their religion is not good. Then we went among the West Europeans, and saw them performing many ceremonies in their temples; but we beheld no glory there. Then we went on to Greece, and the Greeks led us to the edifices where they worship their God, and we knew not whether we were in heaven or on earth. For on earth there is no such splendor or such beauty, and we are at a loss how to describe it. We only know that God dwells there among men, and their service is fairer than the ceremonies of other nations. For we cannot forget that beauty. Every man, after tasting something sweet, is afterward unwilling to accept that which is bitter, and therefore we cannot dwell longer here." Then the vassals spoke and said, "If the Greek faith were evil, it would not have been adopted by your grandmother Olga, who was wiser than all other men." Volodimer then inquired whether they should all accept baptism, and they replied that

7

the decision rested with him. (p. 199)

However, instead of a description of the king's decision, the so-called "Korsun Legend" is presented.[4]

After a year had passed, in 6496 [988], Volodimer marched with an armed force against Korsun [Cherson], a Greek city, and the people of Korsun barricaded themselves therein. Volodimer halted at the farther side of the city beside the bay, a bowshot from the town, and the inhabitants resisted energetically while Volodimer besieged the town. Eventually, however, they became exhausted, and Volodimer warned them that if they did not surrender, he would remain on the spot for three years. When they failed to heed this threat, Volodimer marshalled his troops and ordered the construction of an earthwork in the direction of the city. While this work was under construction, the inhabitants dug a tunnel under the city-wall, stole the heaped-up earth, and carried it into the city, where they piled it up in the centre of the town. But the soldiers kept on building, and Volodimer persisted. Then a man of Korsun, Anastas by name, shot into the Rus' camp an arrow on which he had written. "There are springs behind you to the east, from which water flows in pipes. Dig down and cut them off." When Volodimer received this information, he raised his eyes to heaven and vowed that if this hope was realized, he would be baptized. He gave orders straightway to dig down above the pipes, and the water-supply was thus cut off. The inhabitants were accordingly overcome by thirst, and surrendered. (pp. 199–200)

Although Volodimer had now conquered Korsun, he was not yet ready to accept baptism. He decided to use the conquered city to bargain for something more important:

Volodimer and his retinue entered the city, and he sent messages to the Emperors Basil and Constantine, saying, "Behold, I have captured your glorious city. I have also heard that you have an unwedded sister. Unless you give her to me to wife, I shall deal with your won city as I have with Korsun." When the Emperors heard this message, they were troubled, and replied, "It is not meet for Christians to give in marriage to pagans. If you are baptized, you shall have her to wife, inherit the kingdom of God, and be our companion in the faith. Unless you do so, however, we cannot give you our sister in marriage." When Volodimer learned their response, he directed the envoys of the Emperors to report to the latter that he was willing to accept baptism, having already given some study to their religion, and that the Greek faith and ritual, as described by the emissaries sent to examine it, had pleased him well. When the Emperors heard this report,

8

they rejoiced, and persuaded their sister Anna to consent to the match. They then requested Volodimer to submit to baptism before they should send their sister to him, but Volodimer desired that the princess should herself bring priests to baptize him. The Emperors complied with his request, and sent forth their sister, accompanied by some dignitaries and priests. Anna, however, departed with reluctance. "It is as if I were setting out into captivity," she lamented; "better were it for me to die here." But her brothers protested, "Through your agency God turns the land of Rus' to repentance, and you will relieve Greece from the danger of grievous war. Do you not see how much evil the Rus' have already brought upon the Greeks? If you do not set out, they may bring on us the same misfortunes." It was thus that they overcame her hesitation only with great difficulty. The princess embarked upon a ship, and after tearfully embracing her kinsfolk she set forth across the sea and arrived at Korsun. (p. 200)

But Volodimer had to suffer a dangerous illness before he finally let himself be baptized:

By divine agency, Volodimer was suffering at that moment from a disease of the eyes, and could see nothing, being in great distress. The princess declared to him that if he desired to be relieved of this disease, he should be baptized with all speed, otherwise it could not be cured. When Volodimer heard her message, he said, "If this proves true, then of a surety is the God of the Christians great," and gave order that he should be baptized. The Bishop of Korsun, together with the princess's priests, after announcing the tidings, baptized Volodimer, and as the Bishop laid his hand upon him, he straightway received his sight. (pp. 200–1)

The "Korsun Legend," as presented here, did not find general acceptance in eleventh and twelfth-century Rus'. Therefore the chronicler found it necessary to make the following insert:

Volodimer was baptized in the Church of St. Basil, which stands at Korsun upon a square in the centre of the city, where the people of Korsun trade. The palace of Volodimer stands beside this church to this day, and the palace of the princess is behind the altar.

After his baptism, Volodimer took the princess in marriage. Those who do not know the truth say he was baptized in Kiev, while others assert this event took place in Vasyliv, while others still mention other places.

After Volodimer was baptized, the priests explained to him the tenets of the Christian faith, urging him to avoid the deceit of heretics by adhering to the creeds. (p. 201)

9

Now that Volodimer's personal baptism had finally taken place, he was supposed to be instructed on the basic elements of Orthodox doctrine.[5] This theological exposition takes up three printed pages. Thereupon follows a description of the final act—the general baptism of the Kievans:

> Hereupon Volodimer took the princess and Anastas and the priests of Korsun, together with the relics of St. Clement and of Phoebus his disciple, and selected also sacred vessels and images for the service...
>
> When the King arrived at his capital, he directed that the idols should be overthrown, and that some should be cut to pieces and others burned with fire. He thus ordered that Perun should be bound to a horse's tail and dragged along Borychiv to the river. He appointed twelve men to beat the idol with sticks, not because he thought the wood was sensitive, but to affront the demon who had deceived man in this guise, that he might receive chastisement at the hands of men. (p. 204)
>
> On the morrow, the King went forth to the Dnieper with the priests of the Queen and those from Korsun, and a countless multitude assembled. They all went into the water: some stood up to their necks, others to their breasts, the younger near the bank, some of them holding children in their arms, while the adults waded farther out. The priests stood by and offered prayers. (pp. 204–5)
>
> When the people were baptized, they returned each to his own abode. Volodimer, rejoicing that he and his subjects now knew God himself, looked up to heaven and said [his prayer]. . . . He began to found churches and to assign priests throughout the cities, and to invite the people to accept baptism in all the cities and towns.
>
> He took the children of the best families, and sent them to schools for instruction in book-learning. The mothers of these children wept bitterly over them, for they were not yet strong in faith, but mourned as for the dead. (p. 205)
>
> He had mercy upon us in the baptism of life and the renewal of the spirit, following the will of God and not according to our deeds. (p. 205)

II

I have presented these long excerpts from the tale for two reasons. First, the conversion tale has been regarded for several centuries, by both laymen and scholars, as the reliable, contemporaneous source for the study of Kiev's baptism. It has thereby become part and parcel of the Christian consciousness of the Ukrainian population.

When modern scholarship entered the field during the nineteenth century, it did not discard the conversion tale in its entirety; instead, scholars believed that it consisted of several levels, with differing grades of veracity. They took some elements in it to be historically accurate, since allegedly these went back to the original oral tradition, although they recognized that several subsidiary stories were added by subsequent editors. Among such stories, some scholars believed, was the entire Korsun episode, called by them "the Korsun legend," which appears to be a *deus ex machina*. Modern scholars often blame the conversion tale for not including such vital data as who was appointed the first metropolitan of Rus' and when, and what liturgical language and which script were introduced by Volodimer.[6] But all this is based on a great misunderstanding. One cannot expect a source to provide certain information which transcends its scope.

Like every conversion tale, the one about Volodimer's conversion is a hagiographic narrative, not a historical discourse. The distinctive feature of hagiography is that its products should have a religious character and should aim at edification. A hagiographic work may "assume any literary form suitable to the glorification of the saints, from an official record adapted to the use of the faithful, to a poetical composition of the most exuberant character wholly detached from reality."[7] One may add that during the Middle Ages history was not regarded as an independent social science, but as a branch of rhetoric.[8] The concept of historical truth, as we understand it today, had not yet been born.

The conversion tale in the Kievan chronicle should be read, not as a compilation of narratives, based on oral tradition, that were constantly being enlarged and re-edited, but as a singular literary hagiographic work. Only when one approaches the tale this way can one appreciate the dramatic talent and psychological depth of its author. That writer's main goal was to make his readers understand how it was possible for a pagan barbarian king, which Volodimer certainly was, to decide suddenly to embrace the Christian faith. Since paganism and Christianity were in complete opposition, the pagan king had to be portrayed as a great sinner, especially in his sex life. He was also depicted as slow-witted but sly and cunning and false to his word unless pressed to keep it. He could be impressed and won over to Christianity only by pomp and ostentatious display, rather than by substantive disputations. Naturally, the writer of the tale was obligated to develop two contrasting personalities: Volodimer the pagan *versus* Volodimer the Christian. Whereas Volodimer the pagan was a primitive idolator and an insatiable lecher, Volodimer the Christian became a pious and devoted religious activist.[9]

Volodimer the pagan had to be taught about the superiority of the Christian faith several times. It was necessary to introduce in the tale Volodimer's examination of various religions first at home as expounded by the respective missionaries (this *topos* was first introduced at the end of the ninth century by writers dealing with the conversion of the Khazars to Judaism) and second by emissaries from abroad.[10] In the end, only the miracle of healing the blinded

11

Volodimer could force the savage king to keep his promise. It is clear that such a primitive ruler could not have discovered and appreciated the values of Christianity by himself. He had to be indoctrinated and tutored by the Greeks of the Korsun colony.

The Old Kievan Chronicle, *Povest vremennykh let*, or "The Tale of the Bygone Years," was being compiled in Kiev between 1115 and 1123.[11] Naturally, it had to contain the tale of Volodimer's conversion, but in the first two decades of the twelfth century the conversion was no longer an academic question. The Patriarch Cerularius schism began in 1054, but until the end of the century it made very little progress in Kievan Rus'. With the arrival in Kiev of the intelligent and energetic Greek Metropolitan Nicephorus from Constantinople in 1103, the situation started to change dramatically.[12] Until his death in 1121, Nicephorus used every opportunity to disseminate Orthodoxy of the Byzantine style. He must also be credited with having promulgated the official tale about Volodimer's conversion to Orthodoxy. Since historical veracity plays no role in a hagiographic work, one cannot blame the tale's author for its anachronisms. There are two examples of this. First, in the "examination of religions" episode a Jewish scholar appears and tries to win Volodimer over to Judaism. When the Jew speaks of his land being given to the Christians, it is a reference to the conquest of Jerusalem by the Crusaders in 1099.[13] Second, among the anti-Latin attacks presented in the tale, there is special mention of the controversy over the *azymos* (unleavened bread) which first emerged in the second half of the eleventh century.[14]

Under such circumstances, is it possible to know what really happened in the 980s in Kiev? The answer is yes, but only if one regards matters from a larger perspective and within a larger context, namely, the problems of the Byzantine empire at that time and the rise to power of Rus'.

There are four groups of original, that is, contemporaneous or nearly contemporaneous sources, divided according to linguistic, philological provenance: the Byzantine, the Arabic, the Armenian and the Rus'. Of the Byzantine historians, one was a contemporary (Leo the Deacon, who died ca. 990);[15] two others (Michael Psellos[16] and John Skylitzes[17]) worked in the second half of the eleventh century but based their versions on earlier, probably reliable documents, which may have been contemporaneous with the events themselves.

Two Arabic authors also worked in the second half of the eleventh century. They were the continuators of the "World history" of aṭ-Ṭabarī (who died in 923); one, Yaḥyā of Antioch (who died ca. 1066),[18] was a Christian who also made use of Melkhit-Christian sources; the other, Abū Shujāᶜ ar-Rūdhrāwarī (who died in 1095),[19] was a Muslim who compiled a continuation of the works of his predecessors, covering the years 981–99. A third Arabic author, the historian and geographer al-Marwazī,[20] was writing about 1120, but he usually took his data from earlier, reliable sources.

The Armenian Step^{c}anos Tarōnec^{c}i (Stephen of Taron), called Asołik,[21] died in the eleventh century; he was the author of a "universal" history which gave special attention to invasions of the Caucasian lands by foreigners.

Finally, there are two Rus' sources of the eleventh century worth mentioning. The *Rusin* Ilarion was one of the first Rus' metropolitans. Around 1038–1050 he delivered in Kiev's Cathedral of St. Sophia a sermon on "The Law and Grace" (*Slovo o Zakone i Blagodati*).[22] This was a eulogy to Volodimer in which Ilarion mentioned some problems concerning Volodimer's baptism. Another eulogy of Volodimer was written by the monk Yakov Mnikh ("The Monk") in ca. 1070.[23] It was entitled *Pamiat i pokhvala kniaziu rus'skomo Volodimiru* ("Memory and Eulogy of the Rus' king Volodimer"). There the learned monk, having thoroughly investigated the existing Kiev oral tradition, computed and presented several dates in the lives of Olga and Volodimer.

The 980s were a very troublesome decade for the Byzantine empire. The young ruler Basil II faced internal and external dangers. Social and religious strife was manipulated by ambitious military leaders for their own ends. Two of them, the Domestic of the East, Bardas Sclerus, and the Domestic of the Schools, Bardas Phocas, claimed the imperial throne; by 987 they ruled over all of Anatolia. Basil II and his brother Constantine VIII, the sole representatives of the legitimate dynasty, retained control only over Constantinople. After the rout of Trajan's Gate (near present-day Sofia) the victorious Bulgars controlled all of Thrace. In this situation military support was essential.[24] In previous times the Byzantine emperors had incited one group of barbarians against another, but Basil's predecessor, John Tzemisces (d. 976), had had a very unpleasant experience with Volodimer's father, Sviatoslav. He had enticed the Rus' king to invade Bulgaria, but Sviatoslav, after his victory, refused to return to his own country. The emperor was obliged to bribe the Pechenegs to kill the villainous victor.[25] By 987 the Rus' king Volodimer was Basil II's only possible source of help. The Byzantine emperor's problem, however, was how to secure Volodimer's support without risking a repetition of the scenario with Sviatoslav. The solution was simple. Volodimer should embrace Christianity and receive Basil's sister Anna in marriage. Once he became a member of the imperial family, surely he would co-operate with the emperor for his own sake as well as Byzantium's.[26] Of course, Volodimer was a barbarian, but as the scion of a branch of the Khazar (West-Turkic) dynasty, he was an eligible potential brother-in-law; precedents for such a match were abundant, going back as far as the days of Emperor Heraclius (610–41).[27] Basil II also had no doubt that conversion to Christianity would not trouble Volodimer, who had previously embraced Islam.[28] So in May-

13

June 987, Basil II sent his embassy to Volodimer, which should have arrived in Kiev, after a thirty-five to forty-five-day journey, in either July or August of that year.[29]

What was Volodimer's position in 987? Both his grandfather and his father had been killed in the struggle to secure their realm's future. Igor, his grandfather, had abandoned the Volga, conquered Kiev on the Dnieper, and decided to keep the lucrative, newly established route from the Varangians to the Greeks, that is, the Dnieper route, under his control.[30] However, Igor's Derevlianian Slavic competitors had killed him. Sviatoslav (Volodimer's father) had eliminated the traditional Volga route, after having destroyed the Khazar ports of call, but he had become interested in the economic potential of the Danube-Bulgarians. He, too, had to pay for his ambitions with his life.[31] As ruler of Novgorod, Volodimer accepted Islam (in the 970s) because that move opened trading privileges for the Rus' with the Volga Bulgars, who some decades before (ca. 900) had adopted Islam for the same reasons: their main trading partners were the Central Asian Khwārizmians, Muslims by creed.[32] Volodimer, after he had exchanged Novgorod for Kiev as his capital, could no longer profit by his Muslim connections. The Dnieper route terminated in Constantinople, the centre of Christianity. Volodimer seriously had to consider a shift in his religious allegiance.[33]

The proposal made by Basil II came at a very opportune time; it also served to enhance Volodimer's prestige in his own country, in his new capital (Kiev), among his kin, his retainers, and the Kievans. One should not forget that Volodimer was an illegitimate son of his father. The deal was transacted without delay. The envoys of Basil II left Kiev in September 987 and arrived in Constantinople in October with the first contingent of Rus' troops.[34] Volodimer started the preparations for his baptism as a catechumen. He was certainly helped by one of his wives, the widow of Iaropolk, who was a Greek and had previously been a nun.[35] Since Basil II became godfather *in absentia* to Volodimer, and 1 January marked the feast of his patron saint (St. Basil the Great, Bishop at Caesarea in Cappadocia = Ukrainian Vasyl, d. 379), we can assume that Volodimer's personal baptism took place on 1 January 988, probably at his residence, now renamed Vasyliv, near Kiev. The next step was the official Christianization of Volodimer's retinue and the Kievans. This must have taken place on either 8 April or 27 May, the feasts of Easter and Pentecost, respectively, because these were feastdays with symbolism sufficient for the great occasion.[36]

In the meantime, an expeditionary force of ca. 6,000 men, in 120 to 150 ships (each holding forty to sixty warriors) was being gathered. Immediately after the baptism it set sail from Kiev, along the Dnieper and into the Black Sea, to Constantinople. The expedition probably arrived there in June of 988.[37] In Constantinople, the *porphyrogenita* Anna, equipped for her voyage, was prepared to leave for Kiev. She arrived at the Dnieper rapids, the meeting place between the Byzantine dignitaries and the Rus',[38] in late summer or in early autumn 988.[39] The marriage was celebrated upon her arrival in Kiev, and afterward Volodimer set out for Korsun. Two reasons[40] prompted Volodimer's action. First, Korsun, like Anatolia, had sided with the anti-Basil rebels, and therefore had to be conquered. Second, Volodimer needed priests and church bureaucrats for his new Christian state; they were abundant in Korsun. One of these churchmen, Anastas, played a leading role in the newly created Kiev diocese.[41] Volodimer's capture of Korsun took place not before his marriage to Anna, as the Kievan tale has it, for the sake of dramatic effect, but approximately one year after Anna had arrived in Kiev. A comet that shot through the skies during the capture of Korsun was also seen in Constantinople (by Leo Deacon), and in Cairo (by Yaḥyā of Antioch), in May 989.[42]

There are several important questions about the baptism of Volodimer that cannot be answered on the basis of existing sources. We do not know where and when the first metropolitan see was established or who the first occupants of that high office were. We can be sure that the see was not established immediately after the conversion.[43] First, clergymen had to be imported and the soil prepared. The first Kiev metropolitans surely had a status comparable to the western *episcopi curiae*, that is, they would have been attached to the court of the king or priest.[44] The original seals of eleventh-century metropolitans in Kiev bear the name of the land and people rather than that of the cathedral city: "the Metropolitan of Rus'," and, from the 1070s, the "Metropolitan of all of Rus'," rather than "Metropolitan of Kiev,"[45] which did not appear before the fourteenth century.[46]

Although the sources do not say so explicitly, the Christian clergy in Kiev, since they were imported from Constantinople and/or Korsun, undoubtedly used the Greek language. It was Iaroslav who, after his great victory over the Pechenegs in 1036, first imported to Rus' the Church Slavonic rite and its Slavonic sacred language, which at that time, after the annihilation of the Bulgarian state, was set adrift without an owner.[47] One important matter is certain: there was no "schism" in 988, so Volodimer's Christianity was not confessionally bound.[48]

In summary, the conversion of Kievan Rus' took place in 988, and was achieved through a close co-operation between the Byzantine emperor and the Rus' king. On 1 January, probably in Vasyliv, Volodimer's personal baptism took place. The Rus' elite and the Kievans in general received that rite in Kiev either on 8 April or on 27 May of the same year. The royal marriage of Volodimer and Anna was celebrated in the Cathedral of Our Lady in Kiev, most probably in the late summer of 988.

Why is the conversion of the Kievan Rus', the ancestors of modern Ukrainians, of special significance to universal history? There are two types of human culture, the nomadic and sedentary. Based on mythical thinking,

15

once the nomadic reaches its cyclical height, it is usually replaced by a competing culture and leaves no trace of itself.[49]

The Rus' of the ninth and tenth centuries lived the nomadic pattern under their ruler Sviatoslav. He conquered everything that could be conquered in his time, but when he was killed by the Pechenegs, he left his realm in disarray. Volodimer's baptism changed that pattern of growth, followed necessarily by decay and obliteration. When he swore allegiance to a higher civilization by adopting one of the universal religions based on God's revelation to man, Volodimer assured for his people an eternal place in human development and in universal history.

NOTES

1. The most readily accessible edition of the *Povest vremennykh let* (although not the best) is by Dmitrii S. Likhachev: *Povest vremennykh let*, 2 vols. (Moscow-Leningrad, 1950). See also note 11.

   I quote from Samuel H. Cross's English translation of that work (with small orthographic changes and/or corrections): "The Russian Primary Chronicle," *Harvard Studies and Notes on Philology and Literature*, vol. 12 (Cambridge, Mass., 1930). Quoted by permission of Harvard University Press.

2. This story is taken from the entry under the year A.M. 6488 = A.D. 981. At the end of each quotation, in parentheses, is the page number in S.H. Cross' translation. The form of the name of the Rus' king Volodimer is given as it appears in the contemporary Old Rus' sources.

3. See Aleksei A. Shakhmatov, "*Rech filosofa*" in "'Povest vremennykh let' i ee istochniki," *Trudy Otdela drevnerusskoi literatury* (Moscow-Leningrad, 1940), 4:122–49.

4. Korsun, or Cherson-on-the-Crimea, was an old Greek self-governing colony. Between the fifth and tenth centuries it was the leading manufacturing and trade centre of the entire Crimea and the northern shores of the Black Sea. On the "Korsun Legend," see A.A. Shakhmatov, "Korsunskaia legenda o kreshchenii Vladimira," *Sbornik statei... V. I. Lamanskomu*, pt. 2 (St. Petersburg, 1908), 1029–1153.

5. On these anti-Latin writings, see: A. Popov, *Istoriko-literaturnyi obzor drevnerusskikh polemicheskikh sochinenii protiv latinian* (Moscow, 1875); idem., *Kriticheskie opyty po istorii drevneishei greko-russkoi polemiki protiv latinian* (St. Petersburg, 1878); B. Is. Ramm, *Papstvo i Rus' v X-XV vekakh* (Moscow-Leningrad, 1959). See also Gerhard Podskalsky, *Christentum und theologische Literatur in der Kiever Rus' (988–1237)* (Munich, 1982), 170–84.

6. There is no modern biography of Volodimer the Great. The two existing monographs (after 1930) are not satisfactory, and their scholarship is dated. N. de Baumgarten, *Saint Vladimir et la conversion de la Russie* (Orientalia Christiana, no. 79, vol. 27) (Rome, 1932) and Irenei Nazarko, *Sviatyi Volodymyr Velykyi i Khrestytel' Rusy-Ukrainy* (= Analecta OSBM, sect. I, vol. 4) (Rome, 1954). See also A.P. Vlasto, *The Entry of the Slavs into Christendom* (Cambridge University Press, 1970),

255–81, and G. Podskalsky (see n. 5), 17–24.

7. Hippolyte Delehaye, S.J., *The Legends of the Saints* (Notre Dame: University of Notre Dame Press, 1961), 2.

8. On history and rhetoric, see Charles Sears Baldwin, *Medieval Rhetoric and Poetic (to 1400)* (New York: Macmillan, 1928), and James J. Murphy, *Rhetoric in the Middle Ages* (Berkeley: University of California Press, 1981). See also Herbert Grundmann, *Geschichtsschreibung im Mittelalter* (Göttingen, 1965).

9. On conversion literature, see *La conversione al cristianesimo nell'Europa dell'alto Medioevo* (= Settimane di Studio del Centro Italiano di Studi sull'alto Medioevo, vol. 14), ed. Giuseppe Ermini (Spoleto, 1967), and J.N. Hillgarth (ed.), *Christianity and Paganism, 350–750: The Conversion of Western Europe* (Philadelphia: University of Pennsylvania Press, 1986).

10. On this, see O. Pritsak, "Turkological remarks on Constantine's Khazarian Mission in the *Vita Constantini*," Christianity among the Slavs. An International Congress on the XIth centenary of the death of Saint Methodius, Rome. Pontificio Istituto Orientale, 10 Oct. 1984.

11. O. Pritsak, "The Povĕst' vremennyx lĕt and the Question of Truth," *History and Heroic Tale. A Symposium* (Odense Universitetsforlag, 1985), 133–72.

12. On Nicephorus, see Andrzej Poppe, "Nicefor, metropolita rus. (1104–21)," *Słownik Starożytności Słowiańskich*, vol. 3, pt. 2 (Wrocław, 1968), 369–70.

13. See D.V. Ainalov, "Nekotorye dannye russkikh letopisei o Palestine," *Soobshcheniia Imp. Pravoslavnogo Obshchestva*, vol. 17, no. 3 (1906): 333–52.

14. See M. Cheltsov, *Polemika mezhdu grekami i latinianami po voprosu ob opresnokakh v XI-XII vv.* (St. Petersburg, 1879).

15. Leo Diaconus, *Historiae libri decem*, ed. C.B. Hase (Bonn, 1828).

16. Michel Psellus, *Chronographie ou Histoire d'un siècle de Byzance (976–1077)*, ed. and trans. into French by E. Renauld, 2 vols (Paris, 1926–8). See English trans. by E.R.A. Sewter, *The Chronographia* (London, 1953).

17. *Ioannis Scylitzae Synopsis historiarum*, ed. Johannes Thurn (Berlin, 1973).

18. "Histoire de Yahya-iba Saïd d'Antioche, continuateur de Saïd-ibn-Bitriq," ed. and trans. into French by I. Kratchkovsky and A.A. Vasiliev, in *Patrologia Orientalis*, Paris, vol. 18, no. 5 (pt. 1, 1924) and vol. 23, no. 3 (pt. 2, 1932). See also Baron Viktor R. Rozen, *Imperator Vasilii Bolgaroboitsa. Izvlecheniia iz letopisi Iakhi Antiokhiiskogo* (St. Petersburg, 1883).

19. "Continuation of the Experience of the Nations by Abu Shuja' Rudhrawari, Vizier of Muqtadi," ed. and trans. H.F. Amedroz and D.S. Margoliouth in *The Eclipse of the Abbasid Caliphate* (Oxford, 1921), vol. 3 (Arab. text) and vol. 6 (English translation). See also Ahatanhel Krymsky and Tovfik Kezma, "Opovidannia arabskoho istoryka XI viku Abu-Shodzhi Rudraverskoho pro te iak okhrestylasia Rus'," *Iuvileinyi Zbirnyk na chest akad. D. I. Bahaliia*, pt. 1 (Kiev, 1927), 383–95.

20. *Sharaf al-Zamān Ṭahir Marvazī on China, the Turks and India*, ed. and trans. Vladimir Minorsky (London, 1942).

21. *Step^{c}annosi Tarōnets^{c}woy Asołkan patmut^{c}iwn tiezerakan*, ed. S. Malkhasents^c (St. Petersburg, 1885). See also French translation by E. Dulaurier and F. Macler, *Histoire universelle par Étienne Asołik de Tarôn*, 2 vols. (Paris, 1883, 1917).

22. *Des Metropoliten Ilarion Lobrede auf Vladimir den Heiligen und Glaubenbekenntnis*, ed. Ludolf Müller (Wiesbaden, 1962).

23. The text was published twice: Evgenii Golubinsky, *Istoria russkoi tserkvi*, vol. 1, pt. 1, 2nd ed. (Moscow, 1901), 238–45, and A.A. Zimin, "Pamiat i pokhvala Iakova Mnikha i zhitie kniazia Vladimira po drevneishemu spisku," *Kratkie soobshcheniia Instituta slavianovedeniia* (Moscow, 1963), 37: 62–72.

24. On the situation in Byzantium, see Andrzej Poppe, "The Political Background to the Baptism of Rus'," *Dumbarton Oaks Papers* (Washington, 1976), 9: 197–244. See also Abu Shujā^c (see n. 19), 116–17 (text) and 118–19 (trans.).
25. See Leo the Deacon (n. 15), 155–7.
26. This paper is based on vols. 4 and 5 (unpublished) of my *The Origin of Rus'*. Professor A. Poppe came, on several occasions, to approximately the same conclusions when he analyzed the policy of Basil II toward the Rus' and the Rus' Byzantine policy. See notes 24 and 40.
27. On this first Byzantine-Khazar (Turkic) matrimonial arrangement, see the Patriarch Nicephorus: "Breviarium," in *Nicephori archiepiscopi Constantinopolitani opuscula historica*, ed. Carl de Boor (Leipzig, 1880), 21–2.
28. According to the testimony of Marwazī's sources (see note 20), p. *23 (Arabic text) = p. 36 (English trans.).
29. On the pace of travelling during this period in Rus', see N.N. Voronin, "Sredstva i puti soobshchenia" in B.D. Grekov and M.I. Artamonov (eds.), *Istoriia kultury drevnei Rusi*, vol. 1 (Moscow-Leningrad, 1951), 286.
30. On Igor's conquest of Kiev, see O. Pritsak, in Norman Golb and O. Pritsak, *Khazarian Hebrew Documents of the Tenth Century* (Ithaca, N.Y.: Cornell University Press, 1982), 60–4. Cf. also O. Pritsak, "Where was Constantine's Inner Rus'?" *Harvard Ukrainian Studies* 7 (1984): 555–67.
31. See the evaluation of Sviatoslav's reign by Mykhailo Hrushevsky in his *Istoriia Ukrainy-Rusy*, vol. 1, 3rd ed. (Kiev, 1913), 458–77.
32. On the importance of Khwārizm, see, e.g., Sergei P. Tolstov, *Po sledam drevnekhorezmiiskoi tsivilizatsii* (Moscow-Leningrad, 1948).
33. See note 28.
34. See note 37.
35. *Povest vremennykh let*, ed. D.S. Likhachev (see n. 1), vol. 1, 56 (under the year 980).
36. See also A. Poppe (note 24), 241.
37. See Psellus, ed. Renauld (n. 16), 9 = Eng. trans. by Sewter, 17; Scylitzes, ed. (see n. 17), 336; Asołik, trans. Dulaurier and Macler (see n. 21), 161–5.
38. Iakov Mnikh, ed. Zimin (see n. 23), 72. For example, Iziaslav of Kiev, expecting his Georgian (*iz Obez*) bride, sent his son Mstislav to meet her at the Dnieper rapids in 1154: "Ipatevskaia letopis," ed. A.A. Shakhmatov, in *Polnoe sobranie russkikh letopisei*, vol. 2, 2nd ed. (St. Petersburg, 1908), col. 468.
39. Iakov Mnikh, ed. Zimin (n. 23), 72.
40. They were different from those given in the tale in the Rus' chronicle, but correctly interpreted by the Polish medievalist Andrzej Poppe. See A. Poppe (n. 24), 221–4, 238–9.
41. On Anastas, see Ludolf Müller, *Zum Problem des hierarchischen Status und der jurisdiktionellen Abhängigkeit der russischen Kirche vor 1039* (Cologne, 1959); A. Poppe, *Państwo i kościół na Rusi w XI wieku* (Warsaw, 1968), 46–8.
42. On the comet, see Leo the Deacon, ed. Hase (n. 15), p. 175; Yahyā, ed. Kratchkovsky-Vasiliev (see n. 18), pt. 2 (1932), 432–3.
43. On different hypotheses concerning the hierarchical status of the church in Rus' during the reign of Volodimer, see G. Podskalsky (n. 5), 24–36.
44. One such Episcopus curiae was the German Reinbern, active at the court of Volodimer's son Sviatopolk in 1013. On him, see Andrzej Wedzki, "Reinbern," *Słownik Starożytności Słowiańskich*, vol. 4, pt. 2 (1972), 486.
45. See the date of the "Notitiae episcopatuum" in A. Poppe, *Państwo i kościół na Rusi* (Warsaw, 1968), and Alexandre Soloviev, "Metropolitensiegel des Kiewer

Russland," in A.S., *Byzance et la formation de l'État russe* (London: Variorum Reprints, 1979), no. IXa and IXb.

46. See "Leo's Taxis" in Heinrich Gelzer's "Beiträge zur russichen Kirchengeschichte aus griechischen Quellen," *Zeitschrift für Kirchen-Geschichte* 13 (1892): 247–53.
47. Cf. O. Pritsak, *The Origin of Rus'*, vol. 1 (1981), 30–3.
48. Concerning the Peace of the church proclaimed in Constantinople in June 920 (which lasted until 1054), see Henri Gregoire in *The Byzantine Empire,* pt. 1 (The Cambridge Medieval History, vol. 4), ed. J.M. Hussey (Cambridge, 1966), 137–8. See also Hans-Georg Beck, *Kirche und Literatur im Byzantinischen Reich* (Munich, 1959), 32–5.
49. See O. Pritsak, *The Origin of Rus'*, 1:10–20.

Liturgical Tradition in the Canadian Cultural Context

David J. Goa

Cosmic Ritual
in the Canadian Context

This paper rests on a definition of cosmic Christianity as both a ritual system and a theological perspective of the Eastern Christian tradition. It will examine the symbolic life of the tradition, arguing for its essential cosmic structure, and comment on several changes to this structure which diminish its central form. To illustrate the critical themes I will focus on Vespers, which begins the cycle of services leading to the Divine Liturgy, and on church architecture as sacred space. The range of issues and themes requires a full length study which I have undertaken in a forthcoming book entitled *Ritual and Modernity*. Here we can only highlight several issues.

Cosmic Christianity: Ritual and Meaning

Christian theology and ritual resulted from the crises that shook the fledgling church in the second century. It was through the debate with the Gnostic "heresies" that the church Fathers gradually developed orthodox theology. Their response was grounded in the theology and ritual of Old Testament Judaism. The key insights of Hebrew thought simply could not countenance the Gnostic ideas of the pre-existence of the soul in the bosom of the Original One, the accidental character of Creation, or the soul's fall into matter. The theology, cosmogony and anthropology of the Old Testament understood God to have begun His work by creating matter. Creation was the result of God's energy. His work was completed in creating man, "corporeal, sexual and free, in the image and likeness of his Creator," as Mircea Eliade has put it.[1]

23

Man was created with the powerful potencies of a god. "History" is the temporal span during which man learns to practice his freedom and to sanctify himself—in short to serve his apprenticeship to his calling as god. For the end of creation is a sanctified humanity. This explains the importance of temporality and history and the decisive role of human freedom; for a man cannot be made a god despite himself.[2]

Saint Paul laid the groundwork for this idea of a "sanctified humanity" in his initial discussion of the meaning of the Christ. It is through identification with Christ that the destiny of creation is fulfilled. As he put it, "For anyone who is in Christ, there is a new creation" (2 Cor. 5:17). "What matters," for human salvation, "is to become an altogether new creation" (Gal. 6:15). It is through Christ's life and through identification with him that the faithful enter into the kingdom, into the fullness of human experience.

Where the Gnostic myths call for a return to a primordial purity or unity, the Christian revelation begins by declaring that all human beings, from Adam and Eve to the end of time, have fallen short of what was intended by the Creator. The garden of innocence is lost, the angel stands guard at the gate, and there is no return to a primordial innocence. Nostalgia for Eden is useless. The Gnostic and neo-Platonic doctrines of *return* were countered with a doctrine of creation. And this new creation is sanctified in its totality through the saving acts of the Christ.

Flowing from this early Christian formulation is a theology and ritual system which "glorifies the Creation, blesses life, accepts history, even when history becomes nothing but terror."[3] How is this developed in the symbolic and ritual structure of cosmic Christianity which buttresses the Ukrainian Catholic and Orthodox tradition? The doctrine of Christology and the ritual identification with the Christ is the centre of the faith.

There are two parallel and complementary tendencies that work to this end. The first is to assimilate and give new value to symbols and myths drawn from the scriptures, whether Oriental or pagan in origin. The second, chiefly illustrated by theological thought from the third century on, universalizes Christianity through the help of Greek philosophy, especially neo-Platonic metaphysics.[4]

Saint Paul speaks of baptism as a death to the "old man" (the profane form of being) and the resurrection of the "new being in Christ." This archaic symbolism was elaborated by the early Church Fathers. In both liturgical texts and theology, the baptized soul descends into the abyss for a duel with Leviathan the sea monster, an image modelled on Christ's descent into the River Jordan. Justin, the early Church Father, calls Christ the new Noah, rising from the waters to begin a new race. The baptismal nudity, common to many archaic aquatic rituals, depicts the abandoning of the "old garment" of corruption and sin with which Adam and Eve clothed human beings, and the adoption of a new form, an image of integrity and plentitude. In baptism the monster is slain and the kingdom inherited.[5]

Similarly, with the Cross of Christ, we see the powerful blending of archaic and biblical imagery. The Cross, made of the wood of the Tree of Good and Evil, is identified with the World Tree found throughout human culture. It is described as the tree which "rises from earth to heaven," an immortal plant "that stands at the centre of heaven and earth," a firm support of the universe. It is the Tree of Life planted on Calvary. In theological and liturgical texts, it is compared to a ladder, a pillar or a mountain, all expressing its place at the "centre of the world."[6] Through this cross the entire world is "saved." This is graphically depicted in the icon of the crucifixion common in Eastern Christian tradition. The folklore tradition throughout Eastern Europe tells how Jesus Christ was crucified at the centre of the world, where Adam had been created and buried. Christ's blood flows onto Adam's head directly under the cross. Baptized by Christ's blood, he is restored to life. This image speaks of the sanctification of human nature, not of the biography of Adam. In taking on the full range of human experience, Christ, the incarnation of God and the perfection of human nature, becomes the source of the sacramental life. In him the common human experience of passion, suffering and death is sanctified and the resurrected life is offered to all.

"In short," Eliade argues, "the Christian mythological imagination borrowed and developed motifs and scenarios that belong to cosmic religiosity, but that have already undergone a reinterpretation in the biblical context. . . . "[7]

The emergence of the Cosmic Christ in the theological world of the fourth century took shape through the identification of Jesus as the *Logos*. This highly developed idea in Greek philosophy was understood as "reason," "structure" or "purpose," and has been written about suggestively by Jaroslav Pelikan in his recent book, *Jesus Through the Centuries*:

> For by applying this title to Jesus, the Christian philosophers of the fourth and fifth centuries who were trying to give an account of who he was and what he had done were enabled to interpret him as the divine clue to the structure of reality (metaphysics) and, within metaphysics, to the riddle of being (ontology)—in a word, as the Cosmic Christ.[8]

Pelikan points out that the Church Fathers built on the Gospel of John, which paraphrased the words of Genesis, "In the beginning, God created the heavens and the earth," with, "In the beginning was the Word." The very speaking of God, which is one way to translate *Logos*, made the world possible, intelligible and meaningful. "Jesus Christ as Logos was the *Word of*

God revealing the way and will of God to the world. . . he was also the agent of divine revelation, specifically of revelation about the cosmos and its creation."[9]

We are not speaking here of a "personal" or "historical" faith. The Christian revelation has been understood by the West and particularly by Protestant culture as a set of beliefs and moral practices that provide a pathway for the salvation of the individual soul. In this scenario the historical, indeed, biographical aspects of the life of Jesus become matters of belief upon which the individual's salvation in the after-life is dependent. This is not at all the concern of the Eastern Christian church. Its perspective is of a

> "cosmic Christianity" since, on the one hand, the Christological mystery is projected upon the whole of nature and, on the other hand, the historical elements of Christianity are neglected; on the contrary, there is emphasis on the liturgical dimension of existence in the world. The conception of a cosmos redeemed by the death and resurrection of the Saviour and sanctified by the footsteps of God, of Jesus, of the Virgin, and of the Saints permitted the recovery, if only sporadically and symbolically, of a world teeming with the virtues and beauties that wars and their terrors had stripped from the world of history.[10]

How then does the cosmic structure of Eastern Christianity and thus of Ukrainian tradition, its concern for the sanctification of being within space and time, manifest itself in the ritual tradition?

It is with the early Church Father Origen (Origenes Adamantius) (C.185 to C.254) that the understanding of the essentially cosmic work of Christ takes a critical turn. He argued that God the Father and Creator of all is transcendent and incomprehensible. Christ as the manifestation of the Trinity in human form is the image of God. He shares in the mystery of the Divine and is the fullness of the human nature. "Through the Logos, God creates a multitude of pure spirits (*logikoi*) and favors them with life and knowledge. But with the exception of Jesus, all the pure spirits estranged themselves from God."[11] In this process, they become "souls" (*psychai*; cf. *De principes* 2.8.3), and are provided with corporate bodies and free choice. It is in this condition that they begin to work out their salvation through the pilgrimage which will end in a return to God. "The universal drama might be defined as the passage from innocence to experience, through the tests of the soul during its pilgrimage toward God."[12] This is quite a different return to the original perfection of Creation from that which the Gnostics propounded. Origen understood the *apokatastasis* (restoration of all things) as superior to the original state of perfection the Gnostic idealized, since through the encounter with history and the combat with evil, human beings acquired the "body of the resurrection," the body of Christ. It was in the world of historical experience that the devotee acquired the love of God and came to the sanctified life. This teaching had a rough ride in the church, and was condemned by the Fifth Ecumenical Council in 553, for some theologians took it to mean that all, including Satan, would finally be saved. It was, as many historians of theology have since argued, a preliminary synthesis taken up later by the Cappadocian Fathers, Basil the Great, Gregory Nazianzus and Gregory of Nyssa. The developed tradition of *apokatastasis*, in the words of Eliade, "integrates the work of Christ into a cosmic type of process."[13] It is through the Divine Liturgy that we see this process actualized on the popular level in the lives of the faithful down to the present day.

Liturgy as Rite of Creation

The word *leitourgia* (liturgy) refers to a public work, not a specific set of cultic practices separate from the life of the world. The liturgy of ancient Israel was the corporate work of a chosen few to prepare the world for the coming of the Messiah. The liturgy or public work of the church is to act in the world as the Christ, to bear testimony to Him and His kingdom and, more explicitly, to *be* that kingdom in the world. The liturgical life of the church is a journey, as ancient and modern theologians have noted, *into the dimension of the kingdom*. This does not add a *spiritual* aspect to human life. On the contrary. In the action of the liturgy, creation is fulfilled by "making present the one in whom all things are at their *end*, and all things are at their *beginning*."[14]

In the liturgy of the church the devotees act on behalf of creation. It is a cosmogonic ritual in every sense, begetting the "new creation," restoring the creation to its created purpose. The creation cannot be restored to the Creator except through human beings. In the anthropology of the tradition we are creatures whose essential nature is rooted in adoration. The phrase *homo adorans*, man the adorer, describes the human being's particular place within nature. Adoration is far more essential than our capacity to cultivate plants, use tools, or develop economic systems. It is in offering the creation to its author, an essentially priestly act, that men and women discover who they are. Adoration is the path by which human nature is restored. And, what is even more important, it is precisely in this act that the cosmos, all creation over time, is restored to itself. When we examine the liturgical cycle, it is this action, this drama of offering, that we examine. It is deeply rooted in the symbolic paradigms introduced at the beginning of this paper.

The liturgical cycle is itself a cosmic pattern. Within the daily cycle of services, the organization and meaning of the sanctification of time is laid out. The pattern is drawn from Christ's life on earth, his movement through suffering, death and resurrection. All the other services of the church are a variation on this central theme.

The day begins (the actions of sanctification begin) at sunset. What is patterned in nature is seen as the condition of the human soul. Christian experience begins with a recognition of meaninglessness, of darkness and death. The new day, the new creation, the sanctified life comes out of this recognition. From one sunset to the next, the Divine services flow. In each, the devotee identifies himself with the movement of the Christ through all aspects of life, from the creation to the presence of the redeemed life, the Kingdom of God.

The Vesper Liturgy

The tradition considers the evening Vesper liturgy to be the beginning of the day, as in the Genesis account of Creation. Liturgical time which is part of the cosmic structure of the tradition is not simply a commemoration or reminder of past sacred deeds. The creation of the world by the Word (*Logos*) was completed in the salvific acts of Christ's passion, death and resurrection.

Creation took place in six eons, called days in Scripture. On the seventh day the Creator rested. The Sabbath is also the time of the incarnation of Christ and lasts till his death. Christ's resurrection is the dawning of the eighth day, the new day of creation, in which death is conquered by the death of Christ. It is our day embedded and participating in the eternal. For this reason, the Vesper liturgy begins with the "Creation Psalm" (Psalm 103), in which God is glorified in the new creation.

Bless the Lord, oh my soul, O Lord my God, Thou art very great. . . .
O Lord, how manifold are Thy works! In wisdom hast Thou made them all. The earth is full of Thy creatures. (Psalm 104:24)

In the Vesper liturgy the sanctuary represents paradise. The priest stands before the Royal Doors singing: ". . . the sun knows its time for setting. Thou makest darkness and it is night. . . . " (Psalm 104). This is the first act of worship: the recognition of the Creator. The priest is humanity standing before the Creator in recognition of the wonder of life. But he stands outside the gates of paradise seeking reconciliation, seeking the full union with the Creator. With Psalm 141 the faithful offer up their finitude, their limitations: "Lord, I call upon Thee, hear me, O Lord. Let my prayer arise in Thy sight as incense. And let the lifting up of my hands be an evening sacrifice. Hear me, O Lord." (Psalm 141:1–2) The human condition is not ignored but offered up with hope for redemption. Here we have the cry of the heart of humanity for the perfect union that comes in the return to the Creator. The entrance of the priest through the Royal Doors proclaims that God has welcomed His creation, that the gates of paradise are open to us by Christ, and that the glorious "light of the world" pours forth from the Creator. The response in the Vesper liturgy is:

> O Gladsome Light of the holy glory of the Immortal Father, heavenly, holy, blessed Jesus Christ. Now we have come to the setting of the sun and behold the light of evening. We praise God, Father, Son and Holy Spirit. For it is right at all times to worship Thee with voices of praise. O Son of God and Giver of Life, therefore all the world glorifies Thee.

In Vespers the faithful recall the Creation as the outpouring of God's love. The fall from paradise is called to mind, as the dissonance both within creation and in human experience. The faithful repent and the second outpouring of the love of God, the sending of His son into the world and His restoring of the world to Himself, is invoked. Through the contemplation of creation and the recognition of sin, the pattern of the liturgical action leads to the presence of God's grace and the fullness of life. The faithful enter again the new day of creation, moving into perfect communion with God and the sacramental mystery that awaits them in the Divine Liturgy on Sunday morning. In the midst of the growing darkness, when the fragility and finitude of creation are so keenly felt, the church enacts the cosmogonic rite which speaks of the coming light of Christ.

Vespers in the Canadian Context

Vespers is intended for Saturday evening. The whole symbolic action, the thrust of the sacred language and imagery, is based on the movement of the earth into the darkness of night. When Vespers is downplayed, forgotten about, or simply placed as a kind of necessary preface just prior to the Divine Liturgy on Sunday, the point of its message and the presence it invokes is lost. When Vespers is ripped out of its proper place as darkness begins its ascent at the close of the day, the structure of the liturgical day, the eighth day of creation, the day transformed by the redemptive love of Christ, the eternal day, is broken.

In Canada it has become the norm for both Ukrainian Orthodox and Catholic churches to ignore the Vesper liturgy. Since it is called for by the canons of the church, some inject a short form of it just prior to the Divine Liturgy on Sunday morning. Usually this is done by the priest prior to the arrival of the faithful. This fulfills the legal requirement but renders the cosmic action of the liturgy abstract and perfunctory.

The eternal day the advent of which is typified in Vespers becomes an abstraction, an idea, important perhaps, but one that can be manipulated to fit the social schedule of the community. At worst this suggests the Eternal is a matter of convenience. At best it fails to restore, in an existential manner, the movement of the faithful into the eternal day.

What has been argued about the Vesper liturgy is true of the whole cycle of liturgies within Ukrainian Orthodox and Catholic life. Liturgy is primarily an existential form of meaning: its corporate activity is a *theophany* "showing," as the word implies, the sanctified structure of human experience. When the cosmic form and meaning of the liturgy are displaced by the individualistic and the subjective preoccupations of modernity, the liturgy is radically changed. Of course, the liturgy remains the work of the people; it is the nature of that work that has changed from the re-creative offering of the world to its Creator to acts of personal piety or a formalism uprooted from the rhythm of the day.

The Cosmic Structure of Sacred Space

Mircea Eliade has argued that, until recently, men and women have lived in traditional societies where their existence has been that of *homo religiosus*. They desire "to be, to participate in reality, to be saturated with power."[15] Eliade calls this condition the "nostalgia for paradise," the desire to transcend the human condition, what the Christian would call the state of man before the Fall.[16] This desire is expressed in our wish to exist in both space and time in a completely meaningful way.

The phenomenological study of sacred space suggests that there are several functions which it serves. It is a centre around which a created order takes its form, where human needs may be brought, every failure confessed, guidance sought and power invoked against threat and danger.[17] It is the heart of the real from which the world receives its vitality, its proper organization, and its meaning. Second, it is a meeting point for human and divine beings, "the mooring-post of heaven and earth."[18] Within sacred space is the presence of the divine order, heaven on earth, a microcosm of the sacred. Consequently, the orientation, the proportion and shapes of temples reflect the sacred realm. Finally, it is an immanent-transcendent presence in which the cult of the deity is actualized.

The temple is an *imago mundi*. It reflects the world in the cosmic symbolism of its very structure.[19] There are two methods for ritually transforming a place into a cosmos: (a)assimilating it to the cosmos by the projection of the four horizons from a centre point (in the case of a village) or by the symbolic installation of the *axis mundi* (in the case of a house); (b)repeating, through a ritual of construction, the paradigmatic acts of the gods by virtue of which the world came to birth.[20]

The introduction to this paper discussed the basic significance of the cosmic ritual pattern of Christianity, showing how the central hierophany, the incarnation, passion and resurrection of the Christ, restores the ontological centre of creation.

> To Christians, Golgotha was the center of the world; it was both the top-most point of the cosmic mountain and the spot where Adam was created and buried. The Saviour's blood was therefore sprinkled over Adam's skull buried at the very foot of the cross, and thus redeemed him.[21]

The desire to live at the very centre of this world of meaning is at work in the way Eastern Christian tradition gives architectural form to the cosmic centre.
The church or temple was conceived as the Heavenly Kingdom, paradise and the cosmos. This symbolism was built into the structures:

> The four parts of the interior of the church symbolize the four cardinal directions. The interior of the church is the universe. The altar is paradise, which lay in the East. The imperial door to the altar was also called the Door of Paradise. During Easter (*Pascha*) week, the great door to the altar remains open during the entire service; the meaning of this custom is clearly expressed in the Easter Canon: "Christ rose from the grave and opened the doors of Paradise unto us." The West, on the contrary, is the realm of the dead, who await the resurrection of the flesh and the Last Judgement. The middle of the building is the earth. According to the views of Kosmos Indikopleustes, the earth is rectangular and is bounded by four walls, which are surmounted by a dome. The four parts of the interior of the church symbolize the "four cardinal directions." As "copy of the cosmos," the Byzantine church incarnates and at the same time sanctifies the world.[22]

It is here that the human being participates fully in the reality of the world, is completely surrounded and filled with meaning, and is in communion with the Creator of the cosmos. The gathering of the people of God in the temple, their processions from place to place within it, their movement in tune with the liturgical action, are integrated with the architecture and iconography of the temple. They stand rather than sit; they are co-servers of the liturgy with the priest.

It is clear that following the time of Justinian the liturgy came increasingly to emphasize the Great Mystery: its cosmic shape was firmly established.[23] Equally, the space in which its actions unfolded in the presence of the deity was developed very early as an *imitation* of the cosmos. Indeed, when we examine accounts of the meaning of Byzantine church architecture we see that the church was understood as a type and model of the cosmos. This holds true from the sixth century to the present day.

With what ritual is sacred space, this *imago mundi*, created in Eastern Christian churches? Do we, in fact, have a ritual installation, as the theory suggests, of the four cardinal points, the *axis mundi*, a ritual of construction in which the acts of the Christ, by virtue of which the world has come to be, are manifest?

There are many consecration rituals used in Eastern Christian churches: the turning of the sod, the consecration of the cornerstone, the blessing of the completed structure, and the ritual building of the holy table (altar). All point to the church and the holy table within it as an *axis mundi*. Here the acts of the Cosmic Christ are at play. In the consecration of the holy table, for example, we see clearly the creation of sacred space in all its thoroughness and drama.

The Ritual Building of the Holy Table

The ritual construction of the holy table is presided over by the Bishop. In a cycle of blessings and anointings, he begins the construction of this microcosm, this axis of the sacred, this presence of the Divine. The columns are erected, one for each of the four cardinal directions of the cosmos. In the centre is an axis in which we find the relics of a saint, reminding the faithful that, in Christ, mortality is transfigured. Four nails are used to fix the holy table in place, commemorating "the nailing of Our Lord to the cross."[24] The table is purified with the red wine mingled with rose-water, and the words, "Thou shalt sprinkle me with hyssop, and I shall be clean: thou shalt wash me, and I shall be whiter than snow" are chanted.[25] It is then wiped with sponges, reminiscent of the sponge offered to the crucified Christ. The first covering is placed on the table and bound with a cord. We are told that this is the "winding sheet, wherein the body of Our Lord Jesus Christ was wrapped for burial."[26] A second cloth called the pall represents "the swaddling clothes in which the infant Christ was wrapped at his birth."[27]

The holy table, unlike the altar in the West, was the *presence* of the incarnation as well as the passion, death, and resurrection of Christ. In the West the altar was increasingly seen (until the Second Vatican Council) as a place of sacrifice and the tomb of Christ. The holy table is the tomb of Christ, the place of the "bloodless sacrifice." But it is also the place of the incarnation and "the dread throne of Thy kingdom," as the ritual text notes. The final covering of the holy table, called the *inditia*, of rich and brilliant material, "typified the glory of God's throne."[28] As the seat of God the holy table depicts His presence in the temple. It is the Holy of Holies.

All the liturgies of the church are about the kingdom of God, showing it forth and promising its presence in fullness. This is reflected in the architectural structure of the Eastern Christian Church. Liturgy and architecture are one.

Sacred Space in the Canadian Context

The shape of Ukrainian churches generally followed the norms of the tradition. There are several remarkable examples in Canada of churches, initially built to serve Protestant denominations, which have been acquired by Orthodox and Catholic communities and transformed with considerable success to reflect the meaning described above.[29] In the vast majority of churches, however, we find pews. This innovation is based on the practice of Roman Catholic and Protestant tradition. Pews relegate the laity to a stationary position in which they are encouraged to be passive observers of the priestly action instead of active with the clergy in the serving of the liturgy. The liturgical movement is a living icon. The drama of salvation is proclaimed and enacted in the processions and movements of the faithful. The unity between the microcosm of creation that the temple represents and the action of the liturgy is fundamentally impeded by introducing pews which dominate the nave. The liturgy can now only hint at the journey to the fullness of the kingdom of God. The dramatic movement of the liturgy, a movement of the people, clergy and laity alike, of the redeemed depicted in the icons, is stopped in its tracks.

A similar development occurred with the failure to understand the role of the iconostasis and the icons in shaping the sacred space. Many churches in the Eastern Rite Catholic tradition in Canada did not have an iconostasis built when the church was constructed. It was considered a "decoration," not a part of the essential structure of the worship environment. The liturgical space is an icon, a theophany of the presence of the kingdom of God. It is an invitation to move through a process of sanctification to the fullness of that kingdom. Numerous liturgical scholars have pointed out that the icon of the incarnation (the holy Theotokos and Child) just to the left of the Royal Gates as one faces the iconostasis, and the icon of the Glorified Christ to the right, show us the playground of human experience. All human experience takes place between the Incarnation and the Glorification of the Christ in us. This is not a doctrinal abstraction but a simple description of how the tradition understands the life of the faithful. They are called to live out the process of incarnating the love of God and perfecting it in this life. Through baptism they enter the church and live in the presence of the kingdom. In the liturgical life they are called to the fullness of God's love, to bless and sanctify all creation as typified in the icon of the Glorified Christ.

Without the iconostasis this central ritual movement, an iconographic depiction of the journey to perfection, cannot be clearly "shown" in the liturgical action.

The prominent influence in some parishes of Roman Catholic pieties and symbolic elements diminishes the Eastern Christian symbolic tradition further. The use of statues with their strong personal and sensuous presence con-

33

tradicts the transfigured character of the saints in icons. Stations of the Cross, Benediction and the many other pieties common to the Roman Catholic Church before the Second Vatican Council eat away at the coherent liturgical structure of the Ukrainian tradition.

Orthodox churches have also occasionally been decorated with examples of Protestant religious paintings. Here we see the sensuous qualities of Christ, his agony for example, as the central element. No icon would ever focus on this. The fact that a given painting was a picture of Christ seems to have been enough to include it in the church. At the heart of Protestant devotional art we do not find the theme of the transfigured creation, much less a developed aesthetic capable of speaking about it.

The Eastern Christian church is a temple, not a meeting house. The architectural style, the central place of the iconostasis and icons are all part of the construction of a sacred space in which the liturgy is served by the actions of the faithful.

Conclusion

The tendency in certain parishes of Ukrainian Catholic and Orthodox jurisdictions to "cut and paste" the liturgy has come about for various historical and sociological reasons. Some of them are explored in detail by other papers in this volume. Similarly, the construction of meeting houses, where a temple is prescribed by the tradition, diminishes what, from a symbolic point of view, is the richest tradition in Christendom. Eliade notes that the revalorization of the *parousia* (presence or arrival) initiated by Saint Paul opened up numerous religious paths. The conviction emerged that the spiritual life can move to perfection *in this world* and that history can be transfigured, that historical experience is capable of the perfection and bliss of the kingdom of God. This new interpretation of the sacred, inaugurated by the identification of the kingdom with the people of God living the life of divine love in the world, continues to our day. The kingdom of God does not begin after mortal life has ended. It is entered in the Eternal now.

The paradox is that in the modern world, indeed in many churches we see a multitude of "desacralizations: demythicizations of the Gospel and of tradition, banalization of the liturgy, simplification of the sacramental life, antimystical tendencies and the depreciation of symbolism to the exclusive emphasis on ethical values and the social function of the church."[30]

In Ukrainian religious tradition, Catholic and Orthodox, we see the kingdom of God, the cosmos filled with sacred meanings, present in as complete a way as human beings can imagine. The domes of Ukrainian churches bear witness to a sacred world of meaning. But the desacralization so common in contemporary Canadian culture will continue to challenge the living religious traditions of Ukrainians.

NOTES

1. Mircea Eliade, *A History of Religious Ideas: From Gautama Buddha to the Triumph of Christianity*, vol. 2, translated by Williard R. Trask (Chicago: University of Chicago Press, 1982), 396–7.
2. Ibid., 397.
3. Ibid.
4. See Andrew Louth, *The Origins of the Christian Mystical Tradition from Plato to Denys* (Oxford: Clarendon Press, 1981), for an excellent study of the use the Church Fathers made of Platonic and neo-Platonic thought.
5. Eliade, *A History of Religious Ideas*, vol. 2, 401.
6. These images are found in all the Eastern Christian liturgies. In texts for Holy Week and the Feast for the Elevation of the Cross they are particularly lush.
7. Eliade, *A History of Religious Ideas*, vol. 2, 404.
8. Jaroslav Pelikan, *Jesus Through the Centuries* (Yale: Yale University Press, 1985), 58.
9. Ibid., 59.
10. Eliade, *A History of Religious Ideas*, vol. 2, 405.
11. Mircea Eliade, *A History of Religious Ideas: From Muhammad to the Age of Reforms*, vol. 3, translated by Williard R. Trask (Chicago: University of Chicago Press, 1985), 44.
12. Ibid.
13. Ibid., 45.
14. Alexander Schmemann, *For the Life of the World* (Crestwood, New York: St. Vladimir's Seminary Press, 1973), 27.
15. Mircea Eliade, *The Sacred and Profane: The Nature of Religion* (New York: Harcourt, Brace and Company, 1959), 13.
16. Mircea Eliade, *Patterns in Comparative Religion* (Cleveland: The World Publishing Company, 1958), 383.
17. Eliade, *The Sacred and Profane*, 20.
18. Ibid., 26.
19. Ibid., 53.
20. Ibid., 52.
21. Mircea Eliade, *Patterns in Comparative Religion*, 375.
22. Eliade, *The Sacred and Profane*, 61–2.
23. This development has been brilliantly discussed in the recent book by Rowland J. Mainstone, *Hagia Sophia: Architecture, Structure and Liturgy of Justinian's Great Church* (London: Thames and Hudson, 1988).
24. Isabel F. Hapgood, comp. and trans., *Service Book of the Holy Orthodox Apostolic Church* (Englewood, New Jersey: Antiochian Orthodox Christian Archdiocese of New York and all North America, 1975), 614.
25. Ibid., 498.
26. Ibid., 614.
27. Ibid.
28. Ibid.
29. A notable example is St. Demetrius the Great Martyr Ukrainian Catholic Church, Toronto.
30. Eliade, *A History of Religious Ideas*, vol. 2, 361.

Radoslav Zuk

Sacred Space in Ukrainian Canadian Experience: Tradition and Contemporary Issues

The concept of space in architecture refers to the three-dimensional physical environment within buildings or between buildings. The type of space is defined by its predominant configuration; thus one can speak of horizontal space, vertical space, contained space, flowing space and so forth. Space may also be modified by less easily identifiable factors, that is, amount of light, specific proportions, surface texture and colour. All these attributes combine to imbue a space with a distinct character, which may evoke a specific mood, and make it "sacred" or "profane," Ukrainian or Greek.

To be fully comprehended a space must be experienced directly. Space defies easy simulation in media other than architecture itself. Unlike a painting, which can be reproduced in its true dimension or at a reduced scale by photographic means; unlike an orchestral work or an opera, which can be transferred onto and then replayed with "high fidelity" from a recording or a video tape; unlike the exterior configuration of a building, which can be conveyed by photographs or drawings, architectural space, to be understood, must be walked into, walked through, seen by turning in various directions, and perceived in its true size from a variety of vantage points. A moving picture (film) may partially simulate such experience; a scale model may show the relative sizes of spatial components; a series of photographs may convey the character and sense of details, but the total effect may still remain elusive. How much more difficult it is then to describe space in words. The temptation is to concentrate on easily recognizable features and to enumerate them: the dome, the iconostasis, the style of painting, the colours. Isolated spatial aspects can thus be conveyed, but the actual "experience" of space cannot be satisfactorily communicated. Therefore here, space will be referred to primarily by type, implying the generic nature of a particular spatial experience, rather than by a description of the experience itself.

The architectural means of representing space accurately consists of orthogonal projections in the form of plans, sections and elevations. The first two, in combination, define the exact three-dimensional configuration of space; the last also defines the surface articulation. These are abstractions which need to be reconstituted in the mind into a three-dimensional "spatial" image, which is walked through and seen from a myriad of vantage points in the imagination of the observer. Perspective drawings or photographs only help to simulate some of these many views.

The plan represents the horizontal layout of a building. It thus shows the basis of its spatial configuration, usually determined by functional requirements, types of construction, stylistic precepts, and artistic preferences of the designer. The section completes the representation of spatial configuration by showing its vertical projection. A great variety of possibilities of the vertical configuration can be achieved over a basic plan type. In the examination of the various spatial types of Ukrainian church architecture, initial reference will be made to the plan shape. Reference to the section will be made where applicable. In cases where plans or sections are not available, an assumption as to the spatial configuration will be made, on the basis of exterior photographs of the buildings. Only interior space will be considered. Exterior spaces, which are defined by the grouping of several related buildings or by the position of a building with respect to a street and adjoining properties, as well as exterior spaces generated above the main body of a building by several domes or towers (which may or may not result from the interior space configuration), constitute a related, but distinct, category of architectural space and would require a separate discussion.

An attempt will be made to deal with basic types and thus to isolate principal trends rather than to discuss all possible variants. Examples cited should thus be seen as typifying such trends and not as specific, unique works. The latter usually represent only the wide range of possible interpretations of a basic type. Since the emphasis will be placed on historical trends, the more recent unique cases of new design approaches, which do not fall within the categories identified, will not be considered.

The experience of single elements in a church, that is, the iconostasis, the altar, the tetrapod or the icons, can be relatively easily simulated by means of photographs or drawings. They are usually seen, and meant to be seen, from fixed vantage points in the pews (present in most Ukrainian churches in Canada). While constituting very important features, they normally do not contribute decisively to the configuration of space (except for larger iconostases which may substantially separate the sanctuary from the nave), but help only to articulate it in various ways. Similarly, the wall surface, its texture and colour, the style of continuous wall paintings or a recurrent window shape can be communicated as typical fragments, which the mind can assign to the entire space. They, too, only articulate space, even if substantially. Dark or light of a particular colour, they alter the mood of the space to a marked degree. However, they cannot alter the essence of spatial configuration, although spatial perspective effects painted onto flat surfaces can create a desired spatial illusion from certain vantage points.

Since these elements are easily identifiable, communicable, and classifiable (for example, the familiar composition colour, surface texture of an icon, the typical arrangement of the iconostasis and of its decorative components, the standard location and arrangement of the altar or of the tetrapod, and decorative features of wall paintings), they are frequently considered as sufficient to determine the Ukrainian or sacred identity of a space. The iconostasis, the Byzantine icon, specific Byzantine decorative elements, along with the exterior onion-shaped dome, have evolved into recognizable symbols, often used superficially and arbitrarily, without regard to the overall spatial configuration. Furthermore, usually little emphasis has been placed on the need for an authentic Ukrainian character to these items by commissioning bodies. Any Byzantine feature is accepted, be it Greek, Serbian or other, if the basis of its historical derivation is ancient Byzantine prototypes. It is generally not realized that thereby Ukrainian church art is neutralized and its natural evolution set back some nine hundred years. Referring to history, however, it can be seen that the iconostasis was not introduced until the late fourteenth century;[1] that the decorative schemes in the Renaissance and Baroque periods were typically not in the Byzantine style;[2] and that the great majority of seventeenth and eighteenth-century wooden churches of eastern Ukraine had no wall paintings.[3]

Therefore, in discussing the peculiarities of space in Ukrainian church architecture in Canada it will be instructive to consider them in the context of the historical tradition. This thousand-year-old tradition exhibits a number of distinct spatial types.

The characteristic spatial configuration represented by the Byzantine "cross in square" plan is typical of the late tenth century and extends to the first half of the thirteenth century. Derived from prototypes in Constantinople, it contains the main space in the shape of an equal-arm Greek cross inscribed into a square, with three apses to the east and a narthex to the west. The combination of the three apses and the narthex as integral parts of the main space gives these buildings a somewhat longitudinal direction from west to east resulting, in the lower parts, in a longitudinal central nave and two side aisles, each terminated by an apse.[4] The Church of the Assumption of the Blessed Virgin Mary in Volodymyr Volynsky of the twelfth century and the Church of the Transfiguration of the Saviour in Chernihiv of the eleventh century may serve as typical examples. The Cathedral of St. Sophia in Kiev must be considered as a special and unique case, since it is an extended variant of the basic type, which originally had a central nave and four side aisles.

In Western Ukraine the spatial configuration is quite different in churches which are based essentially on rectangular plans and date from the end of the sixteenth century. It is best exemplified by the Chapel of Three Saints and the Church of the Assumption of the Blessed Virgin Mary in Lviv. The plan of the chapel is a simple rectangle, a typical Renaissance plan shape.[5] The plan of the larger adjoining church consists of a rectangle with slightly accentuated side aisles, a distinct narthex and an apse which abuts almost the entire width of the rectangular nave. The Church of St. Elijah in Subotiv, the so-called Bohdanova Tserkva (Khmelnytsky's church), from the middle of the seventeenth century, has a similar plan disposition. Another typical plan shape is that based on a modified Latin cross, consisting of a central nave, side aisles, strongly articulated transepts, and terminating in one or three apses. While clearly based on West-European prototypes, it can also be considered as an extension of the earlier Byzantine "cross in square" plans.[6] The churches which best exemplify this type are the main church of the Monastery of the Holy Trinity in Chernihiv and the St. Nicholas Church in Kiev, both dating from the second half of the seventeenth century.

The pure Greek-cross type plan which forms the basis of perhaps the most characteristic spatial configuration in Ukrainian architecture of the Baroque era is quite different. As the name implies, it consists of a central area with four equal arms to the east, south, west and north respectively. A shape used in several early (non-Ukrainian) Byzantine buildings, it came into great prominence in the fifteenth century as one of the "ideal" church plans of the Italian Renaissance.[7] In some instances the western arm, which represents the entrance, is modified. The Church of the Protection of the Virgin Mary in Sutkivtsi, of the second half of the fifteenth century, is an early example of this type. The Church of All Saints in the Monastery of the Caves in Kiev, dating from the end of the seventeenth century, or the Church of the Transfiguration in Sorochyntsi, of the first half of the eighteenth century, are classic examples. The Cathedral of St. George in Lviv, of the middle of the eighteenth century with its strongly extended eastern and western arms, can be considered a modification of this type.

Special mention must be made of the tripartite plan where the central space is flanked on the eastern and western sides by equal arms. An outstanding masonry example of this type is the Church of the Protection of the Virgin Mary in Kharkiv, of the second half of the seventeenth century. In vernacular wooden architecture, this type is recognized as the classic plan of Ukrainian folk architecture. It is most frequently found in the Boiko region of the Carpathian Mountains, but exists also in Podillia and in eastern Ukraine. Another vernacular type is the Greek-cross plan peculiar to the Hutsul region in the Carpathians and also to eastern Ukraine where the two lateral arms (the southern and northern arms) appear as an addition to the classic tripartite version. A third characteristic plan type is that of the Lemko wooden churches, also in the Carpathians, of a tripartite division in which each part is distinct. It is strongly related to the tripartite Boiko plan. The vertical spatial definition is, however, substantially different.

This brings us to the important consideration of the vertical, third dimension of space. The vertical projection, together with the horizontal plan shape, determine the actual configuration of architectural space. Thus, examining the sections of various churches, we discover that the space configuration can be quite different over the same basic plan. The typical Byzantine plan can have only one dome, as in the original St. Michael's Church in Kiev, or five domes as in the Church of the Transfiguration in Chernihiv. The rectangular plans of the Church of the Assumption and the Chapel of Three Saints in Lviv are topped by three domes each, while the church of St. Elijah in Subotiv has a cross-vaulted ceiling, without a dome. The modified Latin-cross plans typically have one central dome, sometimes two side domes, and usually two front domes on towers which, however, do not form part of the configuration of the interior space. The typical Greek-cross plan buildings are distinguished by the fact that both the central space and each of the side arms are surmounted by a dome, thus creating a sense of unity and consistency between the plan and its vertical projection. The exceptions here are several mid-eighteenth century churches, for example, St. George's Cathedral in Lviv or St. Andrew's Church in Kiev, each of which has only one central dome contributing to the configuration of the interior space.

In the classic Hutsul wooden churches there is also only one central dome, with the four arms ridged. The Greek-cross wooden churches in eastern Ukraine, however, have on the whole the same spatial scheme as their masonry counterparts. Their space configuration consists of five high, soaring space chambers reaching to the uppermost peaks. In a similar way, their prototype, the classic tripartite Boiko church, has a towering space over each of its three plan divisions (or only over the nave and the sanctuary).

The difference between this type and the Lemko church type, both based on a similar plan distribution, lies in the vertical projection. In the Lemko churches the western part is normally surmounted by a tall tower which is not open to the interior, except for the narthex at its base. The lower nave, concentric in some examples, is vault-shaped in others, the latter version giving the nave a longitudinal, quasi-basilican direction toward the still lower sanctuary.

This great variety of spatial types in Ukrainian church architecture should come as no great surprise. Cyril Mango stated in his recent comprehensive overview of Byzantine architecture that, "While the Byzantine Church developed a theology of painting, it never developed a theology of architecture. . . . it never prescribed a particular architectural form. It was two centuries after the fall of Constantinople that the zealous patriarch Nikon of Moscow decided that one form of church rather than another was demanded by Orthodox worship."[8]

In the older Ukrainian churches in Canada one can discern three basic space configurations. The first is the tripartite type. In plan it follows roughly the Boiko church division, expressing clearly the rectangular narthex, the nave and the semi-octagonal or square sanctuary. In the vertical projection one can trace the often vaulted nave and the low sanctuary to the Lemko precedent. However, the narthex, instead of being under a single tall tower, appears usually as a small, simple gabled structure. In some instances the nave is treated as a square, concentric space. These are usually early, small rural buildings where the size of the nave, approaching a square, was large enough to accommodate a small congregation. The Ukrainian Catholic Church of the Exaltation of the Holy Cross near Innisfree in Alberta (fig.1) may be considered as a characteristic example of this type. The second prevailing type is based on the basilican plan, where the nave is longitudinal in shape, the narthex is often absorbed into the main body of the church, and a single apse is revealed as an extension of the nave (expressed on the exterior or integrated into the main body of the church). In the vertical projection the nave appears as a continuous vault leading from the entrance to the sanctuary. The interior view of the St. Josaphat's Ukrainian Catholic Cathedral in Toronto (fig.2) partially illustrates this configuration.

There are hardly any precedents for this type among the classic historical types discussed previously, with the exception, perhaps, of the St. Elijah Church in Subotiv, where the nave does not have a domed vertical interruption. This type must be seen as an economical response to the need to accommodate a large congregation in a simply constructed shape. There are numerous examples, ranging from relatively small buildings, such as the Sacred Heart Ukrainian Catholic Church in Krydor, Saskatchewan (fig.3) to the large St. Volodymyr and Olga Ukrainian Catholic Cathedral in Winnipeg (fig.4). It may be considered as a unique, Canadian type. The third prevailing type is based on the Latin-cross plan, with an octagonal drum and dome or only a domed ceiling above the crossing, in most cases. St. George's Ukrainian Catholic Church in Prince Albert, Saskatchewan (fig.5) exemplifies the drum and dome configuration, while St. Mary the Protectress Ukrainian Orthodox Church in Winnipeg (fig.6) shows the popular domed ceiling variant. Exact precedents for this type among the classic Ukrainian churches are few. One could consider the Greek-cross Hutsul type, with an extended western arm, as a possible prototype, or perhaps the modified Latin-cross churches of the seventeenth century (but without the pronounced side aisles and occasional side galleries, which produce a rather different space configuration).

The most likely prototypes are the numerous masonry churches built in Western Ukraine in the second half of the nineteenth and at the beginning of the twentieth centuries under the influence of West-European prototypes; for example, St. George's Church in Mychkivtsi and the St. Simon and Anna Church in Naklo.[9] Because of the large volume resulting from such configurations, this type becomes costly when the seating capacity required is large, and this may be the reason why large churches of this type are rare. A number of buildings based on this plan are of considerable architectural interest, especially those designed by Reverend Philip Ruh, such as St. Josaphat's Ukrainian Catholic Cathedral in Edmonton, St. George's Ukrainian Catholic Cathedral in Saskatoon or the Ukrainian Catholic Church of St. Cyril and Methodius in St. Catharines, Ontario (fig.7). Among the many smaller churches St. John the Baptist Ukrainian Catholic Church in Smuts, Saskatchewan, may serve as a typical example (fig.8). While many churches of this type possess more than one dome on the exterior, spatially they belong to this configuration category, as the domes, other than the central one, do not normally participate in the definition of the interior space.

In spite of the many variations of, and some exceptions to, those three types the prevailing number of examples permit the above categorization. In Anna Maria Baran's extensive listing of Ukrainian Catholic churches in Saskatchewan, which covers the period from the beginning of this century to the mid-seventies, of the one hundred and eighty churches illustrated, twenty-two can be considered of the tripartite type, seventy-nine of the basilica type, and seventy-seven of the Latin-cross type (including sixteen churches without a central dome).[10]

One can speculate that it was merely the approximate recollection of a native prototype on the part of the early settlers who built their own churches, and later the lack of proper architectural documentation, that, together with economic limitations and newly available building materials and methods, led to the evolution of such new type variants of Ukrainian architecture. This must also be the reason why these churches do not measure up to the sophistication of the spatial configuration or the geometric rigour of the classic historical monuments.

Along with distinct types of spatial configuration there are also distinct types of spatial articulation which form part of the Ukrainian architectural tradition. The best known of these is the Byzantine mosaic and fresco wall surface treatment dating back to the eleventh century in Ukraine. This tradition of covering entire wall surfaces with images and decorative patterns has persisted through various stylistic interpretations until the present time. Along with the presence of an iconostasis, it became synonymous with the concept of a Ukrainian church interior. However, a number of the finest examples of historical Ukrainian architecture exhibit different types of spatial articulation.

In the Renaissance Chapel of Three Saints in Lviv the treatment of interior surfaces of domes consists of rich ornamentation primarily representing planned motifs, while the images of saints are small in area and are in well-defined locations within strongly articulated framing elements.[11] The baroque Church of the Transfiguration in the Mhar Monastery has fine stucco ornaments enlivening otherwise plain continuous wall surfaces. St. George's Cathedral in Lviv and the Church of the Protection of the Blessed Virgin Mary in Okhtyrka show also predominantly plain interior surfaces with architectural elements as decoration.[12]

The vernacular wooden architecture in Western Ukraine offers a number of outstanding examples of unique wall paintings on wood surfaces; for example, in the Church of St. George in Drohobych,[13] a Boiko-type church, or the Church of St. Nicholas in Serednie Vodiane,[14] a Lemko-type church. In Eastern Ukraine, however, the monumental wooden churches of the eighteenth century, almost without exception, show no wall paintings and display only the texture of wood construction, which underlines the purity of the spatial configuration of the high space towers.[15] The main decorative feature in these buildings is the iconostasis, as is the case in the essentially non-iconographic interiors of the masonry churches mentioned above. This is not to say that the iconostasis did not figure prominently in all the historical churches after the Middle Ages. In many instances it covers the entire opening between the nave and the sanctuary and displays not only masterworks of iconography but also of the architectural framework containing the icons. This framework appears in many variants reflecting the stylistic preferences of the times, for example, Renaissance, Baroque or Neo-Classical.[16]

These types of spatial articulation can also be found in Canadian churches. The Byzantine manner of covering every surface with iconography and rich decoration is perhaps best exemplified by the St. Nicholas Ukrainian Catholic Church in Toronto (fig.9) or by the sanctuary wall of the Assumption of the Blessed Virgin Mary Ukrainian Catholic Church in Montreal. The recent tendency has been to follow the same approach in most of the churches that can afford to undertake new decoration projects. Perhaps it was not only economic limitations, but also deliberate attempts to follow the examples of Baroque precedents, which resulted in a number of churches with predominantly undecorated, plain interior surfaces. The St. Demetrius Ukrainian Orthodox Church in Toronto and the Ukrainian Orthodox Church of St. Sophia in Montreal (fig. 10) may serve as examples of such spatial articulation. Considering the purity and monumentality of these interiors, as well as the significant historical precedents referred to earlier, it may be desirable to maintain them in this state.

The in-between approach, that is, some iconography, some decorative motifs underlining the spatial configuration, and relatively large, substantially unadorned surfaces, seems to be a frequent, rather typically Canadian way of dealing with spatial articulation. It probably comes closest, in spirit, to the articulation of the Church of St. Andrew in Kiev, which shows the Ukrainian preference for rich, geometrically defined, organic or abstract patterns. The St. George's Ukrainian Catholic Church in Prince Albert, Saskatchewan (fig.5) and the Mother of Perpetual Help Ukrainian Catholic Church in Winnipeg (fig.11) may serve as examples of this approach.

Canadian iconostases exhibit a wide variety of types, both in their frameworks, which usually contain derivative historical patterns interpreted freely by local craftsmen, and in the style of the images, which range from strict Byzantine copies, through trite realistic representations, to unique works of considerable artistic value. The iconostasis of the Holy Trinity Ukrainian Orthodox Cathedral in Winnipeg (fig.12) and the details from the iconostasis in the St. Mary's Ukrainian Orthodox Church in Surrey, British Columbia (fig.13), as well as the iconostases shown in some of the previous illustrations, indicate the wide range of the prevailing types.

Neither the historical Ukrainian tradition nor the Canadian experience suggests a simple formula for a single type of sacred space in Ukrainian church architecture. It appears that in Ukraine each region and each epoch developed its own unique interpretations of what the experience of sacred space should be. In the brief history of Ukrainian settlement in Canada, the three basic types of spatial configuration which have evolved have been modified by a great variety of articulation types, each reflecting the interpretation by the respective parishes of what constitutes the Ukrainian tradition. These diverse approaches, which emphasize reliance on literal symbols, such as Baroque-shaped domes or Byzantine icons, have failed, with a few exceptions, to achieve what the majority of historical church buildings in Ukraine demonstrate. Most Canadian examples lack an abstract architectural order which makes a space "sacred," and a basic spatial character which is responsive to the Ukrainian cultural temperament. This character is inherent in specific spatial geometric relationships which have persisted in most of the classic historical configuration types. Although abstract in nature and therefore not easily identified, such geometric relationships are decisive in determining a particular cultural character of architecture.[17]

The challenge in the present-day development of Ukrainian architecture in Canada, or elsewhere, is to understand the processes which operate in the evolution of an architectural tradition. The history of Ukrainian architecture demonstrates that the specific Ukrainian cultural character was maintained in different, internationally current stylistic interpretations and in a variety of configuration types. A new stylistic interpretation, in the contemporary manner, and the development of new creative configuration and articulation types must be aimed for if this tradition is to continue. If characteristic Ukrainian geometric relationships are maintained and if the essential architectural order is achieved, a significant Ukrainian church architecture in Canada could evolve.

NOTES

1. George Heard Hamilton, *The Art and Architecture of Russia* (New York: Penguin Books, 1983), 102.
2. H.N. Lohvyn, *Po Ukraini: Starodavni mystetski pamiatky* (Kiev: Mystetstvo, 1968), 221, 326, 414.
3. *Istoriia ukrainskoho mystetstva,* ed. M.P. Bazhan, 6 vols. (Kiev: Academy of Sciences of the Ukrainian S.S.R., 1966–68), 3 (1968): 154.
4. Cyril Mango, *Byzantine Architecture* (New York: Abrams, 1974), 328–9.
5. Rudolf Wittkower, *Architectural Principles in the Age of Humanism* (New York: Norton, 1971), 108.
6. V. Sichynsky, *Istoriia ukrainskoho mystetstva—arkhitektura,* 2 vols. (New York: Shevchenko Scientific Society, 1956), 1:118.
7. Wittkower, *Architectural Principles,* 3.
8. Mango, *Byzantine Architecture,* 350.
9. Sviatoslav Hordynsky, *Ukrainski tserkvy v Polshchi* (Rome: Bohosloviia, 1969), 11, figs. 47 and 69.
10. Anna Maria Baran, *Ukrainian Catholic Churches of Saskatchewan* (Saskatoon: Ukrainian Catholic Council of Saskatchewan, 1977).
11. Lohvyn, *Po Ukraini,* 223.
12. Ibid., 237, 422.
13. Bazhan, ed., *Istoriia ukrainskoho,* 3:158–62.
14. Ibid., 155–57.
15. David Buxton, *The Wooden Churches of Eastern Europe* (Cambridge: Cambridge University Press, 1981), 164, 167, 171.
16. Bazhan, ed., *Istoriia ukrainskoho,* 3:145–51.
17. Radoslav Zuk, "Architectural Significance and Culture," *Canadian Ethnic Studies* 16, no. 3 (1984):25.

Illustrations are reproduced by permission of Orest Semchishen from his original photographs—figures 3,5,7,8,13 and by permission of Radoslav Zuk—figures 2,4,6,9,10,11,12. Figure 1 is reprinted from *Byzantine Churches of Alberta,* photographs by Orest Semchishen, ed. Hubert Hohn (Edmonton: Edmonton Art Gallery, 1976), by permission of Orest Semchishen.

Fig. 1. Church of the Exaltation of the Holy Cross, Innisfree District, Alberta.

Fig. 2. St. Josaphat's Ukrainian Catholic Cathedral, Toronto.

Fig. 3. Sacred Heart Ukrainian Catholic Church, Krydor, Saskatchewan.

Fig. 4. St. Volodymyr and Olga Ukrainian Catholic Cathedral, Winnipeg.

Fig. 5. St. George's Ukrainian Catholic Church, Prince Albert, Saskatchewan.

Fig. 6. St. Mary the Protectress Ukrainian Orthodox Church, Winnipeg.

Fig. 7. Ukrainian Catholic Church of Sts. Cyril and Methodius, St. Catharines, Ontario.

Fig. 8. St. John the Baptist Ukrainian Catholic Church, Smuts, Saskatchewan.

Fig. 9. Ukrainian Catholic Church of St. Nicholas, Toronto.

Fig. 10. Ukrainian Orthodox Church of St. Sophia, Montreal.

Fig. 11. Mother of Perpetual Help Ukrainian Catholic Church, Winnipeg.

Fig. 12. Holy Trinity Ukrainian Orthodox Cathedral, Winnipeg.

Fig. 13. St. Mary's Ukrainian Orthodox Church, Surrey, British Columbia.

Serge Keleher

Ukrainian Church Iconography in Canada: Models and Their Spiritual Significance

Orthodox iconography is an area of esthetics which has defined principles, so that it can be criticized on foundations firmer than personal preference. This is not merely an ancient Christian art form but rather a crucial expression of Orthodox approaches to God, the universe, the nature of humanity, salvation, and the union with God which the Orthodox call *theosis*, the goal of Christian life. Therefore, just as theologians may not dogmatize according to their own whims or preferences, so must Orthodox iconographers [and those responsible for iconography] ensure that their work both faithfully conveys Orthodox teaching and contributes to the edification of believers [in their faith].

The term Orthodox, or in Ukrainian *pravoslavia*,[1] does not simply mean "right belief" (as is frequently assumed), but also "right glory" or the correct, proper and accurate worship of God, to whom alone glory belongs. This term is far older than the present distinction between Greek Orthodox and Greek Catholic. It makes the same demands upon both sides of that divide since they both share the same worship tradition in which "Orthodox" appears innumerable times. Thus in the technical vocabulary of this paper "Orthodox" includes Ukrainian Greek Catholics.

The theology of the icon has been discussed at length by the Holy Fathers (Saint John of Damascus and Saint Theodore the Studite) and in recent works by Kontoglou, Uspensky, Lossky, and indeed in the material by Archpriest Ivan Syrotynsky and Deacon Michael Barida.[2]

The icon plays a special role in the liturgical worship of the church. One of

47

the best known and most ancient Orthodox icons is the image of the face of Jesus Christ (figure 1), the Face of God which even Moses could not behold. According to tradition, the icon called "Deisis" is always associated closely with the place where the Divine Liturgy is celebrated. It is either over the Royal Doors on the iconostasis or over the High Place behind the Holy Table.

The theme in figure 2 is identical, and the style is very similar. This icon portrays the marriage feast of the Lamb from the Apocalypse of Saint John, which is considered to be a Eucharistic theme and therefore related intimately to the Divine Liturgy. Christ, the Lamb-Bridegroom, is enthroned as at His Second Coming. Theotokos, the figure of the church, the Bride of Christ, stands at His right hand, and Saint John the Baptist, the "friend of the Bridegroom," as he called himself, stands at Christ's left.

There is an authentic, distinct tradition of Orthodox iconography which developed in Ukraine (as in other countries). One of the earliest and best known examples of this tradition is the Icon of the Theotokos called the Icon of the Theotokos (Oranta) in the apse of the Cathedral of the Holy Wisdom built by Iaroslav the Wise in Kiev. This Theotokos (figure 3), shown with her arms raised in supplication for the Church to the Christ-Pantocrator in the dome of the Cathedral, is not Greek; she is clearly a Slavic, Ukrainian woman, the powerful mother, bearing the burdens of her children and able to intercede effectively for her people. This Kiev icon conforms strictly to the canons of Orthodox iconography, and at the same time the Kiev Oranta expresses deep ancient elements of Ukrainian spirituality.[3]

Unfortunately, throughout the Orthodox world, theology and iconography suffered a decline in the seventeenth century, and it was not until the twentieth century that a successful recovery of authentic tradition began. This also occurred in Ukraine, and by the latter part of the nineteenth century, iconography in Western Ukraine was influenced strongly by the religious art of Western Europe. Still, traditional elements persisted, as for example in an iconostasis from the Boiko region of Western Ukraine, now in the Lviv Museum of Wooden Architecture. When the pioneers came from Western Ukraine to Canada, they remembered such churches and sought to build similar ones.

Naturally, they also wanted to emulate in their churches the pattern of divine worship they had known in Ukraine. To this day, it is still possible to find such churches in use in Canadian towns and cities. Where one finds such a church unchanged over the decades, it is likely that one will also find the same pattern of worship. Such a parish will usually have, or have had in living memory, regular Vespers and Orthros (the morning service, which corresponds to Lauds and Matins) and of course the Divine Liturgy. In considering this, we should remember that ordinary people in Galicia possessed books for Vespers and Orthros and used them regularly. Metropolitan Andrei

Sheptytsky, in the 1911 Letter to the Roman Catholic Bishops of Canada, stressed the love of the people for the services of Vespers and Orthros, and their insistence that divine worship be conducted properly, and that, in fact, the cantors often knew the rubrics better than the Priests![4]

This type of iconography found in Canada is my first model. It is the late nineteenth-century "classic" iconography of Western Ukraine and recalls the rich liturgical piety of Ukrainian pioneers, their strong love for and determination to have their own church in the new land. This model is not without its problems, since it comes from a degenerate period of iconography and theology, and is also associated with Jansenism, which encouraged infrequent communion, a bias against intellectual activity, and a fear of novelty. It often refused even authentic, Patristic Orthodoxy. There is often a good deal of folk religion in such parishes. Curious customs and religious practices, such as the particular form of liturgical chants, are preserved there, though forgotten in Ukraine itself. The Ukrainian Catholic Church in Chipman, Saint Barbara's Russo-Greek Orthodox Church in Edmonton, and the Russo-Greek Orthodox Church in Smoky Lake are some examples of this model found in Alberta. This pattern is very prevalent in parishes of the Ukrainian Greek-Orthodox Church as well, although sometimes one can discern a Protestant influence in their iconography.[5] The clergy who served those who remained Ukrainian Catholic (following the schism and creation of the Ukrainian Orthodox Church) were moved by several considerations to develop a new model of iconography, church decoration, and pattern of worship. The greatest threat, in the clergy's view, came from Eastern Orthodox bodies. The problem was that Eastern Orthodox churches and worship looked the same as Greek Catholic churches and worship. If, therefore, a model could be developed which would look more "Catholic," the faithful who became accustomed to that model would be in less danger of feeling "at home" in an Eastern Orthodox church, and would therefore be likelier to remain in the Catholic fold.

This second model is illustrated by Saint George's Cathedral in Saskatoon (figure 4), which almost looks like an elaborate Polish church. Not only is it heavily baroque, but there is no iconostasis (which is considered essential for the Orthodox Divine Liturgy). It has an image of the Sacred Heart of Jesus and the three-dimensional "Stations of the Cross": these devotions are not found in the Orthodox traditions. As we have seen in other illustrations, Orthodox tradition requires that the Icon of Christ the Pantocrator be placed in the central dome of the church. This can be seen in the interior of the dome of the large Redemptorist Church of Our Lady of Perpetual Help in Yorkton, Saskatchewan. Instead of the traditional Pantocrator, this dome is painted with a portrayal of the Trinity which has nothing in common with traditional iconography.

This second model is sad in many ways; often the people have not quite realized what has happened. They have not, for example, perceived the difference between a statue and an icon. This sort of parish usually has a very strong but negative sense of "Catholic" identity and a vehement antipathy toward the Eastern Orthodox Church and anyone or anything that might lead in an Orthodox direction. More recently these parishes have often been proud to retain elements of Roman Catholic devotion that are no longer common among Roman Catholics. For example, such parishes may boast that Roman Catholics attend Stations of the Cross in the Ukrainian church, because the local Roman Catholic priest does not conduct this devotion. Jansenism can also be found in these parishes, but usually the movement for frequent communion (inspired in this century by Saint Pius X and Vatican II among Roman Catholics) has made some progress.

There is a current movement throughout the Orthodox world to revive authentic Orthodox iconography. In Western Ukraine it was encouraged by Metropolitan Andrei Sheptytsky, who organized a museum and a school to promote authentic iconography, and commissioned Petro Kholodny to paint the iconostasis and the entire Chapel of the Holy Spirit in the Theological Academy so as to accustom the students to authentic iconography.

When the Ukrainian "new Canadians" came after the Second World War, some of them carried this ideal of authentic iconography with them and began to organize parishes and churches in accordance with the third model I would like to suggest. The pre-eminent example in Canada is the Church of Saint Nicholas in Toronto, organized through the efforts of the late Protopresbyter Bohdan Lypsky, who had been a Professor in the Lviv Theological Academy. The Iconostasis (figure 5) and the Royal Doors highlight this authentic Orthodox iconographic tradition.

The Oranta and Pantocrator remind us of very early Ukrainian examples from Saint Sophia's in Kiev. The iconostasis of Saints Peter and Paul Church, Montmartre (figure 6), shows how the influence of the third model has been spreading. The older images of the Sacred Heart of Jesus and the Immaculate Heart of Mary on either side of the iconostasis clash with the iconography of Ihor Sukhachiv on the iconostasis itself. The complete "restoration" of this church remains to be done.

The iconography of Saint Michael's Church in Welland (figure 7) also shows some interesting development. The parish is more than fifty years old, but the majority of the present congregation of this parish is drawn from "new Canadians." The exterior of the church, which was built about thirty years ago, shows a rather typical large rural church building, although it has only two domes. When the iconography project began in 1975 the interior was also nondescript and potted plants were the only feature of any interest.

In this movement for authentic, traditional Orthodox iconography that has been termed the third model, two Ukrainian churches outside Canada are particularly important. The "Sobor" of Saints Volodymyr and Olha in Chicago (figure 8) exercises a vast influence, especially in its biweekly bulletin, which is circulated virtually throughout the Ukrainian world, and in the leadership it gives to tradition-minded Ukrainian communities. Saint Sophia's Cathedral in Rome was built by His Beatitude Patriarch Iosyf the Confessor, who insisted on the restoration of authentic Orthodox tradition to all areas of church life. In 1976 Hordynsky executed an iconostasis for the Ukrainian Catholic Church of Saints Peter and Paul in Nutana, Saskatoon, attempting to introduce the third model into a building constructed according to other ideas. A similar problem is faced by the very traditionalist parish of Saint Elias in Brampton, Ontario, which is temporarily using an old Protestant structure. In spite of this difficulty, the community has managed a good iconostasis, which is particularly effective at Pascha (figure 9).

Churches following the third model often lay particular stress on traditional liturgical worship, with an emphasis on the sacraments, regular celebration of Vespers and Orthros,[6] and a restoration of Orthodox usage in many areas of church life. These parishes are often characterized by an integral, holistic approach to spiritual life, which demands a high degree of internal consistency, an increasing theological appreciation of Eastern Orthodoxy, a sympathy toward the ecumenical movement for Catholic-Orthodox rapprochement, a very strong acceptance of the movement for greater autonomy for the Ukrainian church, and a *kerygma* (message) and liturgical life approximating that of Eastern Orthodoxy.

Theologically, this group tends to appeal to the Second Vatican Council's recognition of theological pluralism within the Catholic church and seeks to uphold the position of "Eastern Orthodox in communion with Rome." Since relatively little Orthodox literature is available in Ukrainian, Orthodox theological writing in English is influential in these circles. Nevertheless these parishes usually have a strong Ukrainian national identity. They also tend to sympathize with the first model and appreciate the piety and devoutness of the early pioneers.

A fourth model of iconography emerged in the years following the Second Vatican Council. It appears that some clergy decided that the church needed a pseudo-renewal like that of Roman Catholicism, marked by a secularized worship and the loss of a sense of sacredness. These churches invariably seem bare and empty. Examples of this extraordinary development are Sacred Heart Church in Ituna (figure 10), Holy Cross in Thunder Bay, Saint Nicholas in Winnipeg, and the Basilian Church in Edmonton. These parishes seem to be searching for a "Canadian" religious identity. They often consciously reject many elements of Eastern Christian liturgical and spiritual tradition. Rather they are inclined to a negative "Catholicism," enamoured of all the post-conciliar vagaries, with little regard for the relevant conciliar decrees. They consider the first, second and third models hopelessly outdated.

Finally, I would like to suggest a fifth model, which is difficult to describe. It consists of an attempt to combine all four of the models just described to create a "modernist Orthodoxy." It is somewhat inaccurate to refer to it as a model, as it varies from example to example. One infamous instance involved a priest in full vestments serving what can be loosely termed the Divine Liturgy, on a coffee table, facing his congregation. He was sitting on the floor and playing a guitar while the assembly sang an ersatz folk version of the Jesus Prayer! Such parishes seem to be characterized by the notion that it is possible to take parts from various religious traditions, combining them into an inconsistent and incoherent mix. Sentimental emotionalism and resistance to liturgical principles are the common denominator in this model.

Saint Demetrius Church in Toronto which claims to have a "Byzantine" structure simply because its "dome" resembles a hatbox on top of a rectangle, is a good example of this runaway form. The sanctuary was originally designed to facilitate the celebration of Mass facing the people (following the changes ushered in by Vatican II). The fashion changed, however, and an iconostasis piece, which resembles none other, was installed. A closer look at the sort of iconography favoured at Saint Demetrius (figure 11) shows the passion for combining traditions. The scholastics might have called this a stunning example of the fallacy of composition. It is the sort of muddled thinking which claims steak, lobster, yogurt, aspirin, penicillin, dark beer and chocolate milk shakes are all good. Following the fallacy, if all of these things are combined, the result will be even better! The liturgical and spiritual life of such a parish is likely to resemble the iconography closely—a superficial combination of the most incongruous elements. Perhaps the best that can be hoped for in the short run is that they will cancel each other out.

The third model (authentic and traditional Orthodox iconography) is most consistent with Orthodox liturgy, theology and spirituality. Certain people object that this iconography is not authentically Ukrainian, but rather Russian or Greek. In response to that criticism, however, I offer several examples of magnificent Orthodox iconography from Western Ukraine, from the peak period of the church in those regions. These examples illustrate an iconography at once authentically Ukrainian and authentically Orthodox. The traditional Theotokos, sometimes called the Volhynian Mother of God, comes from the Church of the Holy Protection in Lutsk, and was painted circa 1300. The Holy Face ("Icon not made with hands") comes from the Carpathian Mountains and was painted circa 1500, as does the double Icon of the Annunciation and the Entry of the Lord into Jerusalem. An icon of the Transfiguration appears to come from an early Church of the Synaxis of the Theotokos in the village of Busovysko near Lviv, and was painted in the fourteenth century.[7]

A particularly outstanding example of authentic and pure Orthodox ecclesiastical iconography from Western Ukraine is the stunning iconostasis found in the Church of Saint Paraskeva-Piatnytsia in Lviv, which was recently restored by artists of the Lviv Picture Gallery (the Church is still in daily liturgical use). This iconostasis merits a book-length study.

In Canada this rich tradition is vitally expressed in the icon of the Transfiguration from the iconostasis of Saint Michael's Church, Welland, Ontario, and in a large traditional Orthodox Paschal icon also called the "Descent into Hell," from Saint Nicholas Church, Toronto. A fifteenth-century Paschal icon is from the Church of the Holy Protection in the village of Poliana, near Lviv. There are numerous other examples as well, such as the Dormition of the Theotokos from the iconostasis of Saint Michael's in Welland and one painted circa 1415, from the village of Mińsk Mazowiecki near Lublin.

Article 17 of the Vatican II Decree, *Unitatis Redintegratio,* states:

What has already been said about legitimate variety we are pleased to apply to differences in theological expression of doctrine. In the study of revealed truth East and West have used different methods and approaches in understanding and confessing divine things. It is hardly surprising, then, if sometimes one tradition has come nearer to a full appreciation of some aspects of a mystery of revelation than the other, or has expressed them better. In such cases, these various theological formulations are often to be considered complementary rather than conflicting. With regard to the authentic theological traditions of the Orientals, we must recognize that they are admirably rooted in Holy Scripture, are fostered and given expression in liturgical life, are nourished by the living tradition of the apostles and by the works of the Fathers and spiritual writers of the East; they are directed toward a right ordering of life, indeed, toward a full contemplation of Christian truth.

This sacred Council thanks God that many Eastern children of the Catholic Church preserve this heritage and wish to express it more faithfully and completely in their lives, and are already living in full communion with their brethren who follow the tradition of the West. But it declares that this entire heritage of spirituality and liturgy, of discipline and theology, in the various traditions, belongs to the full catholic and apostolic character of the Church.

Conclusion

Five models of iconography found in Ukrainian churches in Canada have been distinguished:

1. The pioneer model—an accurate reproduction of late nineteenth-century

ecclesiastical art in Greek Catholic churches of Western Ukraine. Many examples can still be found in Western Canada, in Pennsylvania and in Ukraine itself.

2. The "Latinized" model—church interiors designed to look distinctly "Catholic" which appear to strive to cut off the worshipper from the Orthodox roots of the Ukrainian liturgy. Examples in Ukraine are now very scarce, but many can be found in the countries of Ukrainian emigration.

3. The "authentic" model—iconography witnessing to the theological and liturgical renewal and heightened interest in the genuine sources of Orthodox spirituality and worship, with a great stress on historical continuity, theological awareness and liturgical consistency.

4. The "neo-latinized" model—an attempt to imitate the external manifestations of post-conciliar innovations in the Roman Catholic Church. This model also appears to strive to cut off the worshipper from the Orthodox roots of the Ukrainian liturgy. There are no such churches in Ukraine.

5. The "eclectic" model—combining various elements chosen *ad libitum* from a wide variety of religious and non-religious traditions, according to the whim of individuals, usually with no regard for any consistency. Superficially these churches do not necessarily resemble one another, but the underlying idea is the same.

My own conclusion should already be clear: on doctrinal, artistic, theological, liturgical and pastoral grounds, the third model of authentic Orthodox iconography is by far the best suited to the needs of the church, and this model should prevail as the choices facing the Ukrainian churches become clearer. Where the pioneer model has been retained over the decades, it witnesses to an important cultural and folkloric tradition but it can no longer be replicated with the same sincerity.

The second and fourth models are each based on blind imitation of different schools of Roman Catholicism, and as such are completely incongruous with the expressed teaching of the Roman Catholic Church on the universal value and worth of the authentic Orthodox tradition.

Finally, the eclectic model, of course, is nothing more than a freakish fad, and like all such phenomena is ephemeral.

Yet I wish to close with a tribute to the Ukrainian pioneers, who brought their tradition to Canada, and who often defended it at great personal sacrifice. They remind us that our love for the church must inspire all of our efforts, if those efforts are to endure.

NOTES

1. Patriarch Iosyf, "Pro vyholoshuvannia slova 'Pravoslavnyi,'" *Blahovisnyk*, Rome 1961.
2. Vladimir Lossky and Leonide Ouspensky, *The Meaning of Icons* (New York: St. Vladimir's Press, 1981); George Galavaris, *Icon in the Life of the Church* (Leiden: E.J. Brill, 1981); Leonide Ouspensky, *Theology and Icon* (Crestwood, New York: St. Vladimir's Seminary Press, 1978); *The Iconography of St. Nicholas Church* (Toronto: St. Nicholas Ukrainian Catholic Parish, 1977); St. John of Damascus, *On the Divine Images*, trans. David Anderson (Crestwood, New York: St. Vladimir's Seminary Press, 1980); St. Theodore the Studite, *On the Holy Icons*, trans. Catharine P. Roth (Crestwood, New York: St. Vladimir's Seminary Press, 1981).
3. I owe this observation to Petro Bilaniuk; it will appear in a forthcoming article on Marian devotion in his series *Studies in Eastern Christianity*.
4. The 1911 Letter to the Roman Catholic Bishops of Canada from Metropolitan Andrei was republished in Winnipeg (in English) in 1977 by the Patriarchal Society.
5. An example of Protestant influence on iconography in Canada is the image of the "Agony in the Garden" in Saint John's Cathedral, Edmonton. Such images can be found in many Ukrainian Orthodox churches in this country.
6. The Orthros service of the Byzantine Rite combines the services known in the West as Matins and Lauds, or more recently as Vigils and morning prayer. As this combination is unique to the Byzantine Rite, it is best to retain the proper term *Orthros*, rather than adopt one of the Latin terms.
7. For reproductions of these icons, see Sviatoslav Hordynsky, *The Ukrainian Icon of the XIIth to XVIIIth Centuries* (Philadelphia: Providence Association of Ukrainian Catholics, 1973).

All photos courtesy of Serge Keleher.

Fig. 1. The Face of God, St. Sophia's Cathedral, Kiev.

Fig. 2. Deisis, unknown artist of Varivka, 15th century.

Fig. 3. Theotokos Oranta, St. Sophia's Cathedral, Kiev.

Fig. 4. Interior, St. George's Cathedral, Saskatoon.

Fig. 5. Iconostasis, Church of St. Nicholas, Toronto.

Fig. 6. Iconostasis, Sts. Peter and Paul Church, Paris, France.

Fig. 7. Interior, St. Michael's Church, Welland, Ontario.

Fig. 8. Iconostasis, Sobor of Sts. Volodymyr and Olha, Chicago.

Fig. 9. Iconostasis, Church of St. Elias, Brampton, Ontario.

Fig. 10. Interior, Sacred Heart Church, Ituna, Saskatchewan.

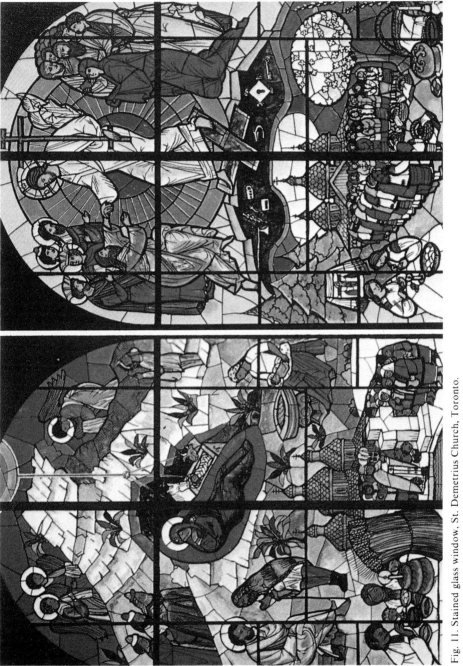

Fig. 11. Stained glass window, St. Demetrius Church, Toronto.

Stephan Jarmus

Changes in the Function of the Clergy from Ukraine to Canada

Introduction

In discussing the function of Ukrainian clergy, I will address the work of the Orthodox and Catholic clergy simultaneously. In Ukraine, their functions were primarily liturgical and, in both cases, the liturgy was and still is the same. Moreover, I will only review the changes here, since I have previously had the opportunity to approach this subject in depth.[1] Because these clergy function in two different worlds—Ukraine and Canada—my task includes the problem of the adaptability of our churches and our clergy to the life and the new conditions in Canada.

As far as the methodology of my discourse is concerned, I intend to deal with it under two separate headings: (1)Old Paradigms of Priestly Ministry, and (2)The Age of Reorientation.

1. Old Paradigms of Priestly Ministry

Though the typically pastoral concerns and pastoral awareness were central to such great liturgical reformers of the seventeenth century as Petro Mohyla and his colleagues, their endeavours and their vision of priestly functions did not prevail in the life of the church in Ukraine. The model for the priesthood which prevailed limited priests to the service at the altar, and left them there for centuries. Thus, for many years the priest served his faithful by means of the proverbial "*Kadylo* and *kropylo*" (by incense and holy water), while the individual needs of people were left unheeded, unattended. Furthermore, there were few preachers in the Greek and the Russian Orthodox Churches, and this situation prevailed even to the modern age. Indeed, for the less educated and simple people, worship was sufficient; it gave them comfort, spiritual strength and hope. Apparently, the very purpose of Eastern Orthodox (or Byzantine) worship was to provide this kind of spiritual sustenance. This situation helped to form a permanent image of the priest as liturgical performer, server and celebrant of the Mysteries (Sacraments). Of course, this placed upon candidates for the priesthood definite expectations. Ontologically, they were supposed to possess the calling for priesthood, though many were simply following in the footsteps of their fathers. Spiritually, they were expected to possess deep faith. Psychologically, they were supposed to love the calling and the people, and to be ready to suffer with them. Moreover, the matter of formal preparation for priesthood will shed some light on the nature of the priestly function at that time.

(a) Preparation of Candidates for Priesthood
Preparation and training of candidates for the priesthood is the constant concern of the church. In the case of the Orthodox church in Ukraine, pastoral preparation ranked rather high, even though the main point of concern was preparation of the priest as a person. This certainly was the case at the end of the nineteenth century. It is exemplified by the holder of the chair of Pastoral Theology at the Kievan Theological Academy, Professor V. Pivnytsky, who wrote three books on Pastoral Theology. One of them, *The Priest, Preparation for Priesthood and Life' of the Priest*, published in 1897, included the following topics (only the titles of major chapters are given here):

Part one: *Preparation for Priesthood*
I. Indispensability of preparation for priesthood
II. Persons in preparation for priesthood
III. Education of candidates for priestly ministry
IV. The Candidate for priesthood after the school

Part two: *Life of the Priest*
I. Fundamental rules
II. Pleasures and entertainment
III. Formal image of the priest
IV. Family life of the priest
V. Home and other occupations of the priest
VI. Priest and his parishioners.[2]

This outline describes thoroughly matters concerning the priest, as a person, and his image. It also includes concern for the personal well-being of the priest, while there is nothing that would suggest concern about pastoral care. However, Pivnytsky's scheme became the model for education in Pastoral Theology for almost a century. This paradigm rules in some schools of theology even in our time. What kind of pastoral personality does such education produce, and what kind of pastoral ministry does it suggest? Clearly, both the priestly and the pastoral personalities and their ministry appear to be incomplete and inadequate. This situation may be illustrated by an interesting phenomenon which emerged precisely at the time, and in the geographical area, of our present concern.

This phenomenon is the uniquely Slavic, very much glorified, phenomenon of *startsi*. This phenomenon appeared sometime in the eighteenth or nineteenth centuries, both in Ukraine and in Russia, where the Orthodox church remained under the order introduced by Tsar Peter I. In that system there was no room for the development of real pastorally minded clergy or pastoral care. It simply was not possible, given the regimentation of civil authorities who seldom were guided by concern for the church, the clergy or the people. The spiritual needs of the people were great, yet there was an obvious absence of sympathetic ministry. It is no wonder, then, that an unusual ministry emerged. The *startsi*, who often were lay persons with little or no education, were people of spiritual wisdom. It was these *startsi* who provided much of the spiritual ministry and counselling which the official clergy simply were unprepared to provide.

There are many stories and legends about these *startsi*. They provided counsel even to the bishops, and later became the pride of the church. This was indeed a great irony, since the church possessed a large clerical population, but few of them were prepared for pastoral ministry other than that of the altar. Indeed, some parish priests behaved like lords. However, the liturgical function of the priests was seen as adequate and satisfactory.

Some pastoral theologians and educators did see the growing need for a ministry in the Orthodox church which would possess a wider pastoral orientation and deeper concern with the well-being of the people. There was little chance to voice these concerns to any meaningful extent, since officially it was not deemed necessary. Indeed, even now, there are few Eastern Orthodox schools of theology in North America which adapt their educational programmes to the requirements of our time. Pivnytsky's model of education of candidates for the priesthood seems to satisfy most Eastern Orthodox educational institutions.[3]

Functions of Clergy in Ukraine
It would be wrong to suggest that theological institutions in Ukraine did not provide an adequate theological education. On the contrary, seminaries and theological academies, collectively, offered programmes that extended through eight to ten years of study, and included all necessary areas of

theological education. However, their educational philosophy was limited and did not prepare candidates for service in the church. There was little or no vision of the pastoral orientation necessary for parish priests. This would have required a philosophy which included pastoral care extending beyond the church and liturgy, designed to accompany the faithful through the pains of everyday life. The old educational system simply did not develop an awareness of pastoral responsibilities and pastoral care. Rather, the notion of priest as pastor was overshadowed by the image of the priest as server at the altar. This placed the priest in a very secure position, but limited his activity to the celebration of various liturgies, and made him inaccessible, or in the words of Archmandrite Constantine, "untouchable" by anything else.[4]

Nevertheless, this image of the priest's responsibility dominated for many years. Accordingly, he was looked upon as the servant of the church and guardian of the welfare of the church—he watched over the flock of his parishioners—but Christ's model of the priest as pastor was overlooked. The priest, as a concerned and caring pastor who risks the welfare of the ninety-nine healthy sheep by searching for the lost one-hundredth person, is still absent from the idea of the Orthodox priest. However, the functions of the Orthodox priest as priest and pastor (connected yet distinguishable aspects of one vocation) are demonstrated before the people every time they attend the Divine Liturgy. Indeed, the Orthodox priest enters into his priestly function precisely and solely during the celebration of the Divine Liturgy, at the moment of his liturgical entry into the Sanctuary at the Little Entrance. It ends when he leaves the Sanctuary after the Communion. The late Fr. Alexander Schmemann described this situation:

> ... the Priest leaves the Sanctuary and with the words: "Let us depart in peace" joins the congregation for a final prayer ("prayer behind the ambon"). Just as, at the beginning of the Liturgy the Priest's entrance into the Sanctuary and his ascension to the Holy Throne (the "high place") expressed the eucharistic movement upwards, his return to the body of the faithful is the expression of this departure, of the return of the Church into the world. But it means also that the eucharistic function of the Priest has come to an end. Fulfilling the Priesthood of Christ, the priest led us to the Heavenly Altar, and from this Altar he made us communicants of the Kingdom. His function was to perform and to achieve the eternal Mediation of Christ, by whose Humanity we ascend to heaven, by whose Divinity God comes to us. And now all this has been achieved once more. Fed with the Body and Blood of Christ, "having seen the True Light and partaken of the Holy Spirit," we are, indeed, His people and His inheritance... There is nothing else to do for the Priest at the Altar, for the Church itself has become the Altar of God and the Tabernacle of his Glory. And thus he joins

the people leading them now, as their Pastor and Teacher on this return into the world for the fulfillment of their Christian mission. . . . [5]

Obviously, the lingering model of the priest's life and function is far from what Schmemann described. It is incomplete, for this distorted image of the priest limits him to his liturgical activity on Sunday. The rest of his life during the week is a void.

According to the old model, the priest serves the church while people's needs are completely bypassed. Therefore, it is not surprising to hear young candidates for priesthood, when asked what motivates such a great decision, reply: "The need to serve the church." As yet, I have not even once heard the answer: "The need to serve the people." Unfortunately the prevailing view of the function of the clergy still invites the services of various self-appointed "*startsi.*" Surely, better ideals and healthier models of pastoral care can and must be developed.

2. The Age of Reorientation

(a) Limitations of Liturgical Ministry
The clergy in Ukraine, Eastern Orthodox and Greek Catholic, were trained for the ministry in a manner that subsumed their pastoral function into their primary liturgical vocation. Tales in folklore and literature provide ample evidence that such ministry was inadequate even in the eyes of the common people. In most cases, a serious class distinction also made the distance between clergy and laity too great. Priests trained in Canada were in a similar situation. The scope of their responsibility was broadened to all areas of life, yet they were expected primarily to pursue cultural (ethnic and material) goals, while their pastoral ministry was limited to the celebration of liturgy and preaching. Here, as well as in Ukraine, the philosophy of theological education did not include the pastoral ministry or pastoral training.

The scope of the priest's responsiblity in Canada is much greater than in Ukraine. This could point to the priest's importance in the community, yet, in reality, he was deprived of much of his priestly authority. He retained liturgical authority but was largely an advisor on matters of parish administration. Unlike the priest in the Ukrainian Catholic Church, he was not a statutory leader. Moreover, in the Consistory and the *Sobor* of the church, he shared equal rights with the layperson. Nevertheless, the statutory limitations of the Ukrainian Orthodox priest in Canada do not affect his spiritual activity. The direct and broad responsibility of the priest for the life of his parishioners provides him with great scope for real pastoral care. Of course, this depends on his pastoral awareness and pastoral abilities.

(b) Pastoral Education in Canada in the Past and Present
For quite a while, the European model of pastoral education dominated the educational philosophy even in Canada. The training institution of the Ukrainian Orthodox of Canada is St. Andrew's College in Winnipeg. During the fifties and early sixties, pastoral theology in this institution was taught by Metropolitan Ilarion. He followed Pivnytsky's model, though he did adapt it to the Canadian situation by including such new chapters as "The Priest and His Work With Youth"; "Priest and Social Work"; "Service to the People is Service to God"; and "Pastor, the Sacrificial Servant."[6]

Adapting to the Canadian context is precisely what pastoral theology and pastoral education should do. Metropolitan Ilarion had the vision to place pastoral theology and pastoral education in the right perspective, but did not venture far enough. His deep pastoral concern is encompassed in his lifelong slogan, *Sluzhyty narodu to sluzhyty Bohu!* (Service to the people equals service to God). Unfortunately, the majority of Metropolitan Ilarion's admirers did not understand his deep philosophical and pastoral concerns and hence failed to transform them into a lasting tradition.

(c) New Direction in Pastoral Education
The traditional liturgical ministry is a specific ministry which is not sufficient for the total care of human beings. We, both Orthodox and Catholics, have not moved far in our endeavours to correct that. Now, however, students of pastoral theology welcome the introduction of new methods and experiences.

For the past fifteen years pastoral theology at St. Andrew's College was my responsibility. Very early in my preparation to teach in this area, I realized that we needed to improve the course work. As a result, instead of one course in pastoral theology, we now have five half-courses with the following titles: Introduction to Pastoral Theology (Orthodox Pastorology), Pastoral Ministry in the Liturgical Context, Pastoral Care in the Context of Human Life, Pastoral Anthropology and Chosen Topics in Pastoral Theology.

A student following the designated programme of pastoral studies certainly should be prepared to function well both as a priest and as a pastor. Of utmost importance to this end is the task of helping the candidates understand human nature, its various needs and strivings, and training them to cope with different situations. Counselling and training in real-life situations also is a very important aspect of this education.

To accomplish this, one course, "Pastoral Anthropolgy," confronts the candidates—future pastors—with the whole spectrum of human needs and helps them to prepare to deal with these. I conceived of "Pastoral Anthropology" as a science. (Let us not forget Matthew 25: 31–46). Christianity teaches that people are unique creations in the very image and likeness of God; and that the individual is the most precious being whose personal worth cannot be compared even with the multitude.[7] This is the point of departure for Christian Anthropology and, consequently, the Christian pastor's consciousness. Such consciousness will, of necessity, influence the caring attitude, and make the pastor aware of the one hundredth sheep that can never be classed as insignificant, regardless of moral or social status.

In Western Christendom, which developed a specifically caring attitude in pastoral ministry, the concept of pastoral anthropology need not be stressed. However, in Eastern Christendom, with its insistence on the individual's duty to belong to the church, to worship, to be charitable, while paying little attention to the individual's needs, developing pastoral anthropology is imperative. We need forms of pastoral care which minister to the total human being. Pastoral ministry is responsible for the whole complex of human needs, including the following categories:

(1) *The physiogenic needs*
These are the impulsive needs that sustain the well-being of the physiological aspect of human life. The latter includes the metabolic and reproductive needs, which are necessary for bodily comfort and physical well-being. The physiogenic order can be nurtured through social and political life, which, like parental care, includes guidance, healing and various kinds of human protection. These needs are a part of pastoral responsibility and, curiously, share in the prophetic tradition of the Bible.

(2) *The psychogenic needs*
The psychogenic order includes a variety of needs such as love, fellowship, freedom of emotional expression, understanding, compassion, support, honest recognition of our creative efforts and acknowledgement of our personal worth. However, no other category of needs is so neglected in Orthodox pastoral education or subjected to such neglect. Some needs are labelled as grave sins and judged rather than treated with therapeutic sympathy. Emotional depression (*Unynie*) is classed as one of the seven deadly sins. While it may be, it deserves our therapeutic skills so healing can occur, not our moralistic judgement and condemnation. Pastoral anthropology, drawing on the insights of modern psychology, can help the Christian pastor to approach these ills therapeutically.

(3) *The noegenic human needs*
Whereas the physiogenic and psychogenic human needs refer primarily to the "immediacy" of human life at its lower level, noegenic needs and their fulfillment point to the higher level dominated by the spiritual intellect. On this level human nature "participates in the noetic realm, and is a companion of the angels."[8] Furthermore, satisfaction of the noegenic needs, and consequently, the development of this aspect of human life, leads us onto the path of *theosis*, and likens us unto God. This is the chief end of human life.

(4) *Ethnogenic and sociogenic needs*
Humans are "social beings" (in Eastern terminology, the "Eucharistic be-

ing").[9] This includes distinct ethnic and social needs that must be recognized by theology and by pastoral anthropology. The Adlerian focus on the human drive for social status[10] is not entirely wrong if placed in its proper perspective. Life is a personal phenomenon, but growth and development depend on a relationship to other human beings. Thus, ethnic and cultural aspects of human life are essential categories. However, they become meaningless if they are deprived of a social context and of its integrity.

Pastoral anthropology should bear responsibility for determining what human needs belong to pastoral responsibility and which should be dealt with therapeutically. However, pastoral anthropology must acknowledge its limits. There are things that must be entrusted to the common pastoral wisdom.

(d) The Problem of Reorientation
Common human needs have not been a concern or pastoral orientation of the Eastern Orthodox Church. The church continues to focus on abstract truth (even though it is often misunderstood and misrepresented)[11] and formal relationship. The faithful, however, experience various pressing demands of modern life, demands which often stand in need of pastoral ministry.

There is a need for change, for placing our pastoral concerns into the very framework of Canadian life. This reorientation has been spoken about for decades as necessary for the life of the church. Failure to act in this area may mean losing our faithful, both Orthodox and Catholic. However, some traditional bind keeps us from doing what is necessary despite a clear perception of the sacred responsibility of the church for the welfare of her faithful.

We hold to the misconception that the people are to serve the church. Yet tradition tells us the church is for the people and that we as its leaders are responsible for the spiritual well-being of all its people. This is where the priesthood can play such an important role. The whole reorientation of the function of the clergy in Canada depends on a healthier perception of this situation, and of the people's needs. Improved pastoral education is necessary to make this service possible.

The change in the function of clergy from Ukraine to Canada was inevitable for purely sociological reasons. Social and family life in Ukraine was guided by a strong patriarchal order. In Canada, the family circle was narrowed to the nucleus of the single unit and by the very force of this new condition became more individualized and liberalized. Naturally, the patriarchal order gradually lost its force and the patriarchal figure disappeared. This process could not leave priests unaffected. The role of the priest also was narrowed, changing from the traditional authoritarian leader to the objective teacher. Now he is evolving further to the impartial counsellor.

Conclusion

The function of clergy, both Orthodox and Catholic, from Ukraine to Canada has, indeed, changed profoundly, and for many reasons. Because of the strong influence of the anti-clerical mentality of the Galician intelligentsia who represented a very small part of the first Ukrainian migration, the authority of the clergy, particularly the Ukrainian Orthodox clergy, was limited and the image of the priest demystified to a great extent. The prevailing secularization of Western culture was an additional factor in this process. This, to a considerable extent, affected the enrollment for theological studies and left the church authorities with little choice in the selection of candidates.

Now, the minimal educational level for entry to the faculty of theology is a bachelor's degree. The normal length of theological education is three years. The Eastern Orthodox theological programme requires a wide range of courses and does not leave time for in-depth studies or specialization. Yet the demand for involvement in a wide range of activities in the Ukrainian community is enormous. Most of these activities require specialization, which cannot be offered.

In light of this, one inevitably comes to the conclusion that our priesthood in Canada is limited and unprepared to meet the many demands that exist. The problem is equally acute for Orthodox and Catholic parish life. Furthermore, most Ukrainian Catholic clergy are educated in non-Ukrainian institutions. This does not enhance their ability to function in Ukrainian parishes.

The concern and issues raised require that we devote our efforts to developing a pastoral anthropology appropriate to the Canadian situation and models of pastoral care that serve the full range of needs present in our parishes.

NOTES

1. See S. Jarmus, "Fate of the Individual and Pastoral Care in Eastern Orthodox Theological Education—Some Steps Towards the Precepts of Pastoral Anthropology" (San Francisco Theological Seminary, 1981).
2. V. Pivnitsky, *Sviashchennik. Prigotovlenie k sviashchenstvu i zhizn sviaschennika* (The Priest. Preparation for Priesthood and Life of the Priest), 5th ed. (Kiev, 1897).
3. An analysis of various manuals on pastoral theology and programmes of pastoral education in the Eastern Orthodox schools of theology in North America is provided in S. Jarmus, "Fate of the Individual and Pastoral Care," 118–40.

4. See his *Pastyrskoe Bogoslovie* (Pastoral Theology), in Russian, Part One (Jordanville, New York: Holy Trinity Russian Orthodox Monastery, 1960), 207.

5. The Very Rev. Alexander Schmemann, "The Orthodox Worship" in *For Better Teaching—Teacher Training Manual for Orthodox Church Schools* (Crestwood, New York: Orthodox Christian Education Commission, 1959), 102.

6. Metropolitan Ilarion, *Pastyrske bohosloviie* (Pastoral Theology), (Winnipeg, Manitoba: St. Andrew's College, 1978). This manual was prepared and edited from notes on Metropolitan Ilarion's lectures by Fr. Hryhorij Udod.

7. Fr. Kallistos Ware, *The Orthodox Way* (Crestwood, New York: St. Vladimir's Seminary Press, 1979), 65.

8. Ibid., 61–2.

9. Ibid., 68.

10. See Alfred Adler, *The Science of Living*, ed. Heinz L. Amsbacher (New York: Anchor Books, 1969).

11. The material on pastoral anthropology and on the nature of human needs is taken from Jarmus, "Fate of the Individual and Pastoral Care," 149–56.

Ecclesiastical Institutions
in the Canadian Cultural Context

Casimir Kucharek

The Roots of "Latinization" and Its Context in the Experience of Ukrainian Catholics in Canada

We may define "Latinization" as the borrowing or taking of certain religious concepts and ritual practices from the Latin Rite Church and introducing them into the Ukrainian liturgical milieu. It is pure and simple hybridization. While this may be advantageous in plant or animal husbandry, it is abhorrent in liturgical matters. An illustration of this phenomenon occurs in the use of languages. If Ukrainian is mixed with English neither language is enriched. The result is only atrocious English or Ukrainian. The same applies to the mixing of liturgical practices and their setting. Liturgy is the external expression of deep inner religious feelings and convictions. It is the "soul" of a people exteriorized in their worship. When one introduces entirely foreign elements into that expression of ritual worship, it distorts and disfigures that worship.

Unfortunately, Ukrainian Catholics and, to a lesser extent, some of the Ukrainian Orthodox, have needlessly done just that. Despite having the richest liturgical heritage on earth, the Byzantine, we do live in the Western world and this is bound to have some influence on the way we do things.[1] By and large, however, there were no good "natural" or cultural reasons to prompt introduction of Latinization into Ukrainian liturgical practice. Rather, the causes of hybridization of Ukrainian liturgical usage by Latinization and, to a lesser degree, by adopting Russian or Muscovite characteristics, were varied and highly complex.

To understand the root causes, one must go back to the Union of Brest-Litovsk, publicly proclaimed in 1596. Before that time, there had been a process of liturgical reforms whose purpose was to standardize Ukrainian church practice. This uniformity had been largely achieved by the time of the Union.[2] Reaction to the Union, of course, was swift and fierce not only on religious, but also on social-political grounds. The enemies of the Union immediately claimed that the idea of reunification with the Holy See was one of Latinization and that the Ukrainian rite and church as well as its canonical prescriptions would become "Latin." In no uncertain terms, they labelled those favouring Union as "traitorous uniates" who betrayed Orthodoxy and their own "ridna," their own "native" church.

This does not square with the historical facts. At the Union its participants, both the representatives of the Holy See and the Ukrainian prelates, neither asked for nor desired any changes in Ukrainian rituals or practices or discipline (for example, married clergy). In fact, the Ukrainian prelates clearly asked for the retention in toto of their rite, liturgical usage and discipline and that all these matters be left in their own hands and jurisdiction. Nor were there any doctrinal or dogmatic difficulties to be resolved. Union with the Holy See, therefore, consisted chiefly of shifting ecclesiastical jurisdictional dependence from the Orthodox Patriarch of Constantinople to that of the Holy Father and the Holy See of Rome.

The Holy See concurred completely on all counts and gladly guaranteed that all liturgical matters would be left to the Ukrainian prelates and their successors. To quote from the official Constitution of Pope Clement VIII of 23 December 1595 regarding the Union: " . . . we receive, unite, join, annex and incorporate our members in Christ, and to enhance more greatly the meaning of our love for all the sacred rites and ceremonies themselves, which the bishops and clergy use, as established by the holy Greek Fathers in the Divine Offices, in the Holy Sacrifice of the Mass and in the administration of the rest of the Sacraments and other sacred functions... with Apostolic graciousness we permit, concede and allow (them) to the same Ruthenian bishops and clergy. . . . "[3] In fact, until the Ukrainian Catholic Church printed its own editions of its official liturgical books, the reunited Ukrainian bishops and clergy used the same books as the Orthodox. Indeed, the Popes hitherto have always maintained that Ukrainian Catholics should preserve their liturgical and ritual traditions. In fact, Pope Benedict XIV severely forbade even the highest Ukrainian prelate to introduce or change anything without the knowledge of the Holy See.

It is not my intention to enter into the various political vicissitudes and pressures during the two centuries before the Union, except to state that as early as 1620, encouraged by the Orthodox Patriarchs of Constantinople and Jerusalem and aided by certain Protestant groups, a dissident hierarchy was set up side by side with the Catholic one. More importantly, the fate of the Catholic Ukrainians varied according to the political powers into whose hands they fell. Eventually, the eparchies which were under the power of

Russia bowed to the persecutions and pressures, especially under Catherine II and Alexander I, and went back to Orthodoxy.

The Ukrainian Catholic Church had to withstand attacks on two fronts: on the one hand, it was criticized by the Orthodox as traitorous and a perversion of Orthodoxy and, on the other, it was viewed with great suspicion and influenced by Latin Catholicism in the Austro-Hungarian empire and later in Poland.

In 1642, a highly polemical work, *Epanorthosis* or *Perspective*, was published in Cracow. Its author, Kasiian Sakovych, was an Orthodox priest who became a Ukrainian Catholic and then embraced Latin Rite Catholicism. The *Epanorthosis* attacked the liturgical usages and ritual of the Ukrainian church, both Orthodox and Catholic. In the example and ideas of Sakovych the Orthodox polemicists had a potent weapon to support their view that joining the Ukrainian Catholic Church ultimately meant destroying the complex of Ukrainian liturgical practices and ritual.

Most of the Ukrainian Catholic clergy were mortified and demanded that Rome put Sakovych's work on the *Index of Forbidden Books*. However, a few were strongly influenced by the work, and began to introduce certain Latinizations into their liturgical practices, notably celebrating the "recited Divine Liturgy." The Polish clergy and civil powers used Sakovych to bolster their view that the Ukrainian Catholic Rite should be just a part of the Latin, while the civil powers saw the book as a means to "polonize" the Ukrainians and ultimately to make the Ukrainian territories an integral part of Poland.

At the risk of oversimplifying a very complicated process, we may say that henceforth the division of Ukrainian Catholic clergy and faithful into two camps had begun: those who favoured Latinization and those who zealously guarded the purity of liturgical practices and rite. In the former camp, most were well-intentioned, but misguided. In their opinion, Latinization would distance the people from Orthodoxy and, therefore, the temptation for them to return to it would be reduced.

The Ukrainian nobility, large landowners and the upper classes, chiefly for socio-economic reasons (either to maintain their positions or to better themselves), became thoroughly polonized and transferred to the Latin Rite despite the decree of Pope Urban VIII forbidding them to do so. Consequently, the intellectual, educated elements had no interest in maintaining the purity of the Ukrainian Rite. Indirectly, this also meant that any social climbers among the clergy tried to emulate the upper classes by favouring Latinization.

As a result, Ukrainian liturgical purity and uniformity was inexorably losing ground. By the time of the Synod of Zamość in 1720 there were many Latinizations. Despite such transgressions and the lack of uniformity in liturgical usages, the Synod itself, because of the delicate nature of the matter, neither sanctioned nor forbade them. The exception was the celebration of the Divine Liturgy and even in this the Synod confined itself to decreeing four points: 1) the Holy Father was to be commemorated in the appropriate points of the Liturgy, 2) the words "and of the Son" (the filioque) were inserted into the Creed, 3) the liturgical sponge was used for wiping the diskos after Communion was forbidden and 4) it was forbidden to practice the *teplota,* the addition of warm water into the chalice prior to Communion. It is unfortunate that the Synod did not forbid further Latinization of the Rite.

Latinization was also enhanced because during the eighteenth and nineteenth centuries the Ukrainian Catholic Church did not have its own major or minor seminaries. Hence the Ukrainian Catholic bishops had to send their candidates for priesthood to Latin Rite seminaries in Poland, Prague, Vienna and Rome. It was inevitable that these future priests and bishops would imbibe the spirit and spirituality of the Latin Rite and this, in turn, would show itself in further glorification and introduction of the Latin Rite in their home eparchies. This led to a number of changes characteristic of Roman tradition.

The amice and alb, for example, were worn instead of the *sticharion* (the inside vestment in the form of a tunic), which is distinctively styled, of any colour, and of any good quality cloth. Royal Doors of the iconostasis were opened from the beginning to the end of the Divine Liturgy. A bell was rung at the consecration before Communion. Kneeling during the reception of Holy Communion became the norm. The *Sluzhebnyk* itself was modelled on the Latin Missal (with all the propers) and, like the Latin Missal, was moved from side to side of the altar at a "low mass." Two washings of the fingers and the sequence of liturgical colours for vestments—unknown elsewhere in the East, which has only two categories, the joyful and sorrowful—emulated the Latin Rite. Concelebration took place only on certain pontifical occasions and the deaconate was increasingly regarded as a transitory state in preparation for the priesthood rather than as a permanent institution. Consequently a deacon or deacons rarely assisted at the Divine Liturgy.

Such Latinizations were practiced extensively in some places, resulting in chaos instead of ritual purity and uniformity. The Synod of Lviv in 1891 missed an opportunity to end that chaos. Its pre-Synodal commission, which included a good liturgist, Father Isidore Dolnytsky, prepared a series of liturgical proposals, especially on the Divine Liturgy and the *Proskomedia.* The entire Title V dealt with this matter. Title V, however, was not even read to the assembly of prelates and clergy, nor was it discussed, and therefore it was not included in the propositions passed at the Synod. A golden opportunity was lost.

When Ukrainian Catholic immigrants came to Canada, they brought with them this chaotic, Latinized state of liturgical affairs. If anything, it was compounded in a Canadian milieu that was either Roman Catholic or Protestant and in a world that was entirely Western in culture and outlook. As in the old country, any candidates for the priesthood had to be trained in Latin Rite seminaries with their attendant Latin spirituality and outlook. Except for the Basilian Fathers, the Ukrainian Catholic Church did not have a seminary of its own until recently.

The Ukrainian Catholic Church in Canada is still feeling the effects of Latinization today. Most of its prelates, for example, still wear Latin cassocks of purplish-red colour, instead of the Eastern *riasa*, Latin skull-caps and pectoral crosses, instead of the panagia. Some even wear white gloves which they remove for the initial washing of the fingers at the beginning of the Pontifical Liturgy. Presumably, since most Ukrainian Catholic bishops still wear pectoral crosses, they frown on ordinary priests who conform to Byzantine tradition. Many Ukrainian Catholic bishops insist on a "bishop's throne" being erected for Pontifical Liturgies during parish visitations (cathedrals have installed permanent ones), forgetting that the bishop's cathedra is the *hornoie sidalyshche*, a seat elevated on a step or two higher than the floor but behind the altar, a tradition dating back to the third or fourth century.

The church in Western Ukraine shared an ancient Eastern tradition of building its architectual church structures according to the liturgical tradition. In Canada, church architecture suffered too. Two domes, aping Latin practice, began to appear on churches. The Byzantine use of one, three, five or seven domes on the churches was lost and forgotten.[4] Many Ukrainian churches in Canada no longer even face the East.

Most of the churches in Canada have no doors from the nave, the church of the faithful, to the sacristies. Hence, people, females included, have to traverse the sanctuary, the very Holy of Holies, in order to consult with the priest before or after the services. Unlike the Latin, Byzantine rubrical prescriptions strictly prohibit females in the sanctuary whatever the reason.

Rectangular altars, aping the Latin, replaced the completely square ones prescribed by the Byzantine Rite. Similarly, three Byzantine altar cloths, hanging to the ground on all sides, were replaced by one, like the Latin, which hangs only from two sides. Latin crucifixes replaced the icon type; Latin style censers were used, instead of the shorter-chained Byzantine type which facilitates the traditional censing style; Latin patens were substituted for the Byzantine diskoses. These latter items were obtained under the pretext that the religious goods stores did not carry the Byzantine ones. Holy water fonts are still evident in Ukrainian Catholic churches, as are the stations of the cross. Their concomitant devotion replaces the moving and beautiful Byzantine Lenten ones.

Far more serious, however, is the nearly total lack of orientation, the interpretation, the "feeling," the "spirit" of Eastern theology. The clergy, most of whom were trained in Latin seminaries, inevitably imbibed Latin ascetic theology and spirituality; the same can be said of moral and dogmatic theol-

73

ogy. Thomism and Scholasticism, unknown in Eastern Christian tradition, became the rule of the day. For example, Cardinal Iosyf Slipy's theological writings are in many places a mere rehash of Latin theology manuals.

Prior to Vatican II, Western liturgical manuals had degenerated into ritual "cookbooks" for seminarians and priests who mechanically followed the myriad rubrics contained therein without regard for their meaning, spirit or historical perspective. Ascetic theology was confined chiefly to Tanquerey and the French school, which was tainted with Jansenism, which exhibited great piety and asceticism, but was harsh and unbending.

Latin moral and dogmatic theology also suffered. Moral theology was permeated with heavy doses of casuistry and its seemingly needless and sophistical distinctions. For example, eating less than an ounce of meat on Friday was venially sinful; more than an ounce, mortally sinful. . . yet the people of Spain and its former imperial territories were not bound to this law. Nor were the wealthy, who could afford lobster, shrimp or crab, because that was not considered to be meat. In Canada, this Latin influence has not ended yet. A married Ukrainian Catholic, who has finished his theological studies, may be ordained in Yugoslavia; then, he can come back to Canada as a married priest, but the person who remains in Canada cannot be ordained as a married man.

Here is another example. Unlike the Eastern perspective, which has always stressed the change of heart, repentance, in confession, the Latins emphasized the number of sins committed, the kinds of sins, not only mortal or venial, but any circumstances which changed the species of sin. Easterners never concerned themselves much with numbers or species of sin: if something was sinful, they did not do it, as all sin wounds Christ and His Mystical Body.

Latin sacramental theology was also debased before the reforms of Vatican II. There was a world of difference between Western and Eastern Catholic understanding and practice of the sacraments, though each believed in the same sacred reality. The Western approach, for example, with its penchant for precision and legalism, with its concomitant tendency to dissect, to break up all phenomena into their component parts and to place them in order, evolved differently from that of the East. The Western outlook was interested more in the "formal," the "technical" aspects, in the "validity" of the sacraments. With the advent of the hylomorphic theory and its near canonization, Western theologians became involved with essential, non-essential, and integral elements of the sacraments to the extent that they ceased to relate the sacraments to the total Christian life, compartmentalizing them as independent units, isolated from the person who receives them. Perhaps such methods developed precision, but it seems that the spirit, the "soul," was very nearly lost.

Nowhere was this more evident than in the meaning of the Eucharist. The abstract, though precise, speculation transformed the most central act of Christianity into the "Eucharistic species," "the species of the Blessed Sacrament," or "Eucharistic elements," as if Christ, who was present there, did not matter. Whole sets of abstract questions formulated by Western theologians were designed, it seems, to compartmentalize the tremendous reality of the Eucharist. The one, organic, living, all-embracing act of Christ and of the whole ecclesia was gradually downplayed or forgotten as interest was concentrated on essential or non-essential parts, elements, moments, formulae, and conditions of validity, to the point that the very notion of the "Eucharist" seems to have become irrelevant. The real meaning of the liturgy receded, obscured in the mists of rubrical prescriptions and measured movements and gestures. This resulted in a worship that was technically correct but internally formalistic; it was mere rubrical technology. Ukrainian Catholic seminarians imbibed such teaching in Latin seminaries and were never educated in the Eastern view.

Eastern theology has always looked to the sacraments in their totality, stressing the hidden, invisible aspects of the "mysteries." This authentic Byzantine tradition is evident in almost every form of liturgical and spiritual life. The iconostasis "hides" the sanctuary, the "holy of holies." The veil of the Royal Doors further hides the most holy, the Eucharist, from the gaze of profane eyes. Even devotion to the Eucharistic Christ tends not to be separated from its central act, the Divine Liturgy. These so-called "Eucharistic" devotions of Roman Catholicism are almost non-existent in the Eastern churches. There is no Benediction of the Blessed Sacrament outside the Liturgy, no special "visits" to the Blessed Sacrament. These devotions are aimed at counteracting the "heresies" of Protestant teaching which deny the true presence of Christ in the sacrament. Eastern Christianity never had to defend itself against such a teaching. God's presence was always perceived in the act of going into a church, which is heaven on earth, and in the mysterious quality of the divine as seen in icons. Iconography itself is permeated with the spirit of "hiding" the sacred: where Western art exposed the Sacred Heart of Jesus or the Immaculate Heart of Mary, Eastern icons simply portrayed Christ the Lover of Humankind.

There is a fundamental difference between the Byzantines and Westerners in the interpretation of sacred images. They are merely art forms in the West, representations however sacred of one whose presence is elsewhere, in heaven. For the Byzantine Christian, the icon is a veritable theophany, a dynamic manifestation of divine energy at work on earth. Hence, the person represented is in some spiritual way actually present through inspiration in the icon. From this presence flow streams of grace upon the sinful world, purifying and sanctifying it. To define this presence is as difficult as explaining the Shekinah or the mysterious presence of Christ amid two or three gathered together in his name (Matthew 18:20).

The mystical teaching concerning icons stems from the idea central to all Eastern typology that the church building is "Heaven on earth." That is why iconography was always much more than an art form. To be worthy of the task, the ancient icon painters prayed and fasted for days before taking up the brush. Only after proper spiritual preparation could they communicate the Divine through their image-making. Icons represent human forms that have been "regenerated into eternity," holy bodies of persons transfigured by grace in prayer and fasting. Iconographers convey these theological meanings through symbolical colours and forms.

The presence in the icons of the holy ones depicted explains their intense veneration by Eastern Christians. Icons would be placed in the east corner of a room, in a small shrine, the *kivot* (holy table tabernacle), encased in glass and lined with silk or velvet. Among Ukrainians this corner was called "red," which is synonymous with "beautiful" in the Old Slavonic language.[5] It is still sometimes used to denote something extraordinary, festive or exceptionally important.[6] Even the most humble peasant tried to decorate this corner with immaculate linen towels elaborately embroidered at both ends. Before the icons, a small altar lamp burned day and night like the sanctuary lamp of Western churches.

Because of belief in the mysterious presence of Christ, His Mother or the saint in the icon, in Christian Russia and Ukraine everyone entering his own home or visiting a friend would bow before the icons and make the sign of the cross before greeting his family or host. The same "presence" forestalled any unseemly conduct, for it was difficult to lie, cheat or to be impure or brutal before an icon, "in front of the saints." How deeply ingrained this feeling was in the lives of ordinary people is shown by the old proverb: before committing a foul deed, "carry out the saints," the holy icons. Reports from the USSR state that even today, after sixty-eight years of atheistic propaganda, many visitors to the museums and art galleries, where so many old icons are exhibited, instinctively take off their caps before the holy images. To them these are not simply museum pieces.

Another spiritual heritage lost to the Ukrainian Catholic clergy, trained as they were in Latin seminaries, was the idea of and devotion to the Kenotic Christ. As the Slavs began to know Christ better, they discovered Him to mean love and compassion, sharing a crust of bread with the hungry, a glass of cool water with the thirsty. His eyes were all-seeing, not only as a stern Judge as the Greeks loved to depict Him, but so that He might notice and remember the smallest good deed performed in His name. He also signified patient suffering and humiliation. Above all, He was gentle and loving. As Dostoevsky, who knew the soul of his people better perhaps than any other, wrote:

THE ROOTS OF "LATINIZATION"

I affirm that our people were enlightened a long time ago, by accepting Christ and His teaching. The people know everything. . . . They learned in the churches where during the centuries, they heard prayers and songs that are better than sermons. . . . Their chief school of Christianity was the ages of endless suffering endured in the course of history when abandoned by all, oppressed by all, working for all, they remained all alone with Christ the Comforter, whom they received then in their soul and who saved them from despair.

Eastern Slavs have admirably combined the ideal of the suffering Christ with a prayer that is at once simple and rich, the Jesus Prayer: "Lord, Jesus Christ, Son of God, have pity on me, a sinner." That is all, but it is repeated over and over again. It combines the plea of the blind beggar at Jericho (Mk 10:48) with the humble request of the publican (Lk 18:13). The word "Lord" confesses Christ's lordship (Pantocrator) over all. The words "Jesus Christ" are an expression of belief in the Lord as Saviour (Jesus) and as Messiah (Christ), the anointed one, who is priest and prince. An explicit confession of faith in His divinity is contained in the words "Son of God." The original expression "have mercy" (the Greek *eleison* and the Slavonic *pomylui*) contain elements of both healing and love in their root forms; hence, they petition Jesus not only for salvation or for healing but also beg for God's love. In English, perhaps a more accurate way of expressing the original content would be to say: "In Your compassion heal me, love me, even though I am a sinner!" Despite the common use of this magnificent traditional prayer, Ukrainian Catholics influenced by Roman practice adopted the rosary, an astonishing substitution.

While Latin theologians spoke of "sanctifying grace gained," the Byzantines spoke of theosis or deification. The Eastern Fathers, basing themselves on the Scriptures, wrote of man's "assimilation to God" (St. Clement of Alexandria), that God became man that man might become God (St. Athanasius); and that Christ would make us as God (St. Gregory of Nazianzus). St. Basil perhaps put it best:

. . . the Spirit is present in each of those who receives Him as if each recipient were the only one, and yet He pours out total and sufficient grace on all men. He is enjoyed by all who share Him according to the measure of their respective capacities. . . .

Shining upon those that are cleansed of every stain, He makes them spiritual by communion with Himself. As bright, transparent bodies, when a sunbeam falls on them, become brilliant too and shine with a fresh brightness of their own, so souls in whom the Spirit dwells, through His illumination, become spiritual and send forth their grace to others. From this source comes... a heavenly citizenship, a place in the chorus of angels, joy without end, abiding in God, the being made like unto God and, highest of all, the being made God (*Theon genesthai*)![7]

Many other Eastern concepts or perspectives on theology were lost to Ukrainian Catholics because their clergy were trained in Latin Seminaries. Simeon of Thessalonika put it well when he wrote to the Latins:

You use evasive arguments, you flourish syllogisms; and I will show that you alter the meaning of the Holy Scripture and the Fathers by false interpretation, that you follow the heathens, not the Fathers. If I wanted to, I could bring forward better syllogisms than yours against your scholastical reasonings—but I do not want to. I ask for proofs from the Fathers and what they wrote; you reply with Aristotle and Plato, or even your new doctors. Against them, I set up the (Galilean) fishermen, with their straightforward sayings, their true wisdom, and their apparent foolishness. I will disclose that mystery of godliness that St. Paul looked on as such strong evidence. I will make foolishness of your wisdom with the words, "Leave these vain matters alone. If anyone proclaims a gospel to you other than the gospel you have received, let him be accursed." Thus will you be brought to confusion, and I shall glory in the glory of my fathers, for the Cross has not lost its power, even though the preaching of it seems foolishness to some.[8]

By discussing the root causes of "Latinization," in contrast to the spirit or "soul" of authentic Byzantine-Slav ritual practice, this paper is meant to be a contribution, however slight, to a better appreciation of the liturgical heritage of Ukrainians.

NOTES

1. For example, in the Western world the colour black is associated with mourning and death; hence, the wearing of black including the priest's vestments at the services for the dead may be more expressive of mourning to Ukrainians living in the Western world than the more traditional Byzantine red (according to Simeon of Thessalonica [*Lib. de Sacra quaestio*, 71], purple; according to Demetrius of Bulgaria [*Praesul Juris Graecorum*, bk. 5], red).
2. The Metropolitan See of Kiev as well as the eparchies of Vladimir, Lutsk and Polotsk. Pinsk and Kholm (Cheom) were reunited with the Holy See in 1596. The eparchies of Lviv and Przemyśl joined later, in 1692 and 1700 respectively.

3. Pontificum Romanorum, Historiam Ucrainae, Vol. I (Rome, 1953), 242–3.
4. In Eastern Christian tradition one dome = one God; three = the three Persons of the Trinity; five = five ancient Sees of the Church or Christ and the four evangelists; seven = seven sacraments; nine = nine choirs of angels; thirteen = Christ and the twelve apostles.
5. So that when the faithful pray, they too face the East like the early Christians. Early Christians regarded the East, whence the sun rises, as the side of holiness and light because Christ had been called the Oriens, the Sun of Justice, the Sun of Truth, the light of the world. They considered the West, where the sun sets, as the side of darkness, the place where Satan dwells. Even the baptismal ceremonial dating back to the fourth century received the renunciations of the devil while facing the West, whereas the syntaxis, the joining of the ranks of Christ, His camp, is always said facing the East.
6. Red Square in Moscow, for example, is not a Communist appellation but the old name of the largest and most beautiful square of the tsar's capital.
7. Basil, *De Spr. sant.*, I, 22 and 23. PG 32, 109AC.
8. (*Dial. adv. Omnes Haereses.* c. 29).

Andrii Krawchuk

Social Tradition and Social Change: The Ukrainian Catholic Church and Emigration to Canada Prior to World War II[1]

The very first Ukrainian immigrants to Canada were peasants. Priests followed considerably later and when they did, the only two classes of Ukrainian society in nineteenth-century Galicia were transplanted to the Canadian context. The reasons for this peculiar social stratification were historical. After four centuries of Polish rule, Ukrainian society had lost most of its native nobility through Polonization. The two classes that were left—the clergy and the peasantry—remained distinct and separate throughout the Austrian period. The Catholic empire had ensured this by granting special privileges to the Greek Catholic clergy that firmly entrenched their superiority over the peasants in the social scheme. Professor Roman Szporluk once referred to that clerical class as a "privilegentsia," and the coinage is appropriate, for indeed Ukrainian priests enjoyed equal status with Roman Catholics, a higher level of education than was available to the peasant, certain legal exemptions, and economic independence from their parishioners (by virtue of their office, priests received from the imperial government small salaries and large tracts of arable land from which profits could be reaped after the peasants had ploughed the soil). All of this instilled political conservatism among the Greek Catholic clergy. They tended to be strongly supportive of a monarchical, hierarchical system of social organization in general and of the Austrian emperor in particular.

Nor did this ideological conservatism limit itself merely to a theoretical acceptance of principles; it was reinforced in practice, in everyday life. For in the Austrian context, in matters pertaining to Ukrainian affairs, the Greek

Catholic clergy were in a position of political leadership. This was manifested in various ways. First, they were recognized by law as superior to the peasants. Second, the lack of a Ukrainian middle class and the tendency of the clergy to discourage their children from marrying outside the class perpetuated their position as a sort of "untouchable" caste. Third, the Greek Catholic bishops were granted a special *ex-officio* status in the Austrian parliament. Finally, most of the Ukrainian secular intelligentsia that emerged after the 1860s were the offspring of clerical families. Thus, they tended to share the conservatism and deference to hierarchical authority espoused by their forebears. This economic, social and political cultivation of a loyal upper class of Ukrainian clerics was a policy that Austria conducted in her own self-interest.

At the same time, the Austrian loyalty of the Ukrainian episcopate had its advantages for Ukrainian immigrants in Canada; it provided a lifeline that linked Lviv, Vienna and the Ukrainian Catholic community in Canada. Like the Ukrainian Russophile movement in Canada, which was supported by the Russian tsar, Ukrainian Catholics were linked through their bishops with the Austrian emperor. This made it possible for interventions to be made on their behalf at the highest level.[2]

The first Greek Catholic priests who served the Ukrainian pioneers in the late 1890s had not accompanied the settlers from Ukraine. Rather, they came to Canada from the United States. Their presence was generally appreciated by the Ukrainian settlers who, given a choice, generally preferred their own priests to French Roman Catholics. Those Greek Catholic priests established the first Ukrainian Catholic parishes in the prairie provinces and promoted the cultural life of the people. The first four priests were Nestor Dmytriw, Pavlo Tymkevych, Damaskyn Polivka OSBM and Ivan Zaklynsky.

This early phase of Ukrainian Catholic life in Canada was short-lived, however, and each of these pioneer priests eventually returned to the United States. Although the purported reasons for their departures may have varied from case to case, they revealed three key factors in the early religious life of Ukrainian settlers in Canada. First, because of their extreme poverty, they could not financially support a parish priest. Second, there were conflicts with the Roman Catholic clergy who considered the Eastern-rite ministry an intrusion into their own jurisdictions. Third, even in the early years of settlement, Catholic-Orthodox tensions among Ukrainians had begun to divide colonies and even, as in the case of Edna-Star, Alberta, split a parish in two. All of these factors discouraged the first Ukrainian Catholic priests from staying in Canada for more than a year or two.

Whether Catholic or Orthodox, the first Ukrainian settlers had to pay unwilling allegiance to ecclesiastical structures that were already established in Canada. Greek Catholics, who were mostly from Galicia and Carpatho-Ukraine, found themselves under the jurisdiction of Roman Catholic hierarchs. Orthodox Ukrainians from Bukovyna and Eastern Ukraine were subsumed under the Russian Orthodox Church. The jurisdictional question affected the Eastern-rite priests as well. Inter-ritual quarrels within the Catholic camp centred on disagreements about the appropriateness of certain ritual practices and about the legitimacy of Roman authority over Greek Catholics.[3] Moreover, Greek Catholic clerics affirmed their allegiance to the Archeparchy of Lviv and, together with their parish communities, were most concerned about retaining the deeds on all church property.

The jurisdictional conflict, an inevitable consequence of the lack of a Ukrainian Catholic bishop in Canada in the early years, had many more ramifications for the religious life of Ukrainian pioneers. Perhaps their single most pressing issue was the prolonged shortage of Ukrainian Catholic priests in Canada. This problem did not exist for lack of clerics in Galicia who were able and willing to emigrate with their own people. Rather, the Roman Catholic Church in Canada took the position of jurisdictional exclusivity and refused to entertain exceptions to its own tradition of 'compulsory priestly celibacy: only those Greek Catholic pastors who were celibate would be admitted into Canada. This was identical to the line followed by the Roman Catholic Church in the United States, and it had the full support of the Vatican.[4] For Greek Catholics, however, such a policy was disastrous because it in effect blocked a badly needed influx of priests from the homeland where, in 1894, only 3 per cent of the priests were celibate.[5] The shortage of priests in Canada became an even more urgent problem in 1898, in the wake of a large wave of immigration from Europe.

Yet, despite the conflict over jurisdiction, Roman Catholics were not insensitive to the difficulties of the Greek Catholics.[6] In 1898, following intensive and successful proselytizing of Greek Catholics by Russian Orthodox clerics, the Roman Catholic Bishop Albert Pascal of Prince Albert travelled to Vienna, Rome and Lviv to request assistance in bringing Ruthenian priests into Canada. Two years later, another Latin-rite priest, Rev. Albert Lacombe, undertook a similar mission to Europe, in the course of which he proposed the formation of an episcopal see for Greek Catholics in Canada.[7] This initiative indicated that some French Roman Catholic priests were not only in tune with the problems and aspirations of Ukrainian Catholics in Canada, but were also willing to promote a constructive alternative.

Throughout the rest of this pre-episcopal period in the history of Ukrainian Canadian Catholicism, the Roman Catholic Church continued to show considerable sensitivity to the spiritual and social welfare of Ukrainians, particularly when it was threatened by sectarian agitation. Such concerns motivated Archbishop Adélard Langevin of St. Boniface to travel to Europe in 1904.[8] In Vienna, Langevin approached the emperor for financial assistance to build churches and schools for Ukrainians in Canada. His efforts appear to have been successful, for on his return to Canada, he funded the construction of a

Greek Catholic church in Winnipeg. Roman Catholics of St. Albert followed his example and assisted the building of another church in Edmonton. As well, the Roman Catholic hierarchy began to call upon its own priests to volunteer for work among Ukrainians.

Another instance of this same sensitivity occurred in 1909, at the first Canadian Synod in Quebec City. It was there that the papal nuncio Donatto Sbaretti read a brief on the situation of the Ruthenian Church in Canada. The brief, entitled "A memorandum on the attempts at schism and heresy among the Ruthenians in Western Canada," had been written by the Redemptorist Achille Delaere.[9] In it, Delaere described how Greek Catholics were joining the Seraphimite Church and the Independent Orthodox Church and proposed that, given the limited ability of the Lviv Archeparchy to supply [celibate] priests for Canada, French priests from Quebec should take up the urgent task of serving Ukrainian Catholics in the western provinces. And, in order to overcome the cultural gap between the two rites, the Roman Catholic bishops of Canada sought Vatican permission for some of their priests to change to the Eastern rite. Such permission was granted in 1906 and by the time of Bishop Budka's installation six years later, nine Latin-rite priests had transferred to the Greek Catholic rite.[10]

The decisive push for a Ukrainian Catholic episcopate came from the church in Galicia. First, steps had to be taken to supply priests for existing parishes and to establish new ones where they were needed. Accordingly, in 1901 Metropolitan Andrei Sheptytsky sent Rev. Vasyl Zholdak O.S.B.M. to study the problems of Ukrainian Catholics in Canada.[11] Zholdak toured Canada for several months, then returned to Lviv with a situation report. He observed that Ruthenian parish communities were strongly opposed to Roman Catholic incorporation of their properties. In addition to Protestant proselytizing, a group of Polish priests had been trying to convert settlers to Roman Catholicism by slandering the Ukrainian priests from the United States and by heaping scorn on Eastern-rite Catholicism in general.[12] Since the American connection was established by the first Ukrainian priests in Canada, the Ukrainian communities saw a constructive alternative in the United States and were placing themselves under the protectorate of the Association of the Ruthenian [Ukrainian] Church Parishes of the United States and Canada. In 1902, Zholdak returned to Canada, with three Basilian priests who proceeded to establish that order in Canada. They were followed in 1903 by two more Basilians, and another two in the following year.

The Basilian mission in Canada was a constructive first step. It provided the first stable foothold for the Ukrainian church in Canada. This stability was provided by the support of the Lviv Archeparchy in Galicia and that of the Ukrainian pioneers in Canada, whose economic status was showing gradual improvement. The mission served also to ease somewhat the tensions between Greek and Roman Catholics. Since they worked as a team, the

SOCIAL TRADITION AND SOCIAL CHANGE

Basilians were not as vulnerable to the criticisms of those who did not understand the nature of Eastern-rite Catholicism. Subsequently, Archbishop
Langevin appointed Zholdak as administrator of the Greek Catholic Church
in Canada, thus conferring a degree of Roman Catholic recognition on that
church.

With the issue of a Ukrainian bishop still unresolved in the first decade of
the century, a movement for an independent Greek Catholic ecclesiastical
province in Canada had emerged. Reflecting the general Ukrainian dissatisfaction with the exclusion of married priests from the country and the apparent lack of progress in installing a Ukrainian bishop, a public manifestation was held in Winnipeg on 28 August 1910. Because it was known that
Metropolitan Sheptytsky was attending the International Eucharistic Congress in Montréal at that very time, the assembly in Winnipeg sent him an appeal outlining the concerns of Ukrainians in Canada. So before he returned
home Sheptytsky travelled to Western Canada and there observed first-hand
the actual religious situation among Ukrainians. Most communities welcomed him respectfully, but in Winnipeg he was careful to avoid the Church
of Saints Vladimir and Olga, which had declared itself independent and did
not recognize any higher ecclesiastical authority. In Vancouver, he was
pelted with rotten eggs by socialists who did not care for his policies in
Galicia and, in particular, objected to his condemnation of the political
violence in Galicia.

On his return to Lviv, Sheptytsky wrote two documents. The first was the
pastoral letter, *Kanadiiskym Rusynam* (To the Canadian Ruthenians, 1911),
in which he urged Ukrainian Catholics to remain faithful to their church, to
show unity, and to respect the laws of Canada. A contemporary observer,
Panteleimon Bozhyk, suggested that this document had a positive effect in
Canada. First, it cut short the exodus of Greek Catholics to Russian
Orthodoxy and Presbyterianism and even encouraged the return of some to
their own church. Some Presbyterians, apparently "too ashamed to return to
Greek Catholicism," at least decided to return to the Eastern rite, albeit in
the form of Russian Orthodoxy. Second, the document gave encouragement
to the sixteen Greek Catholic priests in Canada, whose thankless task was
made all the more difficult by occasionally ungrateful parishioners. Finally,
in Bozhyk's words, the document "also strengthened to a certain extent the
Orthodox Church, especially among the Bukovynians who began to work
and to hold fast to their faith with all the more zeal when they saw that the
Greek Catholics were doing it so well."[13]

Sheptytsky's second document was an appeal to the Roman Catholic
bishops of Canada, in which he developed his own argument for the establishment of a Ukrainian Catholic episcopate in Canada. In his "Address on
the Ruthenian Question," Sheptytsky gave the following breakdown of
Greek Catholic parishes in Canada: one parish incorporated by the Roman

Catholic Church, ten by the Basilian Order, ten referred to simply as "Greek Catholic," and seventy-two undesignated and awaiting a Ukrainian bishop. To emphasize this highly precarious state of affairs, Sheptytsky supplemented these figures with his own assessment of the Eastern mentality:

> In their activity the people of the East move as one body—individuals are hardly ever capable of a thought or an action different from those of the body. . . the pastor wins everything if he succeeds in getting a hold of the mentality of the people and creating an opinion. . . . But if on the contrary public opinion turns against him, and if he does not succeed in subduing it, then his influence, confined to individuals only, amounts to nothing at all in comparison with the totality. The 'hromada' is an idea that is peculiar to the Ukrainian people and refers to the population of a village, which has such a high degree of solidarity that its social and moral unity are so fused together as would allow us to compare it to a large family or to a regiment that adheres to one discipline. The favorite proverb of the Ruthenians is, "The 'hromada' is a great, big person."[14]

In this way, Sheptytsky drove home the point that the urgency of the problem was not simply a matter of a few individuals or parishes. Rather, in his view, the stakes were much higher and could potentially involve the denominational transfer of most, if not all, Ukrainians in Canada, whose numbers he estimated at between 120,000 and 150,000.[15]

Sheptytsky's argument achieved its intended result, for in July, 1911 the bishops of Western Canada sent a letter to the papal nuncio in Ottawa indicating that they no longer had any objection to the establishment of an independent ecclesiastical province for Ukrainians in Canada. In 1912 such a province was instituted and on 6 December of that year Bishop Nykyta Budka arrived in Canada as its first bishop.

Budka had studied theology in Lviv and had pursued doctoral studies at the University of Vienna where, in 1909, he had submitted a dissertation titled "The discipline of the Greek Church in light of the polemics in the period of the schism."[16] Prior to his departure for Canada, he had served as the prefect of the Greek Catholic Seminary in Lviv. He had also been involved in the ecclesiastical judiciary and in emigration affairs, notably through the St. Raphael's Ukrainian Immigrants' Welfare Society. Arriving in Canada at the age of thirty-five, he had full jurisdiction over the newly formed Greek Catholic province in Canada; unlike Bishop Soter Ortynsky in the United States, Budka was completely independent of the local Roman Catholic hierarchy.

The young bishop set out immediately to organize the affairs of his church. First, he incorporated the church as the Ruthenian Greek Catholic Church of Canada under an episcopal charter passed by parliament in 1913. Eighty parishes were subsumed under this church. Most had previously been incorporated with the two religious orders in Canada or with the United States province of Bishop Ortynsky. Now all were re-incorporated under provincial charters.[17]

Also in 1913, Bishop Budka convoked the first Canadian *sobor* (council) of Ukrainian Catholic priests in Yorkton. The *sobor* adopted the Regulations of the Ruthenian Greek Catholic Church in Canada, which were guidelines for the clergy. And in order to counteract the shortage of clergy (in 1912, there were only twenty-two priests), Budka sent a number of Ruthenian students to study at the Roman Catholic seminary in Toronto, under the direction of Rev. Amvrozii Redkevych. He also requested that more priests be sent from Ukraine. In 1913, six more came to Canada.

Unfortunately, these and other constructive efforts by Budka to lay out the organizational foundations of his church were overshadowed by a lack of foresight in external matters. On 27 July 1914, a few days before Canada entered World War I, Budka issued a pastoral letter supporting the Austrian war effort and calling on Ukrainians in Canada to join the Austrian side in Europe.[18] Budka may not have foreseen the implications of this act, but after Canada declared war Canadian suspicions about the real loyalties of former Austrian subjects living in Canada turned into concern for national security. Under the War Measures Act (1914), thousands of Canadian immigrants, including an estimated 5,000 Ukrainians, were designated ''enemy aliens'' and were placed into internment camps.[19] Budka's letter may not have caused this, but it measures clearly did not help matters; nor did his second pastoral letter, a hastily written about-face urging support for Canada.[20] The damage was done, and Budka had incurred the enmity of many who would never forgive him.

This incident, however, must be understood in light of the cultural transition that was behind it. Budka had literally been plucked from the Austrian social and political context and inserted into the Canadian political environment. He could not have been adequately prepared for the transition: there was little time between the Roman Catholic bishops' decision in 1911 and his arrival in Canada the following year. Once in Canada, he devoted his full attention to the internal organization of his church, rather than to resolving the imminent question of loyalty to the British Commonwealth. Thus, when it came to settling external matters, his first impulse was to act as an Austrian loyalist. Indeed, that very sentiment was prevalent in Galicia when the war broke out: Ukrainians believed that a victorious Austria would bow to their national aspirations, and consequently all Ukrainian political parties gave their support to Austria. Budka's judgement clearly rested on the same sort of reasoning, but 1914 was not an opportune time in Canada for such thoughts.

The nature and the extent of the mounting opposition to Bishop Budka can only be understood in light of the social evolution of Ukrainians in the Canadian context. By the time of Budka's arrival in 1912, his pioneer predecessors had developed an unprecedented thirst for independence. Among those with a religious orientation, independence meant an autonomous Ukrainian Catholic Church with Ukrainian priests and a Ukrainian bishop who was not answerable to local Roman Catholic authorities. The appointment of a Ukrainian bishop in the United States in 1908 fuelled this movement in Canada. Moreover, Ukrainians in Canada were generally in solidarity with the movement toward political autonomy in Galicia and began to feel that they, too, should be allowed to stand socially and economically on their own feet in Canada.

A second feature of the social evolution of Ukrainians was a twofold process of secularization that was, up to World War I, uniquely Canadian. It was not the secular current of Galician radicalism inspired by Drahomanov and Franko, some of whose followers emigrated to Canada. Their secularizing work was indeed carried on in Canada, but it was continuous with its roots in Ukraine. Alongside it, a specifically Canadian form of secularization was in progress. The Canadian social context offered upward social mobility, and many Ukrainians became teachers, journalists, editors and lawyers. Thus a new class of educated lay professionals began to emerge in Canada, less dependent on the clergy than the peasants had been. Second, there was a parallel process of secularization at work within the Greek Catholic parish communities. It was the inevitable result of parishes having to do without sufficient priests for almost two decades and was evident, for example, in the "non-aligned" parishes which retained their Christian roots but severed ties with any form of ecclesiastical authority.

The prevailing mood of independence and of secularism among Ukrainians in Canada meant that Galician socialism and radicalism were no longer the only agents of social change and consciousness-raising. The Canadian socio-political setting in which Ukrainians now lived, though initially hostile toward them, nevertheless promised a greater measure of democracy and equality than had been possible under the Austrian monarchy.

The first signs of trouble came when the opposition to Bishop Budka would not abate. Whether or not he deserved it, the Ukrainian public's evolution toward independence and secularism, along with a broader understanding of democracy and equality, led it to perceive Budka's efforts as unduly overbearing and authoritarian. Concern was also voiced about the security of deeds on church property since the episcopal charter that Budka had signed contained no explicit provision for a Ukrainian bishop: it was feared that the pope could arbitrarily appoint a non-Ukrainian as Budka's successor, which would mean the loss of titles on all land holdings of the Greek Catholic Church. Moreover, people were simply fed up with the lack of married Greek Catholic priests, a situation which Budka seemed to be making no effort to change. Finally, the democratized laity fervently desired a more meaningful role in the management of church affairs. Here as well, the bishop seemed impervious to calls for change.

All these concerns came to a head in Saskatoon on 18 and 19 July 1917. It was there that 154 delegates formed what was called the "National Committee," with a view toward establishing an independent Ukrainian Orthodox Church. Most members of the initiating group were associated with the inter-denominational Petro Mohyla Bursa (later the Petro Mohyla Institute) in Saskatoon. The National Committee, led by Vasyl Kudryk, Michael Stechishin and Wasyl Swystun, drew up a series of resolutions that listed in point form their dissatisfaction with the conservative policies of the Greek Catholic Church. The final and decisive cut came in the committee's last resolution, which took an anti-Uniate stand and asserted that the sixteenth-century Union of Brest had been forced upon the Ukrainian people.[21] The organizing principles for the proposed church indicated the social and ecclesiastical concerns that motivated the group. The proposed church was to have a married clergy; bishops were to be elected by a general *sobor* composed of clergy and delegates, congregations would be empowered as trustees to administer church property and finances; and the church would adhere to all the dogmas and rites of the Eastern Orthodox tradition. This organizational structure drew on two main sources of inspiration: the seventeenth-century Ukrainian institution of brotherhoods[22] and the more recent aspirations toward an independent, democratic and national Ukrainian church.

Faced with these events and no doubt anticipating that further Greek Catholic dissent could really get out of hand, Budka resorted to the one source of social stability that he knew—strong leadership of the masses from above. Rather than leading him to revise or at least reconsider his conservative ideas on social organization, the events of 1918 seemed only to have strengthened Budka's resolve to continue on what many considered an undemocratic path. Budka's initial crackdown on dissenting Greek Catholics included such measures as refusing to send priests to dissident parishes, threatening the unrepentant with excommunication, and denial of a church burial.

The Greek Catholic Church, having lost its more progressive members, urgently needed a lay affiliate to rally its remaining faithful and thereby to reassert its weakened authority among Ukrainians. A concrete proposal in this regard came in September 1922 when Osyp Nazaruk, a representative of the Western Ukrainian People's Republic, arrived in Winnipeg.[23] Nazaruk's primary mission in Canada was to raise funds for that government's activities, but during his stay he also became an avid observer of the Ukrainian community and published a number of brochures and articles on the subject. In one of these, he wrote:

The proximity of our people to the sober, even-tempered and highly cultured Anglo-Saxon race must be regarded as one of the greatest blessings
that has befallen us in our thousand year history. This is obviously a race
which learned to control public affairs: cool, firm, practical-minded and
most of all highly cultured . . . . I have been told how the English in Canada
treated our people during the war. I simply couldn't believe that they were
so lenient with our people whom, after all, they considered their enemies
and who often provoked them . . . . [24]

Nazaruk's fascination with Britain and the Anglo-Saxon race was not in-
cidental, but flowed out of his political ideology. He was a Ukrainian monarchist or hetmanist—an adherent of a political programme that was developed
out of a critique of the unsuccessful struggle for Ukraine's liberation. The
critique held that power had been in the hands of socialists and populists who
underestimated the importance of firm leadership. Viacheslav Lypynsky, the
eminent historian and socio-political theorist, in his *Lysty do brativ
khliborobiv* had elaborated on this critique and developed it into a full-
fledged political ideology. He argued that Ukrainians needed the leadership
of a politically sophisticated elite and proposed a three-tiered ideal structure
of Ukrainian society comprising a military class, a working class and an intellectual elite.

The monarchist movement, which preached respect and obedience within
a hierarchical structure of authority, appealed greatly to the Ukrainian Greek
Catholic Church of Canada, which was seeking to restore stability in its
ranks. So, in 1924, an alliance was struck between the two that lasted a
decade. In this period, the Ukrainian Catholic press in Canada—*Kanadyiskyi
ukrainets* and, after its demise, *Ukrainski visti*—were imbued with a monarchist perspective. Both Bishop Budka and his successor Vasyl Ladyka
praised the monarchist organization *Sich*, in which they saw their own hierarchical notion of social organization reinforced. The Greek Catholic-
monarchist alliance lasted until the early 1930s, when lay Ukrainian Catholics organized the Brotherhood of Ukrainian Catholics, while the *Sich* movement continued on a path of militarism.

The social tradition that Galician immigrants brought with them to Canada
had been formed in the conservative world view of Austrian monarchism and
championed by a Greek Catholic clergy that was loyal to it. This tradition of
a hierarchical structure of political as well as ecclesiastical authority underwent dramatic changes in the first period of pioneer settlement in Canada,
when both these vehicles of tradition were suddenly removed. These changes
resulted in a new social consciousness and new forms of Christian social organization which were informed by democratic and egalitarian values as
defined within Canadian society.

So it was that by 1931, 25,781 Canadian Roman Catholics identified themselves ethnically as Ukrainians, while the Ukrainian Greek Orthodox Church in Canada numbered 55,386 members (11.5 per cent and 24.6 per cent respectively of all Ukrainians in Canada at the time).[25] There can be little doubt but that the majority of these people were former Ukrainian Catholics. The prolonged shortage of Ukrainian Catholic priests was likely the decisive factor in both of these processes of denominational transfer. It was largely because of the ban on the immigration of married priests that the Ukrainian Catholic Church simply could not keep apace with the massive immigration of its people into Canada. In the resulting pastoral vacuum, some Ukrainian Catholics turned for spiritual solace to a hierarchically and doctrinally familiar Roman Catholic Church; others, repudiating anything remotely Latin, renounced their Catholicism in favour of an independent church that would be unequivocally Ukrainian. Those, finally, who remained faced the challenge of striking a uniquely Canadian balance between Ukrainianism and Catholicism.

NOTES

1. I am very grateful to Professor Roger Hutchinson for his perceptive and helpful comments on an earlier draft of this essay.
2. Such interventions took a variety of forms, many being directed to the Austrian Ministry of Foreign Affairs: as early as October, 1902, Metropolitan Sheptytsky had written to the ministry with the request that its consulate in Ottawa assist Ukrainian Catholics in incorporating their church as an independent body; in 1904, Archbishop Langevin met with the minister and requested financial aid for Ukrainians in Canada; and in 1906, Metropolitan Sheptytsky wrote a brief to the Foreign Affairs Ministry requesting a subsidy that would enable Ukrainian Canadians to build churches, establish schools and publish a newspaper. Though not all of these interventions were successful, some did bear fruit; thus, for example, Rev. Vasyl Zholdak's second sojourn in Canada (1902–4) was subsidized by the Austrian government. See Bohdan Kazymyra, "Sheptytsky and Ukrainians in Canada," in *Andrei Sheptytsky: His Life and Works*, ed. Paul R. Magocsi with the assistance of Andrii Krawchuk (Edmonton: CIUS, forthcoming). MS: p. 9, n. 16, p. 12, n. 24, p. 13 n. 26.
3. Such particularities of the Eastern rite as the performance of the sacrament of Confirmation by a priest (not by a bishop) and the distribution of the Eucharist under both species were not yet understood by Roman Catholics.
4. Both the imposition of a Roman Catholic jurisdiction on Ukrainian Catholics and the related ban on married priests in North America were policies that had been enacted by the Vatican in 1890. See Victor J. Pospishil, *Ex Occidente Lex. The Eastern Catholic Churches under the Tutelage of the Holy See of Rome* (Carteret, N.J.: St. Mary's Religious Action Fund, 1979), 24–5. With the establishment of a Ukrainian Catholic eparchy in Canada, the jurisdiction question was put to rest; the exclusion of married priests from the country had its loopholes, exceptions to the rule being allowed dur-

ing and immediately after the Second World War. But a related restriction, prohibiting the ordination in North America of married men, remains in force to this day.

5. Jaroslav Petryshyn, *Peasants in the Promised Land: Canada and the Ukrainians, 1891–1914* (Toronto: James Lorimer & Co., 1985), 196; and Paul Yuzyk, "Religious Life," in Manoly Lupul (ed.), *A Heritage in Transition: Essays in the History of Ukrainians in Canada* (Toronto: McClelland and Stewart, 1982), 148.

6. A detailed examination of the Roman Catholic–Ukrainian relationship in the early years of Canadian immigration is given in Gaston Carrière, O.M.I., "Les évêques oblats de l'ouest canadien et les Ruthènes, 1893–1904," *Vie Oblate* 33 (Ottawa, 1974): 95–119; 157–88. See also Francis Morissey, O.M.I., "Relations between Oriental Rite and Latin Rite Catholics in Canada," in *Millenium of Christianity in Ukraine: A Symposium* [Ed. Joseph Andrijisyn], (Ottawa: St. Paul University, 1987), 255–67.

7. Bohdan Kazymyra, "Ukrainski Ierarkhy," in *Almanakh Zolotoho Iuvyleiu 1905–1955* (Winnipeg: Ukrainian Mutual Benefit Association of St. Nicholas, 1957).

8. Metropolitan Andrei Sheptytsky, "Address on the Ruthenian Question to their Lordships the Archbishops and Bishops of Canada" (18 March 1911) in M.H. Marunchak, (ed.), *Two Documents of the Ukrainian Catholic Church 1911–1976* (Winnipeg: National Council of Ukrainian Organizations for the Patriarchate of the Ukrainian Catholic Church, 1977), 9.

9. Achille Delaere, *Mémoire sur les tentatives de schisme et d'hérésie au milieu des Ruthènes de l'Ouest canadien*, (Québec: Imprimerie et Reliure de l'Action Sociale, 1908), 49 pp. Delaere concluded this brief with an impassioned plea for priests, but stopped short of actually proposing the appointment of a Ukrainian Catholic bishop for Canada, contrary to what is suggested in M. H. Marunchak, *The Ukrainian Canadians: A History* (Winnipeg-Ottawa: Ukrainian Academy of Arts and Sciences in Canada, 1982), 104.

10. Morissey, "Relations," 261. The transfer of rite by Roman Catholic priests was not a catch-all solution, for cultural and linguistic barriers still remained. On one occasion, Rev. Josaphat Jean, O.S.B.M. is said to have brought the house down when, during a homily, he mispronounced an exhortation to love the Blessed Virgin as *lupit Matinku Bozhu*: rather than being loved, she was to be given a sound drubbing.

11. Zholdak took along copies of Metropolitan Sheptytsky's first pastoral to Ukrainians in Canada, *Rusynam Osilym u Kanadi*, issued in September 1901. In it, the metropolitan exhorted Ukrainian Canadians to hold fast in their faith and not give in to "false prophets" (non-Catholic priests). The pastoral is reprinted in *Tvory Sluhy Bozhoho Mytropolyta Andreia Sheptytskoho. Pastyrski Lysty (2.VIII.1899 r.– 7.IX.1901 r.)*, "Pratsi Ukrainskoho Bohoslovskoho Naukovoho Tovarystva," Vol. XV, (Toronto: Drukarnia oo. Vasyliian, 1965), 259–66.

12. Marunchak, *The Ukrainian Canadians*, 104.

13. Panteleimon Bozhyk, *Tserkov Ukraintsiv v Kanadi* (Winnipeg: "Kanadiiskyi ukrainets," 1927), 92–3. Bozhyk substantiated his assessment by referring to specific parishes.

14. Sheptytsky, "Address on the Ruthenian Question," 8–9.

15. Ibid., 6–7. Sheptytsky adopted the estimate given in the *Free Press* (Winnipeg, 5 June 1908).

16. Dmytro Blazhejovskyj, *Byzantine Kievan Rite Students in Pontifical Colleges and in Seminaries, Universities and Institutes of Central and Western Europe (1596–1983)*, "Analecta OSBM" Series II, Section I, (Rome: Pp. Basiliani, 1984), 315.

17. Marunchak, *The Ukrainian Canadians*, 110.

18. Pastoral letter of Bishop N. Budka, 27 July 1914, in *A Delicate and Difficult Question. Documents in the History of Ukrainians in Canada, 1899–1962*, Bohdan S. Kordan and Lubomyr Y. Luciuk (eds.) (Kingston: Limestone Press, 1986), 28–30.
19. Lubomyr Y. Luciuk, *A Time for Atonement: Canada's First National Internment Operations and the Ukrainian Canadians, 1914–1920* (Toronto: Civil Liberties Commission, 1987), 1–2.
20. Pastoral letter of Bishop N. Budka, 6 August 1914, in *A Delicate and Difficult Question*, 30–32.
21. Odarka S. Trosky, *The Ukrainian Greek Orthodox Church in Canada* (Winnipeg: Bulman Bros. Ltd., 1968), 15: "... Whereas the present Ukrainian Greek Catholic church is a result of religious union forced upon the Ukrainian nation by Poland in 1596 and which was supported by Austria.... "
22. The institution of lay brotherhoods flourished in Ukraine in the fifteenth and sixteenth centuries, though they had existed considerably earlier. These were parish-based Orthodox organizations, which were exempt from local ecclesiastical authority by virtue of a special privilege conferred directly by a patriarch. The scope of their activity and the extent of their influence grew so much that eventually they came into conflict with local clergy and bishops. Metropolitan Petro Mohyla's reforms in the seventeenth century were an attempt to resolve this problem.
23. The Western Ukrainian People's Republic (WUPR) had been formed in November 1918, upon the dissolution of the Hapsburg Empire. Since Galicia remained a contested area between Poland and the western powers until 1923, the WUPR government continued to function until that time.
24. Cited in Orest Martynowych, "Ukrainian Catholic Clericalism in Western Canada, 1900–1932: Disintegration and Reconsolidation," unpublished paper, 1974, 29. The article by Nazaruk was published in the WUPR organ, *Ukrainskyi prapor* (Vienna, February 1923).
25. *A Statistical Compendium on the Ukrainians in Canada, 1891–1976*, ed. William Darcovich (Ottawa: University of Ottawa Press, 1980), 177, Series 30.2, 30.3. Despite the many concerns that had been voiced about proselytizing by Protestants, Ukrainians who declared themselves Protestant in 1931 were comparatively less numerous: 13,412, or 5.95 per cent of Ukrainians in Canada. Ibid., Series 30.4–11.

Sophia Senyk

Ukrainian Religious Congregations in Canada: Tradition and Change

Today a number of different Ukrainian religious congregations are working among Ukrainian Catholics in Canada. The first to come were the Basilian Fathers and the Sisters Servants of Mary Immaculate, who arrived together from Ukraine in October 1902 in two small groups of four persons each. Some twenty years later the first attempt was made to transfer the Studites, founded in Ukraine at the beginning of this century, to this land of Ukrainian settlements. These three groups came to provide a range of ministries in the Ukrainian settlers' own faith, rite and language.

The members of these three religious congregations continue their work but the religious needs of Ukrainian immigrants also called forth the formation of new religious congregations. Early in this century the work of Belgian Redemptorists among Ukrainians in Canada led to the founding of a Ukrainian branch of this western order which subsequently became active in Ukraine as well. Other groups of Ukrainian Sisters—the Sisters of St. Joseph and the Sisters of Christian Charity—have worked in Canada. Most recently, two Ukrainian Basilian Sisters from the United States began work among Ukrainians in Toronto.

These congregations had manifold achievements but the field must be narrowed somewhat. First, the character of religious life in Western Ukraine in the period of the early Ukrainian immigration to Canada will be sketched. This will help to explain the response of the already existing religious congregations to requests from Canada for missionaries. Then the focus will be on how the members of these religious congregations had to adapt to the different circumstances of their new land. The major portion of this paper will thus deal with the Basilians and the Sisters Servants. It will also consider two other religious congregations: the Redemptorists and the Studites. Their background, and consequently their insertion into the life of the Ukrainian Canadian community, was rather different from that of the first two groups.

In western Ukraine the monks and their monasteries were organized into one body with a common administration, formation and works only after the Western eparchies joined the Union with Rome at the end of the seventeenth century. That process took almost half a century. From the 1740s the Catholic monasteries of western Ukraine formed one province of the Basilian Order, which had the official title of Congregation of the Most Holy Trinity. The Basilian Order was then composed of two provinces: the province of the Intercession [*Pokrova*] of the Mother of God, which comprised Ukrainian monasteries, and the Holy Trinity province, which contained all Basilian monasteries in Belorussia, as well as a few in Ukraine.[1]

The process of organization which formed the Basilians into an order in the western sense did not include the nuns and their monasteries. Women's religious life continued according to the traditional pattern—independent monasteries with no jurisdictional bonds among them—until the destruction of religious life in Ukraine by Soviet authorities in the 1940s. Because their monasteries were not large and because there was no co-ordination among them, it was difficult for the Basilian Sisters to send out members on missions to serve Ukrainian immigrant communities. This explains why it was not the older order of Basilian Sisters, but the newly founded and centralized Sisters Servants who came to Canada.

The Basilians

To understand the circumstances in which the Basilians undertook the mission to Canada, it is necessary to go back to the late eighteenth century, to the period when Galicia fell within the Hapsburg empire at the first partition of Poland (1772). Emperor Joseph II pursued a policy of suppressing all religious houses which could not show activity useful to the state, such as conducting schools. His enactments applied to all religious congregations in the empire, Latin and Oriental. Consequently, within a few years the fifty monasteries of the Basilians were reduced to twenty-six; by 1826 only fourteen of these remained.[2] The number of new members that could be admitted was likewise curtailed.

Although some of the restrictive legislation was abolished after the death of Joseph II in 1790, the Basilians, who had lost a large proportion of their monasteries and monks in the territories incorporated into the Russian empire, were not able to recuperate. The order diminished in numbers and in vitality. Only in 1882, with the help of the Holy See, was a thorough reform carried out, which soon began to bear fruit. Its centre was at the Dobromyl monastery, where the novitiate was established. Membership rose steadily, and the order was able to undertake new works such as wide preaching of missions and developing a religious press in Ukrainian.

When the first Ukrainian immigrants arrived in Canada in 1891, the Basilian reform was only nine years old and was just beginning to yield its first results. There were still very few members of the reformed order who had finished their studies and had been ordained to the priesthood.[3] The field of work that was opening up for them was vast—not only western Ukraine, but the lands of Ukrainian immigration as well. Letters begging for priests to work among the immigrants began to arrive from the United States and Brazil.

As soon as the reformed Basilian order had prepared members who could be spared for foreign missions, in 1897, it sent a priest to Brazil. The order was not able to meet calls to send missionaries to Canada until a few years later. The scarcity of prepared workers and the many fields of work awaiting them, even at home, explains why this mission to Canada was undertaken with some hesitation. Incessant and insistent appeals were made by Canadian bishops, in particular by Archbishop Adelard Langevin of St. Boniface, Manitoba, for Ukrainian missionaries who belonged to a religious order. The Roman Catholic bishop believed that only priests from religious congregations would assure continuity to the mission; if one left, the order could send someone else to replace him. Moreover, there were canonical obstacles to engaging secular clergy, who were mostly married, in foreign missions.

Archbishop Langevin was so concerned about the Ukrainian immigrants, who were deprived of their own priests and hence susceptible to other religious propaganda, that he sent a representative, Father Albert Lacombe, to Rome, Vienna and Lviv to plead with church and state authorities for missionaries. The immediate outcome of this initiative was that Metropolitan Andrei Sheptytsky of Lviv sent his secretary, Father Basil Zholdak, to visit Ukrainian settlements in Canada. Father Zholdak's report described a desperate situation among the immigrants, from the religious point of view. As a consequence, finally in 1902 the first group of Basilian missionaries (three priests and one lay brother) was sent out; with them went one secular priest, Father Zholdak, and four Sisters Servants. The superior of the Basilian group was Father Platonid Filias.[4]

The entire band of missionaries arrived in Montreal on 23 October 1902. As the need for missionaries was greatest in Alberta, they proceeded almost immediately to Edmonton. The work that awaited them there was vastly different from that to which they were accustomed. In Ukraine the Basilians were only auxiliaries to the diocesan parish clergy in pastoral work. The life of the Basilians was centred in their own monasteries. From their monasteries they went out to preach, to give retreats and missions, but they always returned to monastic life.

In Canada the conditions in which the Ukrainian pioneers lived, the absence of other priests, and their own woefully small number forced the Basilians to undertake solitary missionary labours. The Basilians were not auxiliaries in a well-organized parochial system, but instead had to create and provide elements of church organization and religious ministry. They set up churches and parishes and provided basic services—the eucharist, baptisms, marriages, funerals. Even these could not be provided regularly for many years. In other words, the Canadian mission, like the other missions among immigrants, entailed undertaking many duties of the parochial diocesan clergy. These obligations in turn inevitably affected the mode of life of the Basilians. To the early Basilian missionaries from Galicia can be applied the words written in the necrology of Father Matthew Hura, who arrived in Canada in November 1903: "The new environment by its very unfamiliarity compelled the young missionary first of all to be attentive to the different way of life of his brothers across the ocean, to their joys and sorrows, to their particular needs."[5]

The superiors of the order in Ukraine were preoccupied with the changing character of Basilian activity in Canada. They made an attempt to organize it along the same lines as in Ukraine. The highest superior of the order, the Provincial Platonid Filias, knew the situation there at first hand and sought to recall the solitary missionaries to one community, from which they were to go out only on brief mission trips. The Roman Catholic hierarchy protested vigorously. The Roman Catholic bishops, though aware of the incongruity of religious who professed common life, yet were living alone and without community, were concerned about the fate of the Ukrainian immigrants. If Basilian activity were curtailed and the people deprived of their own priests, the bishops feared many would fall away from the church.

When Father Filias decided that Father Antony Strotsky, whose mission base was Rosthern, Saskatchewan, should return to community life in Winnipeg, both the Apostolic Vicar of Saskatchewan, Albert Pascal, and the Apostolic Delegate to Canada, D. Sbarretti, pleaded not only directly, but also through the Holy See against this decision.[6] Removing the solitary Basilian would deprive the Ukrainian population in the area of the ministry of their own priest. The problem being thus stated, Father Filias could not but accede to the requests not to remove the priest from Saskatchewan.

The Basilians brought to Canada the forms of apostolate that had proven successful in deepening the faith and religious practices of the people in Ukraine. Giving missions was a particularly fruitful task.

We can in some measure quantify and summarize the work carried out by these missionaries. There is another side to their activity, however. "Not to have a roof over one's head, nor to be assured of a piece of bread for the morrow, to be deprived of congenial companionship, to bear the soul-oppressing burden of solitariness, persecution, and not infrequently suffering from the attacks and malice of those of other faiths, sectaries and apostates, compelled to undertake continual and long journeys through the settlements"—so Father Filias described the life of these missionaries in a circular letter to all the members of the Basilian order of December 1905.[7] His description of the Canadian mission comes from his own experience.

Seven of our priests in Canada, helped by three brothers of our order, serving about 60,000 faithful, are successfully withstanding not only the Russian schism, but also the far more dangerous sectaries, the so-called *Serafymtsi*. . . . In the province of Manitoba, where there are over twenty churches to be serviced and over 20,000 people, the whole burden of work was carried until recently by only two missionaries. This year [1905], thanks to the arrival of another missionary, a new mission station has been opened at the settlement of Stuartburn, while the station at Sifton was able to have a house built for the priest, and at Winnipeg itself a school has been opened, which shows good promise of development.—In the province of Saskatchewan until recently one of our priests had the spiritual care of over 12,000 faithful and seven churches [the Father Strotsky mentioned above]. Only lately has another of our priests and a brother by their arrival come to his aid; he was being worn out by his labors. In the province of Alberta two of our priests are working, aided by two brothers of our order. In their care they have 20,000 people, about thirteen churches, and in addition two schools.[8]

At that time there were only a few Ukrainian Catholic secular priests in Canada. Unfortunately, this predominance of Basilians in the development of the Ukrainian Catholic Church in Canada, until the appointment of Bishop Nykyta Budka (1912) and even beyond, led to differences between the bishop and the order and to a deplorable rivalry within the church community.

In 1923 the Basilians in Canada opened their own novitiate. This event was more promising for the development of their apostolate in Canada than reliance on receiving fresh members from Ukraine. Henceforth, Canadian-born personnel would be trained to serve their church. There was, however, a new influx of members from Ukraine in the wake of World War II.

The Sisters Servants

The Basilian apostolic spirit, with the characteristics it possessed in the first decade after the Dobromyl reform, brought about the founding of the Sisters

99

Servants and to a large extent formed their spirit. They were the first of a new type of religious congregation in Ukraine. It did not continue the ancient eastern model of monastic life but instead was modelled on western active religious institutes.

The beginnings of the Congregation of Sisters Servants of Mary Immaculate go back to 1891. In that year the pastor of the village Zhuzhel in Galicia, Father Kyrylo Seletsky, organized a mission in his parish. Four priests, two of them Basilians, gave the mission, which lasted five days. Among the participants were several young girls, on whom the mission had a profound effect. They began to live the life of a quasi-religious community and turned to one of the Basilians who gave the mission, Father Ieremiia Lomnytsky, for advice. Father Lomnytsky obtained the support of the pastor, Father Seletsky, and began to take steps to organize a new religious congregation. It would even accept girls with very little education (unlike the Basilian Sisters) and would dedicate itself primarily to the needs of the rural population.[9]

The first Rules of the Sisters Servants (1892), adapted from those of a Latin congregation, stated:

[The Sisters'] task is... to found nurseries for the little children in villages; to care for the sick and the elderly in the village, to serve them and to prepare them for a pious death; to work and labor together with the villagers; on Sundays and holy days to spread a religious spirit among the people by reading them the lives of saints and other spiritual books.[10]

Only ten years after their founding, when they already had over one hundred members, the Sisters Servants heeded the call of their fellow-countrymen who had immigrated to Canada and sent four Sisters. Two more came from Galicia; all other members were recruited locally. In 1910, after eight years, there were nineteen Sisters Servants in Canada; in 1917 there were already forty-seven.[11]

Their case is very distinct from that of the Basilian Fathers. The Basilian Fathers had a long history of being governed from one centre. Their Canadian missionaries relied on directions and fresh help from Ukraine. True, by 1909 some of the missionaries wished to have a novitiate of their own in Canada, but the fact remains that this did not happen for another fourteen years. The Sisters Servants in Canada, on the other hand, were on their own from the very start. They seem to have understood from the first that it was up to those on the spot to work out suitable methods of apostolate and to look after their own future. They were not obliged to give a regular account of their activity and progress to the highest superior of their congregation in Ukraine, nor did they conduct a regular correspondence with their Sisters in Ukraine.

The Sisters Servants accepted the first Canadian girl into their ranks as a postulant only eight months after their arrival, when they were living in great poverty, deprivation and hardship in a log cabin at Beaver Lake. This example—and other parallels could be drawn—shows how adaptable a young, recently founded congregation could be to local circumstances and needs. Being untrammelled by approved procedures helped the Sisters to grow more rapidly.

The superior of the first little group of Sisters was Sister Ambrose Lenkewych; she remained superior of the Canadian Sisters Servants until 1926. She and the Sisters under her direction undertook whatever work seemed necessary or opportune. They had few misgivings about drifting away from the kind of life their Sisters in Ukraine were leading.

For the first few months the Sisters remained in Edmonton, where they began to learn English and taught catechism; one of their members died there after a few months. In July 1903 the remaining three Sisters went out to Beaver Lake. There they were kept busy by farming and other chores of their primitive household and simple religious instruction for the people of nearby farms. In 1905 they were already opening a second mission in Edmonton. This set the pattern for their activities. In broad lines, the Sisters' first task was to teach catechism and the Ukrainian language in evening and day schools. During the summer the Sisters would go out to the farm settlements for the same purpose.

In general, a different approach to their work and different levels of activity developed in Ukraine and in Canada. The Sisters in Ukraine, who at their founding saw all around them pressing social and religious needs in the villages, hastened to satisfy these needs without pausing to consider whether it might not be opportune gradually to raise the horizons of the people to whom they ministered. Thus the Sisters in Ukraine concentrated on developing shelters for children, while their mothers were working in the fields, and later for the orphans of World War I. They also provided elementary nursing aid and did physical work. Much of that was connected to religious needs— looking after churches, working in seminaries, sewing vestments.

The Sisters in Canada were among a population with primary needs, too, but of a somewhat different nature. True, the Sisters had an orphanage in Sifton, but the people above all needed religious instruction and other religious ministry in their own rite and in their own language. When they arrived, moreover, no schooling was being provided for the children on the farms near them. The Sisters at once began to organize a regular system of instruction at Beaver Lake. In the beginning it was of a very primitive character. The classroom was in the same hall that served as the chapel. Of the sixty children attending the school, about half boarded with the Sisters under very cramped conditions. Only in 1913 was a school building begun. It was blessed the following year.[12]

One concrete example characterizes the differences between the Sisters in Canada and those in Ukraine better than any analysis could. In Ukraine the first qualified teacher entered the congregation of the Sisters Servants only in 1919 and only after overcoming strong opposition to her entry. In Canada, in contrast, Archbishop Langevin and Bishop Emile Legal of St. Albert, Alberta, in 1905 urged that the Sisters Servants be trained professionally to teach.[13] Due to the far-sightedness of these bishops, the Sisters were acting on their advice within five years.

This example also shows how ecclesiastical authorities contributed to a difference of outlook on the tasks of the Sisters. In Ukraine the Sisters, in their own view and in the view of church authorities, were simply supposed to help the village population in its daily needs. In Canada, even before the nomination of the first Ukrainian bishop, the Roman Catholic episcopate, at the suggestion of Archbishop Langevin, provided the necessary funds to build the St. Nicholas School in Winnipeg for the Sisters Servants.[14]

The different professional activities and standards of the Sisters in Canada created a certain diffidence among them toward their Sisters in Ukraine. Ties were loosened because of the great distance that separated them, irregular correspondence, the break in communications occasioned by World War I, and the fact that, except for the few pioneer Sisters, the rest had no experience or knowledge of the situation of the Sisters in Galicia. A large number (twenty-eight out of eighty-seven) of the Canadian Sisters in 1931 did not want institutional bonds with the Sisters in Ukraine. They wished to live by the same spirit, to observe the same basic rules, but they did not want to be tied to the same kind of activity. In fact, ten years earlier, in 1921, in a chapter of the Sisters held in Winnipeg the Sisters resolved: "We wish to develop our life without taking into consideration the development of the Sisters in Galicia, but we wish to remain united with the congregation, observing their holy Rule with our own additions."[15]

Thus, as with the Basilian Fathers, members of one religious institute living in different lands and with very different apostolic needs before their eyes found mutual comprehension difficult. The matter took a more extreme turn among the Sisters Servants, who were almost all Canadian-born. The Canadian Sisters naturally considered that just as the Sisters in Galicia were living and developing as best suited the needs of the people they served, so they, too, should have the freedom to work as seemed most profitable to the church and to their people in Canada. The differences in outlook were reconciled in 1934 when the Canadian Sisters entered the Congregation of the Sisters Servants as a separate province.

The Sisters Servants in Canada served the Ukrainian pioneer community with great dedication. The religious instruction they provided enabled many people to preserve their faith. As in the case of the Basilian Fathers, it is not possible to give all the credit and recognition due. Such things as personal dedication, abnegation and self-sacrificing work cannot be gauged or computed.

Although no human endeavour is perfect, to point out shortcomings is not to overlook achievements. The Sisters did have one shortcoming of a religious nature. Those in Canada, who constantly had the example of Latin-rite sisters before them, felt unconsciously, perhaps, the need to emulate them. Religious devotions and chapel furnishings, for instance, were patterned on those of Roman Catholic congregations. Because of the influence of the Sisters, catechetical practices foreign to Eastern tradition and spirit tended to spread within the Ukrainian Catholic Church. What the Sisters passed on tended, generally speaking, to minimize differences between their own and the Roman Catholic Church. This attitude of the Sisters reflected the general cultural impressionability of Ukrainian Catholics when faced with Roman Catholic accomplishments and practices, especially in a country and at a time when they were a small and looked-down-upon minority.

The Redemptorists

An eastern-rite branch of the Redemptorists was founded in Canada when the Flemish Father Achille Delaere, the first Redemptorist missionary among the Ukrainian immigrants, assumed the Ukrainian rite on 21 August 1906. Working among Ukrainians in Manitoba and Saskatchewan since 1899, he had realized that the difference of rite was an obstacle to winning the full confidence of the people. Other members of his order who worked among Ukrainians followed him in assuming the eastern rite. The mission base he had established at Yorkton, Saskatchewan, in 1904 later became the centre of Ukrainian Redemptorist activity.

Father Delaere and his companions worked tirelessly among the Ukrainian immigrants, celebrating religious services, imparting the sacraments, and teaching the faith. He and his fellow-Redemptorists were personal adherents to the eastern rite and to work among the Ukrainian immigrants. Father Delaere, acutely aware of the need for more missionaries, came to realize that instead of relying on individual volunteers to embrace the Ukrainian rite it would be better to found an eastern-rite branch of the Redemptorists.

Such a solution had several advantages. The people, after all, were suspicious of "foreigners," however much they strove to learn the language and to adapt themselves to Ukrainian usages. Missionaries of Ukrainian extraction would thus be more successful working among the immigrants. An eastern-rite branch of the Redemptorists would also assure the continuance of the Redemptorist mission among Ukrainians in Canada. It would give Ukrainian youth the possibility of joining the Redemptorists to serve their own people in their own rite.[16]

Father Delaere's wishes coincided with those of Metropolitan Sheptytsky. In 1913 an eastern-rite branch of the Redemptorists was begun in Galicia. Eventually a number of Redemptorist priests from Ukraine came out to help with the missions in Canada. The Redemptorists in Canada, somewhat like the Basilians, seem in their early years to have depended on fresh forces arriving from Ukraine rather than on Canadian-born members.

For the Redemptorists the problem of adaptation, however, presented itself differently. Their Ukrainian branch had to work out the problem of fitting the traditions of a western order, acquired over more than a hundred years since their founding, with the eastern practices of the Ukrainian church. That it is still not fully resolved is not surprising since, in a sense, the Redemptorists were obliged to perform a double adaptation. They had to adapt a Latin-rite institute with a spirit deriving from Latin traditions to the Eastern rite among a population of that rite in Ukraine. Then they had to take the further step of transposing that experience to Canada, with its own unique situation and problems. It is obvious that there must have been tension between the desire to hold on to features that were felt to be distinctive or characteristic of the Redemptorist order and the necessity to be at the same time "eastern." A synthesis of the two is difficult enough to achieve theoretically, and much more so in practice.

The Studites

Some two decades after the introduction into Canada of the three congregations considered so far, an attempt was made to transpose to Canada a traditional form of eastern monastic life. The Studite monks as an institution were new to the Ukrainian church. But while they were founded only in 1901, they did not look upon themselves as a new foundation. They sought to revive certain eastern monastic traditions which the more apostolic-minded Basilians had relinquished. Thus the Studites saw themselves not as innovators or as a new order, but rather as another branch of the one eastern monasticism.

In 1925, to alleviate the poverty of many peasants in Western Ukraine, a large-scale Ukrainian settlement in northern Quebec was proposed. Among its initiators was Metropolitan Sheptytsky, who tried in this way to improve the situation of his people. In conjunction with the project a Studite monastery was to be established nearby to assure religious ministry to the people.

Arrangements in Canada for the settlement project were entrusted to Father Josaphat Jean, a French Canadian who had adopted the Ukrainian rite and, later, the Studite rule. The site eventually chosen, after a western location had to be discarded, was at Landrienne in the Abitibi area of northern Quebec. Father Jean prepared a house, where he was joined in 1926 by three Studite monks from Ukraine.

Ukrainian families began to arrive at Landrienne, but obstacles to emigration—Polish authorities, the depression and other circumstances—soon caused the entire settlement project to flounder. Soon new arrivals ceased altogether. Problems arose also with the Studite foundation. The Studites who came do not seem to have been sufficiently prepared for the kind of work and life that was awaiting them. Moreover, the locality, because of climatic rigours and isolation, was found unsuitable for pioneer monasticism.[17] Eventually the Studites abandoned Landrienne and Canada. Father Jean entered the Basilian order.

A permanent settlement of the Studites in Canada was made only twenty-five years later. In 1951 a small group of Studite monks, the few who had managed to escape from Soviet-occupied Ukraine, came to Woodstock, Ontario. Their settlement on a farm there exists to this day.

Conclusion

The four Ukrainian religious congregations began their work in Canada under similar circumstances, but from four very different backgrounds. However, the purpose of their coming to Canada in all four instances was the same. Ukrainian Catholic immigrants badly needed and wanted priests and religious people of their own rite to provide religious services and instruction for them. The religious also shared the harsh conditions of life and work of the Ukrainian settlers at large. For each religious community the Canadian experience brought something new, which it had to integrate with its own traditions, even if these were only of recent origin. Except for the Studites, the Canadian branches of the religious institutes took on specific characteristics which were not shared by their fellow members in Ukraine.

The failure of the Studite adaptation was due in large measure to the collapse of the larger settlement project. Once it became clear, at the end of the 1920s, that no further families would be able to arrive and that those who had already settled in the vicinity of Landrienne were thinking of moving elsewhere, there was not much reason for the Studites to remain. The persons involved, moreover, except for Father Jean, do not seem to have had sufficient training for a mission outpost. Thus because of circumstances which were both external (the failure to form a Ukrainian community in the environs) and internal (members did not have sufficient religious training), the Studites at that time were not able to transplant a monastery in Canada.

The first Redemptorists to work among Ukrainian immigrants were dedicated persons of non-Ukrainian origin. It was obviously difficult for them, in spite of their good will, to feel perfectly at home among Ukrainians, and the immigrants felt a certain distrust toward "foreign" religious. Such mutual reserve perhaps is one reason why their community grew slowly in Canada, even after a separate eastern-rite branch had been formed.

The Sisters Servants of Mary Immaculate were a very young congregation when they sent their first members to Canada. Unhampered by set methods and ways of thinking, they were able to fit into any situation where they saw a need they could meet in a certain area or where ecclesiastical superiors called them to a particular work. Their evident adaptability and suitability to the Canadian mission, as well as the example of their spirit of self-sacrifice, soon brought them numerous Canadian-born members.

The Basilian Fathers, like the other congregations, met the challenges of the Canadian mission with great dedication. As an old order, though, with deeply honoured traditions and strong centralization, they sought to adapt to Canadian circumstances in the light of their age-old experience.

In the broadest sense, though, the experience and the task of all these communities was the same. The very fact of coming to work in a new land where everything—terrain, climate, standard of life, political life, foreign cultural context, opportunities for education and work, and social mobility—was different, imposed certain changes on the manner of life of the religious and on their conception of their place in the Ukrainian community and in Canadian life. Their purpose, however, was to help their people preserve their faith and the traditions of their Church.

NOTES

1. The term "Basilian" in its original use simply designated any eastern monk or nun. For further information on the organization of the Basilian order and statistics, see M. Vavryk, *Narys rozvytku i stanu Vasyliianskoho chyna XVII-XX st.* (Rome, 1979).
2. Ibid., tables, 74.
3. Only eleven were ordained up to 1891, though in that year nine others were ordained. Isydor Patrylo, "Narys istorii Halytskoi provintsii ChSVV," *Analecta OSBM*, 17 (1982):80.
4. N. Savaryn, "Misiina pratsia oo. Vasyliian v Kanadi," *Propamiatna knyha z nahody Zolotoho Iuvileiu poselennia ukrainskoho narodu v Kanadi* (Yorkton, 1941), 45–58.
5. J. Skr[uten], "O. Matei Hura," AOSBM, 1, no. 2–3 (1925):302.
6. Iosyf [Giuseppe Mojoli], "Pryizd pershykh Vasyliian do Kanady v svitli dokumentiv," *Propamiatna knyha OO. Vasyliian u Kanadi* (Toronto, 1953), 76–8.
7. Platonid Filias, *Poslannia do Vasyliian* (Zhovkva, 1905), 2.
8. Ibid., 2–3.
9. For the story of the Sisters Servants, including detailed accounts of their activity in Canada, see Atanasii H. Velyky, *Narys istorii Zhromadzhennia SS. Sluzhebnyts P.N.D.M.* (Rome, 1968). Claudia Helen Popowich, *To Serve is to Love* (Toronto, 1971), gives a history of the Sisters Servants in Canada.
10. Popowich, 47.
11. Ibid., 85.
12. Ibid., 75–8, describes the sacrifices entailed in taking on the responsibility for the new school building; see also J. Skwarok, *The Ukrainian Settlers in Canada and Their Schools* (Edmonton, 1958), 28–9.
13. Popowich, 53–4, 56; Velyky, 226. On the qualifications of the Sisters, see also

Skwarok, *Ukrainian Settlers in Canada*, 30, which quotes the *Edmonton Journal* of 1921.
14. Popowich, 65–6.
15. Velyky, 261.
16. For the work of the Redemptorists among Ukrainian immigrants in Canada, as well as for the beginnings and growth of the eastern branch of the order in Ukraine and in Canada, see *Iuvileina knyha OO. Redemptorystiv skhidnoho obriadu* (Yorkton, 1955).
17. About this first settlement of the Studites in Canada, see Bohdan Kazymyra, "Uspikhy i trudnoshchi u velykomu zamiri," *Bohosloviia* 33 (1969): 91–140.

Roman Yereniuk

Church Jurisdictions and Jurisdictional Changes Among Ukrainians in Canada, 1891–1925

The Ukrainian immigration to Canada in the period 1891 to World War I came from the provinces of Galicia (Halychyna) and Bukovyna in the Austro-Hungarian Empire and constituted approximately 150,000[1] on the eve of World War I. The Ukrainians from Galicia were overwhelmingly Greek Catholic, Catholics of Byzantine rite united with Rome. This church was a well-organized and established metropolitanate with four million adherents, organized around the metropolitan of Lviv, two diocesan bishops, approximately 1,200 clergy in 3,000 parishes, and a well-developed Basilian monastic order and other orders of men and women. The Ukrainians in Bukovyna were predominantly member of the Orthodox Church of Bukovyna, headed by the metropolitan of Chernivtsi. This church constituted a larger proportion of ethnic Ukrainians and a smaller number of Romanians. The leadership, however, was in the hands of Romanians or Ukrainian Romanianophiles, but many of the village clergy were dedicated to their Ukrainian and Orthodox roots.

For these settlers in Canada, their religion and church affiliation were most important. In fact, religious identity was clearly asserted and was stronger than cultural and national identities. It was expressed in the institutions related to the parish (*hromada*)—the church building and complex, the emphasis on an indigenous priesthood, the use of the well-rooted Byzantine rite, national religious customs, and language. These were symbols of self-definition, which nourished and preserved the identity of the Ukrainian immigrants. This state of mind was expressed well by Iuliian Bachynsky in 1914:

> Nothing has penetrated nor filled the spiritual life of the Ukrainian peasant-immigrant so thoroughly as did the church and the church rite. Back in his village the church and the rite had become part of him. They became his ethical roadsigns, the guidelines of a pious life here on earth which, as he was taught, led to salvation and rewards after death. . . . There (in the church) his life found spiritual food. There he found and even expressed his own aesthetic feelings, amidst all the light, paintings and glistening clothes of God's servants with their serious, unusual movements of hands and bodies and their incense, bells and singing. This was such unusual beauty, and he was enraptured by it.[2]

Thus the Byzantine-rite church, whether Greek Catholic or Orthodox, was identified thoroughly with the Ukrainian immigrant and, as in the homeland, it accompanied him/her from cradle to the grave. In fact, the existence of social, cultural, educational and family life was unthinkable without the presence of the church.

In the beginning in Canada the immigrants were without church buildings and without clergy, but they managed to celebrate. In each district one of the homes would serve as the centre of the religious ritual and people in the community would gather there on Sundays and feast days. Maria Adamowska aptly described this experience in her memoirs:

> Our poor settlers consulted among themselves and decided to meet every Sunday and sing at least those parts of the liturgy that were meant to be sung by the cantor (*diak*). Since our house was large enough, that was where the meetings were held. On Sunday mornings everyone hurried to our house the way one would to church. . . . And so it was that we were able to gratify, at least partially, the longings of our souls.[3]

Soon thereafter the first church buildings, meagre attempts to copy examples in the homeland, began to appear on the Canadian prairies. In fact within a decade of the arrival of the first settlers, there were already over twenty church buildings, from the Gardenton-Vita area, south of Winnipeg, to the Star-Wostok area, north-east of Edmonton. Initially these edifices stood empty because the village priests remained in the homeland. However the newly arrived immigrants longed for the clergy and began petitioning for them. In 1899, for example, a Manitoba settler wrote to the Greek-Catholic journal *Misionar*:

> Dear Fathers, Life here is very good for our bodies, there is no physical deprivation, but what of that, when there are great deprivations of the soul. There is enough to eat, drink, wear. But our soul is poor, very poor. This is because it has nothing to eat or drink, nothing from which to live, no roof

to stand beneath. It can only shelter itself under strangers' roofs and listen to them, but it does not hear and does not understand.[4]

In some instances, the immigrants received directions from their homeland to embrace the spiritual care of strangers. Alberta Bukovynians received a reply to their request for a priest, sent to the Metropolitan of Chernivtsi: "We are unable to send you a priest due to lack of funds, but there is a Russian Orthodox Mission there which will assign a priest to you. If necessary you should join the mission."[5]

The early immigrants were not satisfied with the spiritual care of other religious bodies, whether Roman Catholic (Latin-rite), Russian Orthodox or Protestant denominations. These only aroused the nostalgia of the settlers for their own rite, customs, language and priests. In a letter sent to Metropolitan Sylvestr Sembratovych of Lviv, the early immigrants of Shenandoah, Pennsylvania, expressed the same nostalgia for their own church and priest as did many Ukrainians in Canada: "We are not entirely the same as we were in our country, because we are missing something. What we miss is God Whom we could understand, Whom we could adore *in our own way.*"[6]

Within fifteen years of the first arrival of Ukrainians in Canada, four different jurisdictions attempted to satisfy the spiritual needs of the people and by 1918 another jurisdiction entered into the competition for their souls. The five jurisdictions which found fertile soil among Ukrainians in Canada included the Greek Catholic Church, the Russian Orthodox Greek Catholic Mission in North America (later referred to as the North American diocese of the Russian Orthodox Church), the All-Russian Patriarchal Orthodox Church (usually referred to as the Seraphimite Church), the Independent Greek Church (referred to as the Ruthenian Independent Orthodox Church by Ukrainians) and the Ukrainian Greek Orthodox Church of Canada. Each of these jurisdictions established itself in the communities of the immigrants, supplied the Ukrainian churches and parishes in the Ukrainian community with clergy to celebrate the "Byzantine rite," and nourished their thirst for worshipping God in their own way. Yet each of these jurisdictions also began competing with one another in the freedom-loving and democratic setting of British western Canada. Each had its own agenda, programme of action, and ideology that it wanted the pious immigrants to accept. Thus after the vacuum of the early years, the Ukrainian immigrant became caught in the crossfire of religious battles and polemics.

At first, and almost simultaneously, the Ukrainian immigrants received the ministry of two competing jurisdictions, the Greek Catholic and the Russian Orthodox Mission. Both slowly developed their following by sending itinerant clergy from the United States but soon established permanent clergy and then formalized their jurisdictions.

ROMAN YERENIUK

The Greek Catholic Church

The first major church to begin pastoral work in Canada was the Greek Catholic. Before the first clergy arrived, the Greek Catholics were ministered to by the French Roman Catholic bishops (Archbishop Adelard Langevin, 1895–1915, and Bishop Emile Legal of St. Albert), who placed them under Polish clergy of Latin rite. This did not satisfy the Ukrainians, who had a deep-rooted dislike, both religious and national, for Poles and the Latin rite of their church. Thus in 1896, Greek Catholics of Edna-Star wrote to the newspaper *Svoboda* and requested aid in seeking a clergyman. Father N. Dmytriv, the editor, answered this in person. In May-June 1896 he travelled through the Canadian prairie visiting communities in Terebowla-Drifting River, Dauphin, Stuartburn and Winnipeg in Manitoba, and Edmonton, Fort Saskatchewan, Rabbit Hill and Edna-Star in the future province of Alberta. The reception he received was most positive. This visit and a subsequent one in 1897 were recorded in *Svoboda*.[7] The visit to Edna-Star, Alberta, however, also provoked a response from the Russian Orthodox Mission, which soon thereafter sent its clergy to the same general area.

Following Father N. Dmytriv, several other Greek Catholic priests ministered to the Ukrainians in Alberta—Fathers Paul Tymkiewicz (1898) and Ivan Zaklynsky (1898) and Damaskyn Polyvka (1899). Despite their small numbers, the clergy encountered difficulties with the Roman Catholic bishops. Although Bishop Emile Legal helped the first Greek Catholic community in Star-Edna to construct its first church, he also introduced a problem that was to create much havoc in the community by having the building registered in the Roman Catholic corporation. This action was opposed by the faithful and the itinerant clergy who believed in trusteeship and eventually they were supported by the Russian Orthodox Mission, which supplied the parish with a priest. The battle over the parish provoked a protracted court case that was fought on three judicial levels—the Supreme Court of the Northwest Territories, the Supreme Court of Canada and the Privy Council in London. The final decision in 1907 was in favour of the church trustees, who at that time were under the Russian Orthodox Mission. This decision created further problems for the Greek Catholic Church because trusteeship became strongly rooted among the Ukrainians and soon developed into a force opposed to the Roman Catholic hierarchy. Trusteeship also became the mode of church incorporation for the St. Nicholas parish in Winnipeg.

However, the Greek Catholics could not be ministered to by the small number of clergy coming irregularly or for short periods of time from the United States. Even the Canadian Roman Catholic bishops realized this, and in 1895 and 1898 they began to petition Rome, Vienna and Lviv for regular priests for the Ukrainians. Very few answered this call, so an appeal was

112

made for missionaries. Archbishop Langevin visited the Redemptorist Fathers in Belgium and received the aid of Father Achille Delaere in 1899. He was joined by three other Redemptorists in 1907—Fathers R. Decamp, Henri Tescher and Ludwig Boske. Archbishop Langevin also approached the French Canadian Congregation of St. Joseph, which responded with five monks: Fathers Adonias Sabourin, Joseph Gagnon, Derise Claveloux, Arthur Desmarais and Joseph Jean. These Latin-rite clergy became bi-ritual, adopting the Greek rite, and worked among the Ukrainian communities on the prairies, although their acceptance was often quite suspect.

Meanwhile Metropolitan Andrei Sheptytsky of Lviv sent Father Vasyl Zholdak to Canada in 1901 to investigate the situation and entrusted him with an epistle to the Greek Catholics of Canada. The fact-finding trip yielded a positive response from the metropolitan. In October 1902, a group of eight—three Basilian priests (Fathers Platonid Filias, Sozont Dydyk and Anton Strotsky), one Basilian monk and four nuns of the Sister Servants of Mary Immaculate—came to Canada to become the first permanent Greek Catholic clergy. They established themselves in Mundare, Alberta. Soon a number of secular clergy arrived in Canada, including some from a dissident movement in the United States, which in 1901 established in Shamokin, Pennsylvania, "The Society of Ruthenian Church Congregations in the United States and Canada." This movement constituted those who resented Latin domination, stood against registering property in the name of Catholic bishops, and disliked how the Roman decrees of the Congregation for the Propagation of Faith placed limitations on the Byzantine rite. Thus the first clergy of the Greek Catholic Church were made up of indigenous Ukrainian, both monastic and secular, as well as French and Belgian missionaries.[8]

The refusal of Rome to allow married secular clergy to come to the New World caused grave problems. Already on 1 October 1890 and 12 April 1894, the Congregation for the Propagation of Faith forbade married secular clergy to serve in North America.[9] These same decrees also stated that all Byzantine-rite Catholic churches were to be integrated into the local Latin-rite dioceses in North America. This double blow against the Greek Catholics caused much harm to the growth and future development of the church. The Ukrainians desired the married clergy they were used to in their villages and longed to have their own separate ecclesiastic-ritual identity. However, during the early twentieth century, Greek Catholic parishes were slowly being incorporated under the Roman Catholic charter with the deed title "The Congregation of the Greek Ruthenian Catholics United to Rome," or they opted for trustee ownership. Married clergy were practically non-existent. The autonomous independent parish in Winnipeg (formerly St. Nicholas and by now Sts. Vladimir and Olga) was soon challenged by the Roman Catholic Archbishop Adelard Langevin, who founded, funded and incorporated under himself a new parish across the street appropriately named St. Nicholas. He entrusted it to the Basilians.

The Greek Catholics in Canada eagerly learned of the arrival of a Byzantine-rite bishop in the United States in 1907 in the person of Bishop Soter Ortynsky.[10] The Greek Catholics in Canada had earlier made requests for their own hierarch, but were turned down. This development in America gave them new hope. The trip of Metropolitan Andrei Sheptytsky to Montreal in 1910 for the Eucharistic Congress enabled him to travel throughout Canada for two months and gain first-hand information on the status of his church. Upon his return home Sheptytsky was able to secure for Canada its first bishop and further clergy. Thus in 1912, Nykyta Budka was appointed as the first bishop (1912–27) of the Greek Catholic Church in Canada, with full jurisdiction over the Byzantine-rite Ukrainians but responsible to the pope. This appointment and episcopate brought to a culmination the formal structure of the Greek Catholic Church as a jurisdiction. He soon thereafter had all parishes incorporated under provincial charters and an episcopal charter was approved by the Canadian parliament in 1913 (known as "The Ruthenian Greek Catholic Episcopal Corporation"). That same year he issued a constitution for his church entitled "Statutes of the Ruthenian Greek Catholic Church in Canada" and in 1914, at a clergy synod in Yorkton, he had a set of regulations adopted, which were known as the "Regulations of the Ruthenian Greek Catholic Church of Canada." These documents were important because they stabilized the Greek Catholic Church and gave it the proper direction for the future.

All of these endeavours, as well as the establishment of a newspaper in 1911 by Archbishop Langevin known as *Kanadyiskyi rusyn*, renamed *Kanadyiskyi ukrainets* in 1919, and the establishment of the St. Nicholas parish school, aided in the normalization of the jurisdiction among the Ukrainians in Canada. By 1912 there were twenty-one clerics in the church—five Basilians, eight secular Ukrainian priests, four Belgian Redemptorists and four French priests. Later that year, this number increased by thirteen secular priests, all celibate, and eight nuns of the Sisters Servants of Mary Immaculate. However no sooner was this status achieved than the 11 August 1913 decree *Ea Semper* of the Congregation for the Propagation of Faith, with its explicit emphasis on celibate clergy, stirred new problems in the religious life of the Ukrainian community.

The Russian Orthodox Mission

Parallel to this first jurisdiction in Canada, a second one developed, the Russian Orthodox Mission. This mission was part of the Russian Orthodox Holy Synod's missionary activity in Alaska, which was established in 1794 but transferred from Sitka to San Francisco in 1872. The Holy Synod's diocese was officially known as the Diocese of the Aleutians and Alaska but in 1900 it was changed to the Diocese of the Aleutians and North America and thus began to follow closely the fate of the Orthodox and Uniate immigration to the United States and Canada. Under the leadership of Bishops Vladimir Sokolovsky (1888–91),[11] Nicholas Zerov (1891–8), Tikhon Bellavin (1898–1907, the future patriarch of Moscow), Platon Rozhdestvensky (1907–14) and Evdokim Mishchersky (1914–7), this church jurisdiction spread its ministry among Ukrainians and other Orthodox of non-Russian origin in both the United States and Canada. In 1905 the diocese transferred its cathedral to New York to be closer to the centre of immigration.

This church considered that it had exclusive jurisdiction over all Orthodox in North America whose roots had been established in Alaska at the end of the eighteenth century. In addition, the Russian Orthodox Church had tremendous financial support right up to 1917 and the Russian revolution. For example, in 1916 the diocese requested $1 million for its work, but was appropriated "$550,000."[12] In this budget were sums for a "vicar See in Winnipeg" as well as for clergy support and institutional support for the parishes in Canada.

The earliest records of contacts of Bukovynian Orthodox with the Russian Orthodox Mission come from the years 1894 to 1896, when Ukrainians in Alberta, having been turned down by the Metropolitan of Chernivtsi, turned to Bishop Nicholas in San Francisco for clergy. In 1897 they did receive aid when Father Dimitrii Kamenev and his cantor, Vladimir Aleksandrov of Seattle, visited Alberta and Father M. Maiarevsky visited Manitoba and Assiniboia. The visit of Father Kamenev to Livia Stone (Limestone, now Wostok), Alberta, provoked the major jurisdictional rivalry that was subsequently fought with the Greek Catholics. The first liturgy there was celebrated on 12 July 1897 and land donated by Theodore Nemyrsky became the site of the first church and cemetery, dedicated on 4 June 1898 to the Holy Trinity. Most of the missionaries visited Canada from either Seattle, Washington (especially into Alberta), or Minneapolis (into Manitoba and Assiniboia, later Saskatchewan). Fathers Vladimir Aleksandrov (1899)[13] and Jacob Korchinsky (1898) laboured in Wostok, and in 1900 the latter established himself in Edmonton and ministered from there. In 1901, Father Constantine Popov visited settlements throughout Manitoba and Assiniboia. Even Bishops Nicholas and Tikhon visited the Canadian mission communities, although little is known of their work here.[14] Later Archimandrite Arsenii Chekhovtsev had considerable success between 1905 and 1911 in both Alberta and Manitoba, and even published a newspaper, *Kanadiiskaia niva*, in Winnipeg.

In 1907 Bishop Tikhon called a council of his diocese to Mayfield, Pennsylvania, which decided to expand missions. Thus, by 1916, this jurisdiction claimed 110 parishes, 64 clergymen and 117,000 faithful in North

America.[15] In Canada they were in Bukovynian communities with some converted Greek-Catholic parishes.[16] Plans were also made to create a vicarate for Canada. Bishop Alexander Nemolovsky was appointed in 1916,[17] but this was short-lived and in 1917 Archimandrite Adam Filipovsky became the administrator for Canada.

The Russian Orthodox Diocese of the Aleutians and North America took advantage of the movement of religious independence among Ukrainians and exploited their cultural and ethnic confusion. Nonetheless, with the Russian revolution in 1917, the finances came to end, priests and parishes soon established themselves in other jurisdictions and the church witnessed a fast decline.

The All-Russian Patriarchal Orthodox Church (Seraphimite)

In early 1903, a third jurisdiction was founded in Canada, the so-called All-Russian Patriarchal Orthodox Church, headed by the monk-impostor and founder Stephan Ustvolsky or, as he called himself, Metropolitan Seraphim.[18] His church subsequently was referred to as the Seraphimite Church. An itinerant monk with falsified documents of consecration, he initially attempted to establish himself in the United States among Greek Catholics. However, with the support of Canadian immigration agent Cyril Genik, he soon made his way to Winnipeg. Here a young group of Ukrainian intelligentsia, the so-called Bereziv Trinity (John Bodrug, John Negrich and Cyril Genik), had become disenchanted with both the Russian Orthodox Mission and the Greek Catholic Church. They believed that Seraphim could be exploited for their own purpose, which was to create a new Ukrainian national church, independent of all foreign influences.

Initially, Seraphim appealed to the pioneers and very quickly answered their need for clergy. Within a short period, he had ordained fifty priests and deacons and had extended his jurisdiction into numerous parishes on the prairies with close to 60,000 faithful. Seraphim often ordained men who were semi-literate and of low social rank in the community. However, he also ordained the future leaders of the Independent Greek Church—John Bodrug and John Negrich. Seraphim espoused trustee ownership of churches and a jurisdiction independent of all patriarchs, popes, ecclesiastical centres such as Rome, or the Holy Synod in St. Petersburg. Yet he and his assistant, Makarii Marchenko, went on drinking sprees, constructed the "tin can cathedral in Winnipeg" and made further indiscriminate ordinations. That soon provoked a strong reaction against his self-created and self-styled jurisdiction.

The enlightened clergy convinced Seraphim in the fall of 1903 to return to Russia to receive new support for his church. During his absence, the enlightened clergy, supported by the Presbyterian Church, established a new contender in the jurisdictional rivalry among Ukrainians—the Independent Greek Church. On his return in 1904, Seraphim realized a coup had taken place and excommunicated all those behind it. Meanwhile Seraphim himself, as well as his clergy, were excommunicated by the Russian Holy Synod, which realized the hoax. In 1908, Seraphim again left for Russia, never to return, and was succeeded by his eccentric assistant, Makarii Marchenko, who declared himself "Arch-Patriarch, Arch-Pope, Arch-Tsar, Arch-Hetman, and Arch-Prince." He soon excommunicated the pope in Rome and the entire Russian Holy Synod.

The short-lived jurisdiction headed by Seraphim and Marchenko had answered a number of immediate needs of the Ukrainians, but was soon discredited. At the same time, Seraphim's work in Canada spawned a new competitor for Ukrainian allegiance.

The Independent Greek Church

The fourth jurisdiction to seek the support of Ukrainians was the Independent Greek Church (the Ruthenian Orthodox Independent Church in Ukrainian). During Seraphim's absence the enlightened clergy and laity—Cyril Genik, John Bodrug[19] and John Negrich—took control of the church. Founded on a hybrid foundation of Presbyterianism by content and Byzantine-Rite by form, the new jurisdiction considered itself autonomous and independent of all foreign religious influences.[20] The three leaders had, in fact, reached an accord among themselves and then secretly had made arrangements with the Presbyterian Church. The original three plus Michael and Alexander Bachynsky constituted its first jurisdictional consistory. The distinguishing features of the Independent Greek Church were its emphasis on trustee ownership, church government according to democratic principles, a synodal form of government consisting of both clergy and laymen, and a consistory responsible for ordaining clergy. In 1908 their constitution was completed.

On 26 June 1904, the new church was officially established at a four-day synod with a large number of delegates. John Bodrug was elected superintendent (bishop) while the consistory members were Father Alexander Bachynsky (president), Father John Danylchuk (secretary) and Wasyl Novak (treasurer). This church was supported financially by the Presbyterian Church of Canada. The Presbyterian Board of Home Missions undertook a number of projects to assist the new church. In 1905, the Ukrainian publication *Ranok* (Dawn) was established, classes in theology at Manitoba College were started, and residence schools (*bursa*) were set up in Winnipeg, Teulon, Sifton and Vegreville, as were hospitals in Teulon and Vita.

Notwithstanding excommunication by Seraphim in 1904, the Independent Greek Church took over numerous parishes that formerly had belonged to him, so that by 1907 the new church claimed some thirty clergymen and

30,000 to 40,000 faithful. However, the Independent Greek Church began to experience difficulties in 1907 and 1908, when the Presbyterians demanded further reforms in theology and the abandonment of the Byzantine-Rite practices. The church quickly lost a number of clergy who objected due to the openness of Protestantism and anglicization. The masses in turn followed their leaders. This led to a number of lawsuits and court cases over the possession of church properties in places like Portage La Prairie and Gimli in Manitoba; Vegreville and Rate in Alberta; and Goodeve in Saskatchewan.[21] Most of the rulings went against the trustees, and vested ownership with the Presbyterian Church. The last remnant of this church survived until 1912, when the remaining twenty-one clergy were given the choice to leave or to transfer to the Presbyterian Church.

The major obstacle for the Independent Greek Church was the manipulation of the Presbyterians. The Byzantine Rite, once abandoned, easily gave way to anglicization and the spirit of protestantism, for which the masses were not ready. John Bodrug himself did not enter the Presbyterian Church but continued his labours among Ukrainian evangelicals. In his memoirs he commented on the failure of the church:

> For the first time in its history, our nation had lived to see a Church of its very own, founded on the Word of God, a Church that could be administered according to its own wishes, without feeling over it the patronage of Rome, or of the Patriarchs. This church could not function without outside help. The Presbyterian Church, a creation arising out of the spirit and culture of the Scottish people, however genuinely Christian and highly cultured it may be, was [sic!] NOT UKRAINIAN. Every people has its own peculiar psychology and culture and every church must fit the psychology and culture of a given people. And when reform does come to a given church, such reform must take place step-by-step, according to the spiritual growth and traditions of that nation.[22]

Ukrainian Greek Orthodox Church of Canada

The last jurisdiction to enter into the forum of religious competitiveness was the Ukrainian Greek Orthodox Church of Canada.[23] It was established in 1918, but the movement began earlier. The leading figures were characterized by their loyalty to the people, their open espousal of Ukrainian cultural identity, and their intense opposition to clericalism. They strongly believed in higher education and many became school teachers in order to mould the masses into an identifiable group. These, in fact, were the *narodovtsi* (populists)—active defenders of the Ukrainian heritage and culture, strong supporters of the Ukrainian communities' solidarity, and active defusers of the Canadianizers, whether Protestant churches or the public school system.

They were also the promoters of bilingual (Ukrainian-English) schools on the prairies in the second decade of the twentieth century.

The *narodovtsi* were nurtured in the Ruthenian Training School, established in Winnipeg in 1905 and later in Brandon in 1907, and the School for Foreigners in Regina in 1909 and Vegreville in 1913. The 250 graduates of these schools, many of them subsequently bilingual teachers, became the fertile source of the movement. In 1907, the leaders organized themselves into the Ukrainian Teachers Association of Canada. As well, the leaders were instrumental in establishing a newspaper, *Ukrainskyi holos* (Ukrainian Voice), to popularize their ideals. This was the first newspaper in North America to bear the name "Ukrainian" on its masthead.

Among the early challenges for the group were activities against some of the policies of the Greek Catholic Church. The *narodovtsi* could not tolerate non-Ukrainian clergymen and challenged the incorporation of Ukrainian churches under the Roman Catholic hierarchy and, later, the Greek Catholic. The former challenge was seen as a threat of latinization and de-Ukrainization while the latter was considered a usurpation of the communities' labours and freedoms. In 1913 with the decree *Ea Semper*, a new issue was raised—only celibate clergy would be allowed to serve in Canada. For the *narodovtsi* this was another intrusion into the community and thus they began an appeal for clergy "just like in our homeland."

Having raised these issues, the leaders of the group began to rally for "a return to the faith of our forefathers," and to establish a Ukrainian National Church in Canada. Their position was epitomized in an editorial in *Ukrainskyi holos*: "... in Catholicism as well as Russian Orthodoxy, Ukrainian patriotism is not compatible. The one and the other desires to make a Ukrainian a servile slave and not a patriot, not even a man, but only a blind tool of their own interests."[24]

Next, Bishop Nykyta Budka himself came under attack by the *narodovtsi*. His newly created "Ruthenian Greek Catholic Episcopal Corporation of Canada," and subsequent "Statutes of the Ruthenian Greek Catholic Church of Canada," and the newly proclaimed "Regulations of the Ruthenian Greek Catholic Church of Canada" of 1914 alienated this group of Ukrainians, who saw in these documents strong, legalistic Roman Catholic influence. The *narodovtsi* concluded that the Greek Catholic Church was insufficiently national for their leaders to support it as the "National Church of Ukrainians in Canada."

Still further, this group feared that Greek Catholics would lose the content and substance of the Byzantine Rite and its accompanying Ukrainian national character. This fear intensified as the decade unfolded. However in reaction to this fear, the intelligentsia started to crystallize their own ideas on a "Ukrainian National Church." Beginning in 1914, the movement began to move in the direction of Ukrainian Orthodoxy—the Orthodox Church in

Ukraine of the tenth to seventeenth centuries associated with Ukrainian princes, hetmans, Kievan metropolitans and brotherhoods. At the same time, the group strongly objected to the Russian Orthodox Missionary Diocese in North America and saw in it the continued expansionist policies of Russian tsardom and the Holy Synod at the expense of the Ukrainian nation, its culture and its church. World War I interrupted the immediate development of this "National Church," but it re-emerged in 1917–18.

In 1916 another dimension of the debate between the *narodovtsi* and Greek Catholics arose in the Ukrainian community and its newspapers. Ukrainians developed the *bursa* (student residences in major university cities—Adam Kotsko Bursa in Winnipeg, P. Mohyla Institute in Saskatoon and M. Hrushevsky Institute in Edmonton). At the P. Mohyla Institute, established in 1916 as a non-sectarian institution, the problem arose. Soon after its founding, Bishop Nykyta Budka attempted to have it incorporated under his episcopal charter. To counter this encroachment, the institute incorporated itself on 28 January 1917, according to Canadian statutes. However, Budka continued to promote his cause, and the matter of the institute became hotly debated in the Ukrainian press. Budka refused to recognize the secular nature of the institution while the board and administration of the institute rejected any submission to the bishop, and the whole conflict reached the point of an impasse—no compromise was possible. Mohyla Institute became the most important centre of the *narodovtsi*, an island of Ukrainian nationalism with a number of "nationally thirsting students."

The major thrust to establish the "Ukrainian National and Democratic Church" began in late 1917 as a movement of *narodovtsi* to establish a Ukrainian Orthodox Brotherhood on Canadian soil. The three key leaders were law students Wasyl Swystun (also rector of P. Mohyla Institute), Michael Stechishin and Wasyl Kudryk (editor of *Ukrainskyi holos*). In December 1917, seven hundred delegates gathered in Saskatoon for the second national convention of Ukrainians, recognized as the "unofficial Ukrainian parliament." Representing the "Ukrainian national soul," they censured the Greek Catholic Church and Bishop Nykyta Budka and gave a vote of confidence to Swystun, Stechishin and *Ukrainskyi holos*. This action exasperated the two sides and provoked further heated debate on the pages of *Holos* and *Rusyn* between the "Saskatoon clique and its national parasites"[25] and the "Budka circle with its fraternalizing [sic] pro Roman and anti-national stand."[26]

A number of events in their homeland aided the *narodovtsi* during the years 1917 and 1918. The collapse of imperial Russia and the subsequent Ukrainian revolution, the establishment of the Ukrainian Central Rada and later the Ukrainian People's Republic, and the movement in Ukraine to create a Ukrainian Orthodox Autonomous Church gave credence to the *narodovtsi* in Canada. Also at this time a series of articles, including a draft of a constitution, written by the *Narodnyi sviashchenyk* (national priest) in the pages of *Kanadyiskyi farmer* prepared the way.

On 18–19 July 1918, a conference was convoked in Saskatoon by Wasyl Swystun and endorsed by a national committee of thirty prominent prairie community leaders. With 154 delegates in attendance, a decision was reached to establish a Ukrainian Greek Orthodox Brotherhood. The function of the brotherhood was "to conduct all the church activities until the time when there will be a legally elected and consecrated bishop in conformity with the eastern Orthodox Church."[27] The brotherhood elected a nine-member presidium, three per prairie province, to guide affairs until the first *sobor*. No bishops or clergy were involved in this development, which began as a lay movement.

Participants at this conference again condemned Bishop Budka and adopted a five-point programme which included: communion with other Eastern Orthodox Churches, a married priesthood, trustee ownership of church property, bishops to be elected by the *Sobor*, and parishes to accept and discharge clergy. The decisions of this conference were quickly disseminated across Canada with an appeal to all Ukrainian people. The first step had been taken, but the polemical battle also began anew with accusations and rebuttals in the partisan press of both sides.

However, the new movement had to legitimize its position, so it began to search out a bishop and clergy. At first, dialogue was begun with Archbishop Alexander Nemolovsky of the Russian Orthodox Mission. Initially accommodating, he soon changed his position and refused to offer pastoral leadership to the Ukrainian Orthodox Brotherhood because it had adopted a very strong Ukrainian national position. The Brotherhood certainly was not going to become another pawn for the Russian Orthodox Mission's expansion work. This attempt nonetheless fuelled the opposition against the newly created Brotherhood.

Six months after the Saskatoon conference, the third Ukrainian National Conference was convoked in Saskatoon in December 1918. The leaders of the Brotherhood also used this occasion to convoke the first *Sobor* of the Ukrainian Greek Orthodox Church of Canada on 28 December 1918. At this *Sobor*, the establishment of the church was approved and confirmed and a committee was struck to draft a church statute and charter. At this *Sobor*, the first four priests, all formerly from the Russian Orthodox Mission, took an oath of allegiance to the new church and were assigned to four prairie areas. They soon broke with the church, however, leaving the Brotherhood in the same position as in mid-July 1918.

The lay leadership of this church again commenced negotiations with the Russian Orthodox Mission, but this time with Metropolitan Platon who, after the revolutionary upheavals in the Russian Empire, returned to America in 1919. He was favourably predisposed to the Ukrainian Greek Orthodox

Church and negotiations had progressed to the point that a joint nineteen-article agreement had been formulated on 16–17 July 1919. However, the two parties, after lengthy debate in both camps, negated the document. The Russians' dismissal of Ukrainian nationalism and the embarrassment of the Brotherhood over this action, which the Greek Catholic circles used for their own end, led to the mutual termination of discussions.

Meanwhile, the Brotherhood began to investigate new ways to establish its legitimacy. The arrival of the learnèd Father Lazar German in Canada brought to the attention of church leaders the availability of Metropolitan Germanos Shegedi, a Syrian Orthodox prelate in the United States. Negotiations with Metropolitan Germanos progressed quickly and at the second *Sobor* of the church (held first in Winnipeg on 27 November 1919 and later continued in Edmonton, 4 December 1919, and Saskatoon, 10 December 1919), an agreement was reached for the Ukrainian Greek Orthodox Church to come under his spiritual care until a Ukrainian Orthodox bishop could be consecrated. The metropolitan was to have authority over matters of dogma, ecclesiastical discipline and rite, while the consistory was to handle the general administration of the church. Sixteen resolutions were adopted at this *Sobor*, and a consistory to have three priests and four laymen was established. Metropolitan Germanos subsequently appeared at the *Sobor* and then, in a pastoral letter of 29 November 1919, ratified this decision.

At this time only six clergymen served the church on the prairies. However, in March 1920, the first three students of the church's Saskatoon Seminary graduated and were subsequently ordained by Metropolitan Germanos. The three new priests (Fathers S. W. Sawchuk, D. Stratychuk and P. Sametz) joined the former six to proselytize on the prairies.

In 1920, the third *Sobor* of the Ukrainian Greek Orthodox Church of Canada was held, again in three centres (Winnipeg, 11 November, Saskatoon, 18 November and Edmonton, 25 November). At this time the *Sobor* decided to elect an administrator and establish a newspaper. When positive reports of the church's growth and need of more clergy were received, the *Sobor* empowered the church to enter into discussions with the movement of the Ukrainian Autocephalous Orthodox Church in Ukraine.

The Ukrainian Greek Orthodox Church in Canada was able to achieve wide popularity in a very short period, since a significant number of parishes of the Greek Catholic and Russian Orthodox Mission changed over to the new church. This again provoked heated accusations in the Ukrainian newspapers. The Ukrainian Greek Orthodox Church in Canada subsequently adopted Ukrainian as the liturgical language in 1922; launched a newspaper in 1924, *Pravoslavnyi Visnyk,* edited by Father W. Kudryk; accepted the jurisdiction of the Archbishop Ivan Teodorovych in 1924; and in 1929, became officially incorporated as the "Ukrainian Greek Orthodox Church of Canada."

Analysis

The five church jurisdictions each laboured through an initial developmental stage, subsequent consolidation, and eventual acceptance or, as in the case of the Seraphimite Church and the Independent Greek Church, extinction. Through these years, the local Ukrainian parishes and communities continued to be ministered to by the clergy of the various jurisdictions and sometimes they passed from one jurisdiction to another, or, in some cases, even to a third.

The jurisdictional changes and upheavals in the religious life of Ukrainians in Canada occurred primarily for ten reasons.

1. The rise of Ukrainian nationalism from political or religious identification as Galicians, Bukovynians, Austro-Hungarians, Ruthenians, Greek-Catholics or Greek-Orthodox. The immigrants slowly developed a national consciousness as Ukrainians. Events in the homeland greatly aided this development and influenced the immigration experience in Canada. Parishes and communities wished to have a clergy which was nationally as well as spiritually conscious and all foreign influences, including clergy, were considered detrimental to the proper self-definition of the immigrants. Notably the liturgical language of the Ukrainians was Church-Slavonic in the Ukrainian redaction in all the jurisdictions, but beginning in 1922, the vernacular Ukrainian was adopted by the Ukrainian Greek Orthodox Church of Canada.

2. The democratic nature of Canada deeply influenced the parishes and parishioners when they decided their religious affiliation. The freedoms offered by Canada were unheard of in their homeland. Thus they took full advantage of the new climate and began to question anything and everything that limited their freedom. As a result, the Ukrainians wanted to be active participants of their religious heritage. They wanted to decide the fate of their church property, the selection of clergy, and the administration of the local and national church. The Ukrainian Greek Orthodox Church of Canada was most receptive to this and its leaders openly challenged the Greek Catholic Church.

3. Ukrainians had a deep attachment to the Byzantine Ukrainian Rite and its manifestation in the liturgy and church life. To this were attached the Christian cultural traditions among Ukrainians. All five jurisdictions attempted to maintain the Byzantine Rite, but deviations from the rite were found. This is illustrated by the changes forced by the Presbyterian Church upon the Independent Greek Church and to a lesser extent by Latin-rite influences upon the Greek Catholic jurisdiction.

123

4. A number of jurisdictions received financial support to operate their ecclesiastical affairs. The Independent Greek Church was supported by the Presbyterian Home Missions; the Russian Orthodox Mission in North America was supported by the Holy Synod in St. Petersburg; and the Greek Catholic Church was supported in part by the Roman Catholic dioceses and bishops. All acknowledged the value of this assistance. For example, the Russian Orthodox Mission was for all practical purposes self-sufficient and did not have to depend on the support of the local parishes and parishioners. However, when this came to an end in 1917, the jurisdiction rapidly declined and a number of its parishes passed on to other jurisdictions. At the same time, financial assistance also meant that the "sponsors" could influence or even at times dictate church policy.

5. All the jurisdictions had dynamic and strong-willed leaders at the helm. Bodrug, Seraphim, Budka, Swystun, Tikhon and others were strong-willed, charismatic and outspoken personalities. While they could attract and enthrall a community or parish, they also had major detractors. Most often these individuals were perceived as either heroes or villains, and people who accepted one or the other became associated with that particular church or jurisdiction. Some of these individuals were able to attract parishes to their respective jurisdictions.

6. The Ukrainian Byzantine Rite has always had room for married, as well as secular and monastic celibate clergy. Yet in their homeland, Ukrainians felt a greater attachment to the married clergy who shared their pattern of life. In Canada, this same attachment was popularized. The Greek Catholics, under the influence of the Vatican, established an almost exclusively celibate clergy, both secular and monastic. The other jurisdictions all emphasized the married priesthood. This, along with other reasons, provoked some jurisdictional changes.

7. The placement of church property either under ecclesiastical or episcopal corporations, or vesting it in the members of the community provoked many difficulties. The latter was supported by nearly all jurisdictions. Even the Greek Catholic Church had members who challenged the episcopal corporation and argued for a policy of trustee ownership of church property. Among a number of Greek Catholic parishes, the incorporation of church properties to centralized church authority contributed to jurisdictional change.

8. An appeal to the courts was used on occasion by various jurisdictions to assert their authority within the community. However, this was very expensive and exhausting. The classic example was the court battle over

the parish in Edna-Star, Alberta, that was finally decided by the Privy Council in London in favour of the Russian Orthodox Mission. Similar court cases were fought between the Independent Greek Church and the Presbyterian Church in a number of centres on the prairies.

9. Ukrainian newspapers were the pulse of community life. The various jurisdictions, with the assistance of funding bodies and institutions, enlisted the aid of newspapers to assert their respective positions in the lobbying for the souls of the Ukrainian Canadians. Such newspapers as *Kanadyiskyi farmer, Ukrainskyi holos, Kanadyiskyi rusyn* (later renamed *Kanadyiskyi ukrainets*), *Ranok, Pravoslaviie* and *Pravoslavnyi visnyk* all contributed to influencing the masses. Some of these newspapers were able to influence certain groupings of people to change jurisdictions.

10. The Ukrainian immigrants realized the importance of education to improve their social condition. Early eagerness to pursue studies whether at the Manitoba College or the Ruthenian Training Schools opened new horizons for youth and young adults. Many of them became important cultural and religious figures in the Ukrainian community. A more enlightened community was always willing to challenge the established norms and question certain practices as well as ingrained "truths." Thus the "enlighteners" sometimes aided the mobility of Ukrainians from one jurisdiction to another.

Conclusion

The church jurisdictions over Ukrainians in Canada from 1891 to 1925 form a most important chapter in the social history of Ukrainian Canadians. In addition, they show a most dynamic and energetic community that was challenged to maintain old world values but at the same time subjected to the New World's freedom and liberty. In certain instances accommodations were made to the new circumstances and an evolution was accomplished. However, selections were also made, which established priorities in the religious life of the settlers. The lively debates between jurisdictions provoked deep challenges that eventually witnessed the survival of some and the demise of others. If anything, the jurisdictional rivalry was able to foster the strong maintenance of the Ukrainian language and culture in Canada. Although the jurisdictional battles of the first thirty-five years in Canada involved a number of issues that today may seem trivial or secondary, nevertheless in their time they were of prime importance. Today's surviving jurisdictions, the Ukrainian Catholic Church and the Ukrainian Orthodox Church, had the ability to resolve satisfactorily the challenges of their time and accommodate themselves to the new situation in a creative way. In the ensuing years these two jurisdictions developed parallel to each other throughout Canada. Each continued to challenge the other in an informal way and together they represent the traditional spiritual values of the Ukrainian people.

NOTES

1. The exact number is difficult to ascertain because of the variety of names under which they were recorded in Canadian records—Galicians, Bukovynians, Austrians, Poles, Ruthenians, Russians et al. See W. Darcovich and Paul Yuzyk, eds. *A Statistical Compendium of the Ukrainians in Canada, 1891—1976*, Series 31.
2. Iuliian Bachynsky, *Ukrainska Immigratsiia v Ziedynenykh Derzhavakh Ameryky* (Lviv, 1914), 256.
3. Maria Adamowska, "Beginnings in Canada" in Piniuta, *Land of Promise* (Saskatoon, 1981), 74.
4. *Misionar* (Zhovkva), 1899.
5. Quoted in C. J. Tarasar (ed.), *Orthodox America, 1794—1976* (New York, 1976), 69.
6. Quoted in L. Myshuha (ed.), *Propamiatna knyha Ukrainskoho Narodnoho Soiuzu* (Jersey City, 1976), 32.
7. See *Svoboda*, 22 April 1897—3 January 1898.
8. The best study of the Greek Catholic Church is P. Yuzyk, "The History of the Ukrainian Greek Catholic (Uniate) Church in Canada" (M.A. thesis, University of Saskatchewan, 1948).
9. In the United States, these decrees caused a major movement to Russian Orthodoxy led by Father Alexis Toth in Minneapolis, who was responsible for at least fifty parishes uniting to Orthodoxy. See K. Russin, "The Right Reverend Alexis G. Toth" (M.A. thesis, St. Vladimir's Seminary, 1971).
10. Soter Ortynsky was a suffragan bishop and was responsible to cach Latin hierarch in whose diocese he served. For his biography, see B. P. Procko, "Soter Ortynsky: First Ruthenian Bishop in the United States 1907–1916," *The Catholic Historical Review*, LVIII, no. 4, 513–33.
11. Bishop Vladimir received Father Alexis Toth and his parish in Minneapolis into the Orthodox faith in 1891.
12. C. J. Tarasar (ed.), *Orthodox America*, 129–30.
13. His report on this visit is found in ibid., 74–5.
14. Reported in ibid., 31 and 70.
15. P. Yuzyk, *The Ukrainian Greek Orthodox Church of Canada 1918–1951*, 47.
16. For a list of parishes, see Tarasar, *Orthodox America*, 348–9.
17. Ibid., 130 and 174.
18. Unfortunately no major study exists of this figure. For details on his jurisdiction, see Panteleimon Bozhyk, *Tserkov ukraintsiv v Kanadi* (Winnipeg: Kanadiiskyi ukrainets, 1927), 25–45.
19. See the memoirs of John Bodrug, *Independent Orthodox Church* (Toronto: Ukrainian Canadian Research Foundation, 1982).

20. See Vivian Olender, "Symbolic Manipulation in the Proselytizing of Ukrainians" in this volume.
21. Yuzyk, 51.
22. Bodrug, *Independent Orthodox Church*, 119.
23. Two major studies exist of this church: Odarka S. Trosky, *The Ukrainian Greek Orthodox Church in Canada* (Winnipeg, 1968) and Paul Yuzyk, *The Ukrainian Greek Orthodox Church of Canada 1918–1951* (Ottawa: University of Ottawa Press, 1981).
24. *Ukrainskyi holos,* 27 May 1914.
25. *Rusyn,* 17 July 1918.
26. *Ukrainskyi holos,* 31 July 1918.
27. Ibid., 7 August 1918.

Historical Factors
in the Maintenance of
Religion and Ethnicity

Dennis J. Dunn

The Vatican, the Kremlin and the Ukrainian Catholic Church

When the Ukrainian Catholic Church was established at the Union of Brest in 1596, the Vatican was supportive and enthusiastic. The Papacy relished the opportunity to extend the Catholic writ further into Eastern Europe, particularly among the large Ukrainian population located between Muscovy, Poland, Austria and the Ottoman Empire. The Ukrainian ecclesiastical leaders under Poland's sway were also receptive for the most part. Their choice seemed to be between assimilation into an Orthodox world which was increasingly dominated by the Russians or following their Orthodox traditions within the embrace of Rome under Poland. There was a third choice, of course, and that was to try to remain Ukrainian Orthodox. Many Ukrainians did this, although they soon found Russia, their culturally expansive neighbour, pressuring them.

For those Ukrainians who chose union with Rome, soon there was disillusionment and disappointment. They had been guaranteed equal status with the Latin rite of the Polish Church, but once the union was effected, the Ukrainian Catholics, clergy and laity alike, were treated as second-class citizens by the Polish church and political officials. Their treatment, perhaps, encouraged Bohdan Khmelnytsky to seek help from Tsar Aleksei in the Union of Pereiaslav in January 1654. The Vatican, however, did not agree with Polish church policy and issued documents supporting the Ukrainian Catholic Church's autonomy and importance, but Polish church officials paid no heed.[1] Latinization was pushed, and even Rome adopted some measures, especially in the training of clergy, which worked against the equality of the Ukrainian Catholic rite.

Once Poland was partitioned by Russia, Prussia and Austria, the Ukrainian Catholics found themselves divided, mainly between the Russian and Austrian empires. The most inauspicious development, from the point of view of the Ukrainian Catholics, was the emergence of the Russian empire as the major power in Eastern Europe. The Vatican was also disturbed by this, but it eventually adjusted to the new reality.

From the moment of its inception in 1596, the Ukrainian Catholic Church was slated for obliteration by Moscow. The Russian government viewed the Catholic church as an heretical faith. Traditional Russian feelings in this matter were clearly reported by Olearius, a German traveller in seventeenth-century Muscovy. Catholics "and their religion," he wrote, "have been a kind of abomination in the Russians' eyes." Indeed, "even the name [Catholic] is detested."[2] Of course religious differences were not the sole, or even the main, reason for Russia's hatred of the Ukrainian Catholic Church. There was also politics. The Ukrainian Catholic Church enabled the Papacy, once the Tsar annexed Ukrainian Catholic lands, to circumvent Moscow and maintain a tie with the Ukrainian and Belorussian peoples on the Eurasian plain. For the suspicious and authoritarian government of Russia, this tie between its subjects and a foreign centre was deeply disturbing.

Furthermore, the Ukrainian Catholic Church was a troubling example of an Orthodox-type religious institution which Moscow did not control. That in itself was bad enough, but, even worse, it could stimulate thoughts of autonomy within Orthodox breasts. The Ukrainian Catholic Church was, at minimum, an example of a church which used the Divine Liturgy of St. John Chrysostom and was free from Moscow. The Russian Orthodox Church had not always been completely identified with the state. It was only in the seventeenth and eighteenth centuries that the tsars had been able to subordinate it and, in many ways, pervert it for the political purposes of Russification. Although Russian Orthodoxy excoriated Catholicism, a church independent from the government had an innate appeal to Orthodox churchmen. Patriarch Nikon, who pushed for a freer hand and who paid for his temerity with dismissal, might perhaps have been influenced by the Union of Brest.

Finally, the Ukrainian Catholic Church eventually became a catalyst for Ukrainian nationalism. In the nineteenth century the very threat of forcible conversion to Orthodoxy fuelled national sentiment. In the twentieth century the Ukrainian Catholics in the Austrian empire acted as a beacon of Ukrainian nationalism. The church there supplied spiritual and organizational support for the Ukrainian nation.[3] The example of the Ukrainian Catholic Church, perhaps, also sparked national feelings among Ukrainian Orthodox Christians who chafed at being religiously subordinated to the Russian Orthodox Church and politically subordinated to the Kremlin. From Moscow's point of view, the Ukrainian Catholic Church and its leaders were a dangerous island of irredentists which could arouse the entire Ukraine. It was for the same reason that Stalin feared Nazi control of Carpatho-Ukraine in 1939.[4]

Unlike several other religious groups, the Ukrainian Catholic Church was persecuted unremittingly by the Kremlin authorities. That suggests the campaign against it was primarily political. Attacks against Roman Catholics were only sporadic. They were discriminated against for jobs and educational opportunities, their dioceses reorganized and their ties to Rome severed. The Roman Catholic Church, like the Orthodox Church, was also forced to answer, in virtually all matters, to a secular government official. Jews were also discriminated against but, like the Roman Catholics, the persecution was inconsistent. After the Polish Partitions, Jews were kept in a Pale of Settlement whose eastern border coincided with the boundary of the old Polish Republic, but there were only brief periods, under Nicholas I and Alexander III, when they were pressured to convert to Orthodoxy. In contrast, Ukrainian Catholics were constantly abused and attacked. The pernicious and all-out campaign against Ukrainian Catholics in the twentieth century is paralleled only by Stalin's terror in the 1930s. The persecution was brutal, unrelenting and intent upon total destruction. The Ukrainian Catholics were seen not as heretics but as traitors.

Sizable numbers of Ukrainian Catholics, for the first time, came under Moscow's rule in the latter part of the eighteenth century when Catherine the Great, working with Austria and Prussia, divided the Polish state and took as Russia's share the former Polish provinces of Volhynia, Podolia and Ukraine. The partitions placed five Ukrainian Catholic dioceses under Moscow's control: Brest-Litovsk, Pinsk, Lutsk, Polotsk and Kiev, where the metropolitan see was located. Catherine turned the army loose on the hapless Ukrainian Catholics. In one of the most brutal religious persecutions ever recorded in history, the Ukrainian Catholic Church lost 9,000 of 11,000 parishes, 145 monasteries, and more than 8,000,000 believers. Cossacks were stationed in Catholic villages, and allowed to threaten, plunder and murder until the peasants acquiesced. Catholic priests were tortured into submission or killed. Parents were intimidated by the kidnapping or disfigurement of their children. Turncoats were richly rewarded. "Along a trail strewn with blood and humiliation, with mass suicides and unrecorded martyrdoms, the missionaries of the Empress effected the confiscation of most of the Uniate Churches, and the nominal conversion of some four-fifths of the Uniate population."[5] By the end of her reign, only 1,500 churches remained in Union with a total congregation of approximately 2,000,000, only one Catholic bishop was left, and the church hierarchy was subordinated to a consistory controlled by the state.[6] Nicholas I continued the attack. Books were burned; priests were murdered; the army forced mass conversions to Orthodoxy; churches were obliterated. In 1839 Nicholas staged a farcical reunion between the Ukrainian Catholic Church in the Russian empire and the Russian Orthodox Church and cut all ties between the Ukrainian Catholics and the Papacy.[7]

The remaining concentrations of Ukrainian Catholics were located in the Kholm (Cheom) diocese in the Kingdom of Poland—the last bastion of Ukrainian Catholicism in territories controlled by Moscow—and in Galicia and Transcarpathia in the Austrian empire. The Kholm diocese was annexed in 1875 under Alexander II, leaving only the Ukrainian Catholic centres in the Austrian empire. The Union of Brest was officially annulled by Moscow in all lands of the Russian empire in 1875. After the Revolution of 1905, Nicholas II permitted a Russian Uniate Church to be organized. The papacy appointed as its initial head the metropolitan of the Ukrainian Catholic Church, Metropolitan Andrei Sheptytsky, who resided in the Austrian-controlled city of Lviv. He, in turn, eventually named a Russian, Leonid Fedorov, to head the incipient church, but it did not last very long under the Bolsheviks. As for the Ukrainian Catholic Church in the Russian empire, it had been so devastated by Moscow's inveterate hostility that it could not take advantage of the brief respite of toleration between 1906 and 1914.

When World War I broke out, Nicholas II showed that the hiatus between the October Revolution and 1914 was entirely expedient. Russian soldiers swept into the Austrian territory of Galicia and immediately set about attacking Ukrainian Catholics. Metropolitan Sheptytsky was placed under house arrest until he was liberated following the fall of the tsar in March 1917.

From the time that the Russian empire had emerged as the dominant power in Eastern Europe and annexed large parts of the Polish state, which included Ukrainian lands and people, 'the Russian government was bent on the total destruction of the Ukrainian Catholic Church. By 1917 it had virtually succeeded in destroying the church in the Russian empire. What was the policy of the Vatican during this period of persecution? It was, to say the least, ambiguous. Although some debate revolves around the motivation of specific popes, it is an established fact that the Roman Curia did not even persuade Ukrainian Catholics they had good intentions. To be sure, the Vatican continued to uphold the Ukrainian rite and it objected to the persecution of the Ukrainian Catholics, but at the same time it showed itself to be inattentive, if not inimical, to Ukrainian Catholic suffering and aspirations. Disturbed by the connection between nationalism and radical political movements, the Vatican's general approach in Eastern Europe was to support the status quo. "Render unto Caesar" was uppermost in the minds of Vatican officials when it came to the Catholic subjects of the tsar. Of course, the popes had no way directly to force a change of policy in Moscow, but the failure to condemn Moscow publicly and continuously or to seek help for the beleaguered Ukrainians among the major powers cut deeply into the Vatican's moral authority. In the age of Machiavellian politics the pope's only weapon was and is his moral authority.

The Bolshevik Revolution ushered in a new era of persecution for the Catholic church, Ukrainian and Roman rite alike, which persists to this very day. The Bolsheviks hated the Ukrainian Catholic Church for the same reasons that the tsars detested it, but they also had another motive. The Bolsheviks were atheists who pummelled religion enthusiastically. They spared no religion initially, cutting away with equal abandon at Russian Orthodoxy and the minority faiths. Lenin soon, however, reverted to the tsarist policy and subordinated the Russian Orthodox to the policy aims of Soviet government. The Communists continued to attack Orthodoxy, though, until Stalin halted the persecution during the war when he found the church was a key generator of nationalist feeling and thus an essential support for his regime. After the war, Khrushchev again attacked the Orthodox church, and the Communists still might alienate their government from the religious nationalism of the Russian people.[8] Although policy toward the Russian Orthodox Church was checkered, there was no inconsistency toward the Catholic Church and its various rites. It was attacked uniformly.

As of January 1917, of course, the major branches of the Ukrainian Catholic Church existed outside the Russian empire in Austria-Hungary. With the defeat of that state at the end of World War I, they found themselves under the jurisdiction of Poland (Galicia and western part of Belorussia) and Czechoslovakia (Carpatho-Ukraine and the Prešov diocese in northeastern Slovakia). There were also Uniate Catholics in Romania and in the Križevci diocese in Yugoslavia.

In 1918 the Communists nationalized Uniate Church property and schools, disenfranchized and heavily taxed the clergy, and removed the civil rights of clergy. They also denied juridical status to religious groups and ruled that church buildings and equipment could only be used by "councils" which consisted of twenty or more people over the age of eighteen who were licensed by the government. In 1919 the government outlawed religious instruction (other than by parents) of children under the age of eighteen. In 1920 a drive to close monasteries began. The exarch of the incipient Russian Uniate Church, Leonid Fedorov, was incarcerated along with most of the Roman Catholic bishops in 1922–3. They were found guilty of anti-Soviet activities, counterrevolutionary conspiracies, inciting unrest, and undermining the dictatorship of the working class.[9] Most were sentenced to long prison terms, but one Catholic leader, Mgr. Constantine Budkiewicz, the dean of the Catholic clergy in Petrograd, was executed. The small Russian Uniate Church was soon dismantled.

Persecution was also the fate of the Roman Catholic Church. The hierarchy and the bulk of the clergy were removed by 1924. The French Jesuit bishop Michel D'Herbigny, who was in the Soviet Union to discuss Vatican-Kremlin problems in 1925, secretly consecrated eleven bishops and apostolic administrators. The Soviet government, however, expelled D'Herbigny and quickly cashiered the new leaders. Ukraine, of course, was forcibly annexed by Moscow in 1921 and the suppression of the small Ukrainian Catholic Church there soon followed.

During the Nazi-Soviet alliance from 1939 until June 1941, the Soviets held the Ukrainian Catholic dioceses of Lviv, Stanislav, and Przemyśl with roughly 3,200,000 believers.[10] Stalin chose not to move against the church at this time. Conditions were too uncertain and dangerous with the war raging and the alliance with Berlin weakening. Communications between Ukrainian Catholic officials and the Vatican confirm that the Communists were more tolerant then.[11]

The German invasion of the Soviet Union in 1941 forced the Soviets to retreat, but in 1944 they again pushed into Eastern Europe. By the end of the war the following Ukrainian Catholic peoples and regions were under Soviet sway: Western Ukraine with over 3 million believers, one archbishop-metropolitan, seven bishops, 2,400 priests, more than 1,000 nuns, and 600 monks; Carpatho-Ukraine with nearly 500,000 believers; Prešov diocese in Slovakia with 356,000 believers; and Western Belorussia with 30,000 believers. In addition, they held the Romanian Uniate Church with 1.4 million believers. The Ukrainian Catholic Church in Western Ukraine and Western Belorussia was forced to join the Russian Orthodox Church in 1946. The "Reunion Sobor," which was held to give legitimacy to the suppression of the Ukrainian Catholic Church in Galicia, was both arbitrary and uncanonical. There is even growing evidence that the Ukrainian priest who worked with the Soviets to orchestrate the farce, Reverend Kostelnyk, was operating under duress.[12]

The Uniate Church in Romania was coerced into joining the Romanian Orthodox Church in 1948. The Ukrainian Catholic Church in Carpatho-Ukraine had to merge with Russian Orthodoxy in 1949. Finally, the Ukrainian Catholic Church in Slovakia was obliged to adhere to the Orthodox church in 1950.[13] By the beginning of the 1950s, the only surviving Uniate diocese in the Communist bloc was found in Yugoslavia, and owed its survival primarily to the Tito-Stalin break. During the Prague Spring in Czechoslovakia in 1968, the Prešov diocese with its 356,000 Ukrainian Catholics was permitted to re-establish itself. In addition, a significant Ukrainian Catholic Church in diaspora continues in Western Europe, Canada and the United States. A sub rosa Ukrainian Catholic Church exists in Ukraine and, despite its lack of priests and bishops, it is a potent religious and political force in Western Ukraine.[14] There is also a small Ukrainian Catholic community in Poland which is protected by the powerful Roman Catholic Church.

The attitude of the popes since World War II toward the Ukrainian Catholic Church cannot be conveniently generalized. Of course, there are some general characteristics, but the modifications are so many that it is better to describe the positions of the popes individually. Pius XII was a bitter foe of

Soviet Communism, and during the war he predicted what would happen in Eastern Europe if Germany were to be levelled and the western democracies were to pursue a policy of concessions toward Moscow.[15] He was hamstrung, though, by his unwillingness to step forward in defence of national movements in Eastern Europe and by his public reticence over German atrocities. He demonstrated that characteristic phobia of the Catholic Church for nationalism. He also had a low standing with the leaders who were heading the war effort in the United States and England. As far as the Ukrainian Catholic Church was concerned, he publicly condemned the forced union with Orthodoxy and he looked upon Russian Orthodoxy as a tool of Moscow. He also held the traditional Catholic position that even if Orthodoxy were not a puppet of the Kremlin, it was still a schismatic faith which would have to look to union with Rome. The East European hierarchy, from Cardinal Wyszyński to Cardinal Mindszenty to Cardinal Slipy, all agreed.

Pope John XXIII ushered in a new era when he took a different approach to Orthodoxy and Moscow. He believed the church should be working toward religious freedom in Eastern Europe, not the supremacy of the Catholic church. He also believed that the USSR under Khrushchev might be abandoning its campaign against religion and that it was time to try dialogue rather than confrontation. John was a warm, tolerant pastor, but he was politically naive and he epitomized the church's traditional antipathy toward nationalism in Eastern Europe. Unbeknown to him, just as he was making overtures to Moscow, Khrushchev was orchestrating a brutal campaign against religion, the like of which had not been seen since before World War II. The Ukrainian Catholics were not informed of the pope's change of heart about Orthodoxy. In effect, he was implying that the Ukrainian Catholic Church was not a model for Orthodoxy and that it might be an impediment to understanding between Rome and Zagorsk. He did achieve the liberation of Cardinal Slipy but that Ukrainian leader soon felt himself to be a prisoner of the Vatican.[16]

Paul VI and Archbishop Agostino Casaroli formally elaborated the policy of *Ostpolitik*. Rome's position now was quite clear: pursue religious freedom in Eastern Europe without regard to the primacy of one religion; work to build the hierarchy of the Roman Catholic Church; negotiate and pursue dialogue with Moscow since it was the established political power in the East and held the keys to peace, order and religious freedom; open discussions with the Orthodox church with the aim of pursuing common religious objectives, including keeping the peace and working for a free religious environment. The rationale for papal *Ostpolitik* was summarized by Paul VI in 1965 when he argued that it was a policy based upon Christian patience and, more importantly, on the prevention of a greater evil.[17]

Ukrainian Catholics were in a hopeless situation. They had legal and moral right on their side, but compared with their Russian protagonists—the Russian Orthodox Church and the Kremlin—they were politically impotent. It was a fatal combination. Ukrainian Catholic leaders were shocked and hurt at the Vatican's new orientation. They were bitter that the Ukrainian Catholic Church, the most persecuted church of all, should now be a secondary consideration of the Vatican. Most of them failed to perceive that even conservative churchmen in the West were enthusiastic about a modus vivendi with the USSR, and that Ukrainian Catholic complaints, precisely because they were unanswerable, were bound to provoke the kind of irritation and contempt that is often the product of bad conscience. Ukrainian Catholic leaders hoped for public protests over their treatment and, eventually, for a patriarchate. Cardinal Slipy cried out in 1971 that "no one defends the Catholic Ukrainians."[18] The pope was privately sympathetic, but made it clear in 1971, 1975 and 1976 that to elevate Slipy to Patriarch of Ukraine would be imprudent.[19]

Many of the Ukrainian Catholics in diaspora, able to speak freely in contrast to their brethren in the Soviet Union, objected to the Vatican's general line. The Vatican, however, paid them little heed. Pope Paul VI was convinced that the policy of *Ostpolitik* was paying dividends and would ultimately work for the benefit of the Catholic church generally in Eastern Europe.

The Vatican's position is open to criticism. First, it misunderstood nationalism in Eastern Europe. Nationalism is the major force in Eastern Europe, and nationalists there, in contrast to the West, are not anti-religious but pro-religious. The church is flying in the face of an incredibly powerful ally in order to support, in effect, the Communist status quo. Because of past problems with nationalist forces around the world, the church has been understandably reluctant to support nationalist movements in Eastern Europe. So often such movements have been anti-religious or only expediently pro-religious. In addition, of course, support might lead to a confrontation between the authorities and the nationalists that could end in violence. Further, the church is not dedicated to national states, but to a religiously unified Europe, indeed, world, which would approximate the religious unity of Christendom. In Eastern Europe, however, there seems to be a strong case for backing the nationalists. They are very pro-religious. They believe in the concept of Europe unified around Christianity, and they have the support of the people.

Secondly, in terms of evaluating the efficacy of papal *Ostpolitik*, the church has made only marginal gains in Eastern Europe as a result of its pursuit of detente with the Communist authorities. The major showcase, namely the strength of the church in Poland, had nothing to do with Vatican policy. On the contrary, under Cardinal Stefan Wyszyński, the Polish hierarchy pursued a policy of toughness toward the Communists and it paid rich dividends. The strength of the church in Poland owes much to the hierarchy's absolute unwillingness to compromise over essentials.[20] Indeed, it is not because of papal *Ostpolitik* that a Polish pope was possible,[21] rather, it was in spite of it.

Thirdly, the Russian Orthodox Church persists as merely a pawn of the Soviet government. Orthodox believers, of course, should not be written off, but the hierarchy is another matter. Dimitry Pospielovsky outlines a damning indictment of the Orthodox leadership, especially Patriarch Pimen.[22] Fourthly, Ukrainian Catholics have suffered terribly for their Catholicism. It is unconscionable for a spiritual pastor to treat them shabbily and make only *private* remonstrances over their fate. Fifthly, the Ukrainian Catholics are a logical model for the reunion of Orthodoxy with Rome. Rather than neglecting them, the Vatican should see them as a bridge to the East. The Ukrainian Catholic Church is unique in its perseverant use of the common ritual of Ukrainian Churches (Orthodox and Catholic) and its acceptance of Rome's leadership. Of all churches in Europe, it could most easily address the religious needs of the persecuted Orthodox believers of the Soviet empire.

Finally, it is doubtful that the Vatican's policy of *Ostpolitik* is preventing a greater evil. The Ukrainian Catholic Church is already suppressed in the USSR. Its underground believers and clergy are hounded and arrested when found. The Communists cannot do much to the churches in the other satellites of Eastern Europe. If they opened up a campaign of violent persecution, they would give propaganda advantages to western critics, create martyrs who could change religious feelings into a political challenge, clearly show everyone that they are imperialist occupiers and that the church is the protector of the national heritage, and risk confrontations like those which continue to emanate today from Poland.

When the present pope, John Paul II ascended the papal throne in 1978, he appeared, initially, to be an advocate of Paul VI's policy of *Ostpolitik*. He courted the Russian Orthodox Church and the Soviet government and, like his predecessor, turned aside Cardinal Slipy's request to be named Patriarch. However, by 1980, there is some evidence that John Paul II was reevaluating the official position of "benign neglect" toward the Ukrainian Catholic Church. In a document called "On February Seventeenth," issued in February 1980 by the pope and at the Ukrainian Vatican Synod in March 1980, a measure of self-government was given to the Ukrainian Catholic bishops. Although it is a matter of debate as to whether the latter event established a Ukrainian Patriarchate, it nonetheless gave the Ukrainians a framework for episcopal continuity. Then in November-December 1980 the Ukrainian Catholic bishops held a synod in Rome and passed a resolution called "The Solemn Repudiation of the Legality of the So-Called Lviv Synod of 1946." In effect, the Ukrainian leaders announced that the Lviv Synod which forced their church to join the Russian Orthodox Church was illegal. Since the meeting was held with the pope's approval and the pope made no effort to disassociate himself from the resolution, the Russian

Orthodox Church immediately objected. Patriarch Pimen wrote the pope on 22 December 1980 that the "synod of the Ukrainian Catholic bishops held recently in the Vatican with Your blessing" was disturbing and its "resolution may, in the fullest sense of the word, annul all those greater achievements in the sphere of rapprochement between our two churches." Further, it "creates dangerous tensions in the relations between the Roman Catholic and Russian Orthodox Churches." Its "content and spirit. . . are alien to the spirit of ecumenical brotherhood that exists between us, and what is more, it endeavors to revise and destroy the structure of the Russian Orthodox Church." Pimen went on to demand that the pope unequivocally denounce the resolution.[23]

The pope replied on 24 January 1981. While he said the resolution did not have an "official character," he was vague enough so he did not, in effect, endorse Moscow's position on the Lviv Synod of 1946.[24] For Moscow these events were undoubtedly upsetting.[25] In the context of the unfolding contest between Solidarity and Moscow's satellite government in Warsaw, in which the pope, ipso facto, was an inspiration to Solidarity, the Ukrainian Catholic developments were ominous. Might the pope be preparing to open the Pandora's Box of East European nationalism? Ukrainian nationalism is a powerful force which, if stoked by the pope, could challenge Moscow where it is most vulnerable, on its denial of political rights to the nationalities within its empire. Indeed, the pope's hand could also, to the suspicious mind, be seen in the Catholic ferment in Lithuania and even in Czechoslovakia. Of course, to some Ukrainian church leaders the pope was giving very little, if anything at all, but there was a real change, at least in tone and spirit, from *Ostpolitik*. It would be obvious to sensitive, suspicious minds in the Kremlin.

Ultimately, I think, the attempted assassination of the pope in 1981 was tied to Moscow's fear that he might abandon *Ostpolitik* and initiate a new policy, which we might call "religious rollback."[26] It is really impossible to say whether Moscow's fears were justified, but, if they were, the attempted assassination nipped the pope's initiative in the bud. Since the assassination attempt, the pope has been very careful with regard to the Ukrainian Catholic Church as well as other religious/nationalist forces in Eastern Europe. For the Ukrainian church, when Cardinal Slipy died, he chose a leader with whom he could work, but to whom some Ukrainian nationalists objected. He really had no other choice, for if he publicly elevated the unofficial leaders of the Ukrainian Catholic Church he would be setting them up for removal. It is clear that he holds the Ukrainian Catholics dear and hopes to help redress past grievances without compromising what little progress has been made.

His very positive stand toward the Ukrainian minority in Poland is encouraging. He supports a clerical administration for the Ukrainian Catholics in Poland, but the problem to be resolved is how to set up such a hierarchy without precipitating repression from Moscow. The Lublin seminary trains

Ukrainian Catholic clergy under a Roman Catholic guise. Since 1981 Catholic organizations that had sprung up as part of Solidarity have been rebuilding Ukrainian churches in Poland which were destroyed in 1947. In the summer of 1983 at Castel Gandolfo, a choir of Ukrainian girls from Poland performed for the pope.[27]

The future is difficult to predict, but the triangular relationship between Moscow, Rome and the Ukrainian Catholic Church is, I believe, a key to understanding the future of Eastern Europe. It should be watched carefully.

NOTES

1. Victor J. Pospishil, "The Saga of the Ukrainian Churches," in Miroslav Labunka and Leonid Rudnytzky, (eds.), *The Ukrainian Catholic Church, 1945–1975* (Philadelphia: St. Sophia Religious Association of Ukrainian Catholics, 1976), 16.
2. Samuel H. Baron, ed. and trans., *The Travels of Olearius in 17th-Century Russia* (Stanford: Stanford University Press, 1967), 282–3.
3. Bohdan R. Bociurkiw, "Institutional Religion and Nationality in the Soviet Union," in S. Enders Wimbush, (ed.), *Soviet Nationalities in Strategic Perspective* (London and Sydney: Croom Helm, 1985), 188–90.
4. Adam B. Ulam, *Expansion and Coexistence: Soviet Foreign Policy 1917–73*, 2nd ed. (New York and Washington: Praeger, 1974), 264.
5. Norman Davies, *God's Playground: A History of Poland*, 2 vols. (New York: Columbia University Press, 1982), 2: 210.
6. Wasyl Lencyk, *The Eastern Catholic Church and Czar Nicholas I* (Rome and New York: Ukrainian Catholic University Press, 1966), 15, 19–20.
7. Ibid., especially chapters VII and IX.
8. Bociurkiw discusses the crisis at length in his "Institutional Religion and Nationality," 197–9.
9. Francis McCullagh, *The Bolshevik Persecution of Christianity* (New York: Dutton, 1924), 142–276, 364–5; see also Boleslaw Szczesniak, *The Russian Revolution and Religion* (Notre Dame: University of Notre Dame, 1959), 113–26; also see N. V. Krylenko, *Sudebnye rechi, 1922–1930* (Moscow, 1931), 18.
10. Pierre Blet, *et al. Actes et documents du Saint Siège relatifs à la seconde guerre mondiale.* Vol. III: *Le Saint Siège et la Situation Religieuse en Pologne et dans les Pays Baltes (1939–1945),* 2 Parts, Part One (1939–1941) (Città del Vaticano: Libreria Editrice, 1967), 3–4.
11. Ibid., 79, 144, 297, 565 note 1.
12. See Bohdan R. Bociurkiw, "The Suppression of the Greek-Catholic Church in the Post-War U.S.S.R. and Poland: A Comparison," unpublished preliminary draft of paper presented at the Third World Congress for Soviet and East European Studies at Washington, D.C., 30 October—4 November 1985.
13. The best treatment of the Uniate Church in the postwar period is Bohdan Bociurkiw, "The Uniate Church in the Soviet Ukraine: A Case Study in Soviet Church Policy," *Canadian Slavonic Papers* 7 (1965): 89–113. A crucial document on the suppression

of the Ukrainian Catholic Church in Ukraine is *Diiannia Soboru Hreko-Katolytskoi Tserkvy, 8–10 bereznia 1946, u Lvovi* (Lviv, 1946). Also see D.J. Dunn, *The Catholic Church and the Soviet Government, 1939–1949* (New York: Columbia University Press, 1977).

14. See the following studies on this theme: the *samvydav* document from Ukraine called "The Life of the Ukrainian Catholic Church in the Catacombs," *Ukrainian Review* 31, no. 1 (Spring 1983): 27–40. Also see Lev E. Dobriansky, "The Religious Revolution," *Ukrainian Quarterly* 38, no. 4 (1983): 360; Bohdan R. Bociurkiw, "The Catholic Church and the Soviet States in the 1970s," (unpublished ms.), 21; D.J. Dunn, *Detente and Papal-Communist Relations, 1962–1978* (Boulder, Colo.: Westview Press, 1979); "Increasing Activity of the Ukrainian Catholic Church in the Western Ukraine," *Radio Liberty Research Bulletin*, 119/83, 16 March 1983. *The Chronicle of the Catholic Church in the Ukraine* is a fascinating source of recent information. For an analysis, see Andrew Sorokowski, "The Chronicle of the Catholic Church in Ukraine," *Religion in Communist Lands*, 13 (Winter 1985): 292–7.

15. Dunn, *Catholic Church and Soviet Government*, 89–101.

16. Hansjakob Stehle, *Eastern Politics of the Vatican 1917–1979*, trans. Sandra Smith (Athens, Ohio: Ohio University Press, 1981), 318.

17. Ibid., 312.

18. Ibid., 367.

19. Ibid.

20. Dunn, *Detente and Papal-Communist Relations*, 100–22.

21. This argument can be found in Stehle, *Eastern Politics*, 391.

22. Dimitry Pospielovsky, *The Russian Church Under the Soviet Regime 1917–1982*, 2 vols. (Crestwood, New York: St. Vladimir's Seminary Press, 1984), 2: 470–1.

23. Russel P. Moroziuk, *Politics of a Church Union* (Chicago: *Chicago Herald*, 1983), 112.

24. Ibid., 112–13.

25. Ibid., 114. The pope's correspondence was published in *Zhurnal Moskovskoi Patriarkhii* (April 1981) 4: 6–7.

26. For more information on the attempted assassination and its connection to events in Eastern Europe, see Paul Henze, *The Plot to Kill the Pope* (New York: Charles Scribner & Sons, 1983); Claire Sterling, *Time of the Assassins* (New York, 1983); and Alex Alexiev, "The Kremlin and the Pope," *Ukrainian Quarterly* 34, no. 4 (1983): 38–84.

27. Interview with Norman Davies, Washington, D.C., 1 November 1985.

Bohdan R. Bociurkiw

Soviet Suppression of the Greek Catholic Church in Ukraine and its Impact on Ukrainian Catholics in Canada

Since the Union of Brest of 1596 (and in Transcarpathia, the Union of Uzhhorod of 1646),[1] the Greek Catholic (Uniate) Church has evolved into a national institution of central importance in Western Ukraine, although it was suppressed by the Russian authorities in the rest of Ukraine (and Belorussia) in the course of the nineteenth century. Prior to World War II, the Ukrainian Greek Catholic Church embraced four dioceses and one Apostolic Administration, with over four million faithful.[2]

However, in March 1946, the Ukrainian Greek Catholic (Uniate) Church was officially suppressed in Galicia by the Soviet state. To create the fiction of a "voluntary" ecclesiastical suicide, Stalin's police, with willing help from the Moscow Patriarchate, staged a pseudo-sobor in Lviv, after eleven months of anti-Uniate terror. Devoid of any representative character or canonical authority, this gathering "voted" to dissolve the 350–year old Union with Rome and to "reunite" with the Russian Orthodox Church. Repression of the Uniates was extended to Carpatho-Ukraine, where the church was banned in 1949 without the benefit of any "sobor."[3] Forcible "reunion" of the Mukachiv diocese with the Moscow Patriarchate was re-enacted a year later in the adjoining Prešov diocese in Slovakia.[4] In Poland, the Greek Catholic Church was implicitly "de-legalized" by government decrees in 1947 and 1949, after the deportation and dispersal of the Ukrainian population from southeast Poland.[5] By 1950, whatever remained of the Greek Catholic Church was driven underground in all Ukrainian-populated lands annexed or controlled by the Soviet Union.

143

I shall attempt to re-examine, firstly, the factors which shaped the Soviet decision to destroy the Ukrainian Greek Catholic Church, as well as the circumstances, methods, and immediate and long-range consequences of its forcible "reunion" with the Russian Orthodox Church.[6]

Secondly, I will briefly survey the fate of the illegal Uniate Church during the subsequent four decades. My focus will be primarily on Galicia. Thirdly, I will try to assess the impact of Soviet suppression of the Uniate Church within the USSR on the Ukrainian Catholic Church in Canada, focusing on the period from 1945 until the 1963 release of Metropolitan Iosyf Slipy from the USSR.

I

It can hardly be doubted now that the long-range Soviet objective in suppressing the Greek Catholic Church was to promote Sovietization and eventual Russification of West Ukrainians by depriving them of their national church, their oldest and only surviving ethno-religious integrating structure. The other goal was to cut the links between the local church and the Vatican, which was perceived as an international ideological centre of anti-Communism and anti-Soviet subversion, determined to inspire a Western crusade against the USSR and its satellite empire. The more immediate objective was to facilitate the Soviet struggle against the massive Ukrainian nationalist resistance movement led by the UPA and OUN. These groups had been significantly undermining Soviet war efforts in Western Ukraine and frustrating attempts to establish effective Soviet control over the less accessible areas of Galicia.

The Uniate Church's refusal to assist the Soviet authorities to bring about the surrender of UPA partisans and the surfacing of the nationalist underground[7] affected both the Soviet decision to destroy the church and the time chosen for its implementation. The timing—after an initial period of benevolence toward the Uniate Church, from July 1944 to early 1945— might have been determined by the decision of the Yalta Conference in February 1945, which awarded Western Ukraine to the USSR, by the now certain victory of the Soviet armies over Germany, and by a favourable assessment in the Kremlin of the progress of its campaign against the UPA partisans and the nationalist underground network. The decision to proceed with the suppression of the Ukrainian Greek Catholic Church must have been reached in the Kremlin sometime between January and March 1945. The Moscow Patriarchate was brought into the action only afterward, when it was realized that Soviet policy objectives would be better served by the absorption of the Uniates into the "patriotic" and well policed Russian Orthodox Church.[8]

The main role in the "conversion" of the Uniates was assigned to the Soviet security organs (NKGB/MGB), assisted by the local administrative and propaganda apparatus.[9] After several days of vicious anti-Uniate propaganda, the NKGB on 11 April 1945 arrested Metropolitan Iosyf Slipy and four other bishops in Lviv and Stanislav. Several weeks later, some 100 leading clergymen were swept away by the next wave of arrests.[10]

Installed in May, after the arrest of the episcopate, the "Action Group for Reunion of the Greek Catholic Church with the Russian Orthodox Church," led by Rev. H. Kostelnyk, was arbitrarily assigned the functions of provisional administration of the Uniate Church in Galicia by the government.[11] Its task was to "persuade" the priests to abandon the Union with Rome and provide a semblance of a "spontaneous," "voluntary" movement of the clergy for reunion with Moscow. No attempts were made to recruit a mass lay following for this cause. Clergy who remained unmoved by the arguments and sanctions of the Action Group were harassed, arrested by the security organs, and threatened with Article 58 (counterrevolution) of the criminal code, *unless* they agreed to adhere to the Action Group and its objectives. "Converts" were rewarded with instant release and reinstatement to ecclesiastical posts. In this way, by March 1946, slightly over 50 per cent of the Galician clergy had been "won over" to the cause of reunion,[12] especially after several hundred of their fellow pastors who would not succumb to terror were sentenced *in camera* to lengthy prison-camp terms.

When it became clear that none of the arrested Ukrainian Catholic bishops would renounce the Union and preside over the church's reunion with Moscow,[13] two leaders of the Action Group (Frs. Pelvetsky and Melnyk) were quietly ordained in Kiev as Orthodox bishops after the Groups's thirteen core members were "received back" into the Russian Orthodox Church in February 1946.[14] The purpose of this ordination was to "meet" the canonic requirement of episcopal participation in church sobors.

The "Reunion Sobor," which met in the cordoned-off St. George Cathedral in Lviv, in the presence of Soviet movie cameramen and delegates from the Moscow Patriarchate, was chaired by Rev. Kostelnyk and the two freshly ordained Orthodox bishops. It was a carefully stage-managed affair, with all 216 delegates appointed by the Group, no agenda, no rules or resolutions of the sobor circulated in advance, and the very event withheld from public knowledge until the sobor resolved by an open "vote" to dissolve the 350-year-old Union of Brest and join the Russian Orthodox Church. Only then was the new rank of Pelvetsky and Melnyk revealed to the delegates, along with the news of the Group's prior conversion to Orthodoxy. By hastily publishing the official *Proceedings* of the Lviv sobor, the Group leaders supplied first-hand evidence of the arbitrary and uncanonical nature of this gathering.[15]

Paradoxically, the reunion campaign did not encounter serious challenges from the then beleaguered Ukrainian resistance movement. It was not until *after* the Lviv sobor, in August 1946, that the nationalist underground (at least in certain parts of Galicia) issued its ultimatum to the reunited clergy to renounce their apostasy. While some clergy complied with this demand or tried to explain to the OUN network the involuntary and, therefore, invalid nature of their conversion, others would not risk Soviet reprisals.[16]

The assassination of Fr. Kostelnyk in September 1948, blamed by Soviet propaganda on the underground, was evidently engineered by the MGB itself.[17] There is evidence that Kostelnyk (as well as Pelvetsky and Melnyk) formed the Action Group under duress—after he had become convinced that the Kremlin would not tolerate the Uniate Church under any conditions. He accepted the prospect of formal "reunion" with the Moscow Patriarchate only because it seemed a lesser evil than the complete Soviet elimination of the network of intensely patriotic parish clergy. He apparently thought that perpetuation of their unique social and moral leadership role in the war-devastated Galician society would thus be assured.[18] His pragmatic response bitterly divided the clergy and the faithful.

While the Moscow Patriarchate now extended its jurisdiction to the once uniformly Uniate Galicia, it was prudent enough neither to hasten the "Orthodoxization" of the local rite and religious custom, nor to proceed with the Russification of its new Galician dioceses. In fact, the formally Orthodox Church in Galicia has been able not only to retain its distinctly ethnic Ukrainian character, but also, as Khrushchev's anti-religious campaigns devastated the Russian Orthodox Church in central and eastern Ukraine,[19] to preserve its numerous and populous parishes. Thus there has been a dramatic increase in the relative weight of Western Ukrainian parishes, priests, and candidates for clergy within the Ukrainian Exarchate.

One reason for this development was the continuing, albeit illegal, existence of the Ukrainian Catholic Church, which directly benefited from Khrushchev's de-Stalinization campaign. The return in 1955–6 from Soviet prison camps and internal exile of two surviving bishops (Mykola Charnetsky to Lviv and Ivan Liatyshevsky to Stanislav [Ivano-Frankivsk]), as well as of hundreds of priests and monastics, has markedly strengthened the catacomb church. Some of the reunited parishes have even repudiated Orthodoxy.[20] Widespread expectations that Khrushchev's regime would permit legalization of the church failed to materialize in the face of vocal opposition from the Moscow Patriarchate[21] and its highly placed patrons. The authorities' concern that mass closings of the "reunited" churches in Galicia and Transcarpathia would drive believers back into the arms of the Uniate Church had, no doubt, spared the local Orthodox dioceses from the brunt of the 1958–64 anti-religious campaign.

Another, more fundamental, reason for both the manifestly Ukrainian character of the Orthodox Church in Galicia (in contrast to Eastern Ukraine), and the survival of its illegal counterpart (the Ukrainian Catholic Church) has been an intimate overlapping and interdependence of intense religious and national consciousness which has long characterized Western Ukrainians.

II

Since the mid-1950s the catacomb Ukrainian Church in the USSR has had an unbroken succession of several bishops, of whom three would surface to ordain, direct and discipline the clergy in the archdiocese of Lviv (headed by an exarch of the exiled Metropolitan Slipy), the Soviet-annexed two-thirds of the Przemyśl eparchy, and the Ivano-Frankivsk (Stanislav) diocese (the component parts of the Galician metropoly);[22] there was also a bishop for the Mukachiv diocese,[23] and, for some time, one bishop for Ukrainian Catholics in Central Asia.[24] Estimates for the illegal Uniate clergy in Galicia have varied from as few as 300–350 to as many as 1,000.[25] In Lviv alone, according to Anatolii Levitin-Krasnov, there were about 80 Uniate priests in 1974.[26]

In cities, the old territorially defined parishes were replaced long ago by functional networks involving one or more "after-hours" priests, usually assisted by secret nuns and lay activists, who minister to small gatherings of trusted believers. In villages, some of the once numerous churches and chapels to which the Uniate believers refused to admit Orthodox priests or the churches deprived of an Orthodox pastor have been (with the local authorities looking away) used for services by visiting Uniate clergymen. In other cases, where no priest, Uniate or Orthodox, was available, believers themselves celebrated parts of the services and devotions, often in front of the padlocked church built by their ancestors. Regular Ukrainian Catholic broadcasts received unjammed from Radio Vatican have supplemented the work of the catacomb clergy with radio church services for many Ukrainian Catholics, otherwise unable to partake in Uniate liturgy.

Alongside the secular clergy, the three monastic orders—the Basilians, Redemptorists, and Studites—have been training candidates for priesthood in very difficult conditions. While the identities of the older clergy are known to the Soviet police, who frequently subject them to searches, fines, confiscations, temporary detentions and lengthy interrogations, it is the secretly ordained new clergy who have been particularly preyed upon by the KGB. The most successful of the catacomb church's components have been female congregations of Sisters Servants, Basilian and Studite nuns, as well as those of St. Joseph, St. Josaphat, St. Vincent and Holy Family. They have had numerous new vocations and have been particularly active among the sick and elderly, as well as in religious instruction of the young.[27]

While the unconditional submission to state control has had a profoundly corrupting effect on the Russian Orthodox Church, the illegal Uniate Church, however closely supervised from without, has managed to preserve its spiritual integrity and maintain credibility with its increasingly better educated and more critical-minded flock. Some old divisions between the "Easterners" or "Reformers" (rite purifiers) and the "Latinizers" or "conservatives" (adherents of the established blend of Eastern and Latin influences)[28] have come to overlap. New tensions within the catacomb church have been created by differences over liturgical language, the Vatican's relations with the Orthodox, and the issue of the Ukrainian Catholic Patriarchate. The issue of legalization and the price to be paid for it has also had a divisive impact on the church, as has the question of the most appropriate strategy: a low-profile, limited but tolerated activity versus a high-profile confrontational, dissident line designed to mobilize Western support for the restoration of the church's legal rights.[29] Soviet authorities have apparently attempted to exploit and manipulate some of these divisive tendencies in order to weaken the church's base in Ukraine and undermine its support abroad, most notably through the *Pokutnyky* (Penitents) movement that eventually repudiated not only the post-Pius XII Vatican, but even the illegal Ukrainian Catholic Church.[30]

After several waves of repression, including one which followed the legalization of the Uniate Church in Czechoslovakia in 1968, Soviet treatment of Ukrainian Catholics worsened with the ascendance of Karol Wojtyła (John Paul II) to the throne of St. Peter. This was apparently due to his open support of the Ukrainian church's cause, as manifested by his appointment of Archbishop Myroslav Lubachivsky as coadjutor and successor to Archbishop-Major Iosyf Slipy, which ensured that the Lviv see would not become vacant after Cardinal Slipy's death, and by his authorization of the convening of world Synods of Ukrainian Catholic bishops under the Archbishop-Major.[31] Developments in Poland and the prolonged succession crisis in the Kremlin added to the regime's concerns about the visible activization of the Uniate Church in Western Ukraine and soon erupted in a campaign of selective murders, arrests and harassment of some Ukrainian Catholic clergy and a massive counterpropaganda campaign against the *ouno-uniaty*.[32]

III

Soviet suppression of the Ukrainian Greek Catholic Church has had a number of immediate and delayed or indirect consequences for Ukrainian Catholics in Canada and other countries of Ukrainian diaspora. Isolated from the mother church since September 1939, they found themselves after World War II nearly completely cut off from the historical and spiritual centre of the Uniate Church, its imprisoned hierarchy, its dissolved theological academy and seminaries, monastic novitiates and minor seminaries; its dispersed monastic orders; its confiscated or destroyed storehouses of knowledge, culture and art; its publishing houses and periodicals and other resources that helped in the past to nourish the diaspora church. To be sure, the escape to the West of 250,000 Ukrainians, including 200 Greek Catholic clergy and about fifty theology students[33] and numerous Ukrainian Catholic intellectuals, provided an important substitute for the loss of contact with Western Ukraine. Eventually, during the 1945–54 decade, 33,835 displaced Ukrainians emigrated to Canada, the great majority of them Greek Catholics, including some sixty priests or about-to-be-ordained theology graduates.[34]

While the new Ukrainian Catholic emigration was not the consequence of the church's suppression in Ukraine, it helped substantially to strengthen the sentiment voiced by Ukrainian Catholic spokesmen in Canada that after the mother church had been banned in Ukraine, the church in Canada must become a "Piedmont," an outpost of Ukrainian Catholicism in the West that will speak for the silenced church, carry on the struggle for its restoration in Ukraine, preserve the purity of rite and tradition, and train the cadres of priests and lay activists that one day will be necessary to rebuild the church in the motherland.[35]

The combined effect of the church's persecution in Ukraine and the influx from Europe of the Ukrainian Catholic clergy and laymen weakened assimilationist pressures upon the church, prepared the ground for the rite-purification and autonomist/patriarchal movements within the church, and frustrated, for some time, nativist sentiments for the use of the English language within the church and for its formal de-ethnization (as a "Byzantine-Rite" or "Eastern Catholic" Church).

The suppression of the church in Galicia and the expected influx of new Ukrainian immigrants to Canada may have figured prominently among the Vatican's motives for expanding the Ukrainian Catholic hierarchy in Canada and giving it a regular territorial base. Following a visit to Canada by Cardinal Eugène Tisserant, Secretary of the Congregation for Eastern Churches, the Ukrainian Catholic exarchate in Canada, headed by Bishop Vasylii Ladyka, in 1948 was divided by the Holy See into the three exarchates of Central, Eastern and Western Canada.[36] A fourth exarchate was established for Saskatchewan in 1951, and in the same year, the Protohegumen of Redemptorists in Canada, Rev. Maxim Hermaniuk, was appointed auxiliary to Archbishop Ladyka in Winnipeg.[37] In 1956, reorganization of the Ukrainian Catholic Church in Canada was completed with the transformation of the four exarchates into residential sees united in a separate church province (Metropoly) under Archbishop-Metropolitan Hermaniuk of Winnipeg.[38] In 1974 a fourth diocese—New Westminster—was established for British Columbia.[39] The significance of these developments lay in how they made the canonical status of the Ukrainian Church, functioning under its own Eastern

canon law, equal with that of the Roman Catholic Church in Canada.[40] The
Conference of Ukrainian Catholic Bishops in Canada joined with its equi-
valents in the United States and other countries in the West to form the
diaspora Bishops' Conference, which significantly strengthened the Ukrainian presence in the Vatican. The importance of this for the "Silent Church"
in Ukraine greatly increased when the Holy See opened the door to dialogue
and closer relations with the Moscow Patriarchate. The Ukrainian hierarchy's demands on behalf of the prohibited Uniate Church in Ukraine at the
beginning of the Vatican II was one of the several factors which stimulated
complicated negotiations among Pope John XXIII, President Kennedy and
Nikita Khrushchev. The result was the release from lengthy Soviet captivity
of Metropolitan Iosyf Slipy,[41] who was recognized by the Vatican as
Archbishop-Major of Ukrainian Catholics, and Cardinal.

The Kremlin's release of the head of the Ukrainian Catholic Church gave a
new, authentic and more powerful voice to the catacomb church before the
Pope and world Catholicism as well as the governments and public opinion
of the West. It attracted international attention and offered unprecedented opportunities and challenges for unifying and co-ordinating the activities of the
church in captivity and the church in the West, under the powerful, charismatic figure of the Confessor-Metropolitan. To what extent the potentialities
for change in the status of the Uniate Church in the USSR were explored and
realized lies beyond the scope of this paper.

One aspect of my topic remains to be discussed. The Kremlin's persecution of the Uniate Church in Ukraine, its refusal to restore legal status to the
church after Stalin's death, and its resumption of slanderous attacks against
the Uniates after a marked resurgence of Ukrainian Catholic activities in
Galicia since 1955–6 have aroused in Canada strong feelings of sympathy
for and solidarity with the persecuted church since 1945. Public protests, appeals on behalf of fellow Greek Catholics in Ukraine to the Roman Catholic
Church, the Canadian government and the media; manifestations; publications; continuing pressure on the Vatican not to subordinate its public support
for the persecuted church to the exigencies of its *Ostpolitik*; various direct
forms of support for the banned hierarchy and clergy in Ukraine—all these
activities of the Ukrainian Catholic Church (and of various representative
Ukrainian Canadian institutions) have attracted predictable Soviet responses.

Through its Ottawa embassy-distributed propaganda and through publications mailed directly from the USSR (particularly the "Ukraina" Society's
pamphlets and newspaper *News from Ukraine*), the Soviet regime has embarked on an increasingly slanderous disinformation campaign. This
campaign is designed not only to cover up its religious persecution, but to
besmirch its victims. It attacks the Ukrainian Catholic Church in Canada (and
in the West in general) as an allegedly anti-communist, warmongering, nationalist organization, which harbours in its ranks "fascists" and "Nazi col-

laborators," who seek to sabotage East-West detente and normal Canadian-Soviet relations.[42] Even the Orthodox Metropolitan of Kiev and selected bishops and clergy from the Ukrainian Exarchate have been deployed in this campaign, especially while visiting Canada or receiving Canadian visitors in Kiev. At the same time, in their ecumenical exchanges with Rome, representatives of the Moscow Patriarchate—serving at the same time as proxies for the Kremlin—have been quietly attacking the Ukrainian Catholic Church as an obstacle to true East-West ecumenism. Some of them even hint at prospects of a much closer unity between Russian Orthodoxy and Roman Catholicism, were it not for continuing papal support for the "remnants of Uniatism" in Western Ukraine and the "nationalist émigré churchmen" in the West. The impression of wavering Vatican resolve on the issue of Uniate rights in Ukraine was especially manifest in the activities of the Secretariat for Christian Unity under Cardinal J. Willebrands. His failure to respond to the act of ratification of "reunion" of Uniates with the Russian Orthodox Church, an act read in his presence at the 1971 Local Sobor in Zagorsk, was particularly disturbing to Ukrainian Catholics both in Ukraine and abroad because it seemed to give *de facto* recognition of the Soviet suppression of the Greek Catholic Church.[43] This perception that papal *Ostpolitik* involved sacrificing the persecuted Ukrainian Uniates could not but reinforce anti-Vatican sentiments (as did such other issues as married clergy and the Patriarchate), and divide Ukrainian Catholics in Canada.

The complex interrelationship between the Ukrainian Catholic Church in Canada, Ukrainian Catholicism in the West, the Vatican, and the still banned and persecuted mother church in Ukraine is undergoing slow but inevitable changes as the old generation of Ukrainian Catholic hierarchy, clergy and laymen passes away, and as both the Papal See and the post of Archbishop-Major of Lviv and Halych have new incumbents who are quite different from their predecessors. The critical and most exposed link in this changing relationship will remain the church in Ukraine, where the ranks of clergy ordained or trained before 1945—now in their sixties and older—are being rapidly depleted both in the illegal church and among the legal pseudo-Orthodox clergy under the Moscow Patriarchate's jurisdiction. The generational change in Ukraine and the lack of proper conditions to train new Uniate clergy are likely to weaken the effective influence, if not legitimacy, of the Ukrainian Catholic Church, despite the striking improvement in the position of Greek Catholic Ukrainians in neighbouring Poland. This makes the legalization of the church in Ukraine an extremely critical issue, though it is not necessarily politically achievable at this time.

NOTES

1. See Rev. A. Pekar, *The Bishops of the Eparchy of Mukachevo with Historical Outlines* (Pittsburg: Byzantine Seminary Press, 1979), 5–7. In 1721, the Union was extended to Máramaros district.
2. They were served by eight bishops, 2,741 secular and 156 regular priests, 160 monasteries and convents with 350 brothers and 982 sisters, a theological academy and four theological seminaries with over six hundred students, and 2,668 parishes with 3,982 churches. The above figures do not include Prešov diocese. Statistical data are derived from *Shematyzm dukhovenstva Lvivskoi Arkhieparkhii 1938* (Lviv, 1938); *Shematyzm hreko-katolytskoho dukhovenstva zluchenykh Eparkhii Peremyskoi, Sambirskoi i Sianitskoi na rik bozhyi 1938–1939* (Przemyśl, 1938); *Shematyzm vseho klyra hreko-katolytskoi Eparkhii Stanyslavivskoi na rik bozhyi 1938* (Stanyslaviv, 1938); *Shematyzm hreko-katolytskoho dukhovenstva Apostolskoi Administratsii Lemkovshchyny* (Lviv, 1936); and *Annuario Pontificio per l'anno 1965* (Vatican City, 1965), 288.
3. See Vasyl Markus, *Nyshchennia hreko-katolytskoi tserkvy v mukachivskii ieparkhii v 1945–50 rr.* (Offprint from "Zbirnyka prysviachenoho pamiati Z. Kuzeli," *Zapysky N.T.Sh.*, vol. CLXIX (Paris, 1962).
4. Julius Kubinyi, *The History of Prjasiv Eparchy* (Rome, 1970) Editiones Universitatis Catholicae Ukrainorum S. Clementis Papae, XXXII, chs. XII-XIV.
5. Decrees of 5 September 1947 and 28 September 1949 confiscated the property left by persons "resettled to the USSR." There is no published decree explicitly banning the Greek Catholic Church in the P.P.R. *Dziennik Ustaw*, no. 59 (1947): 989–90; and no. 53 (1949), 1023–4.
6. This part of my paper draws on my earlier study, "The Suppression of the Ukrainian Greek Catholic Church in Postwar Soviet Union and Poland," published in Dennis J. Dunn (ed.), *Religion and Nationalism in Eastern Europe and the Soviet Union* (Boulder, Colo.: Lynne Rienner, 1987), 97–119.
7. Nevertheless, in late February 1945, the Lviv metropoly arranged for a secret meeting between representatives of the Soviet forces and the UPA Command, which failed to end hostilities in Western Ukraine, as the Soviets demanded unconditional surrender by the Ukrainian insurgents. It was bound to be turned down by UPA/OUN (Metropolitan Iosyf Slipy, "Zhaloba," a complaint to a minister of the Ukr. SSR, dated 17 February 1961, written while the Metropolitan was in the Kiev prison undergoing another interrogation). A copy of this document was received from Cardinal Slipy in late 1981. Cf. Lev Shankovsky, "Bolshevyky pro UPA," *Visnyk O.O.Ch.S.U.* XXII, no. 6 (1968): 18; and his "Fantazii Moskvy pro roliu Vatykanu u borotbi UPA," *Patriiarkhat* XI, no. 3 (March 1978): 15–16; and S.T. Danylenko, *Dorohoiu hanby i zrady* (Kiev: Naukova dumka, 1972), 260–2).
8. This is suggested by the absence of any appeal for "reunion" with Russian Orthodoxy in the first published attack on the Greek Catholic Church on 6 April 1945 by "Volodymyr Rosovych" (pseudonym of Iaroslav Halan), "Z khrestom chy nozhem?," in the Lviv daily *Vilna Ukraina*, and by a highly publicized meeting in the Kremlin, on 10 April 1945, between Stalin and Molotov, on the one side, and Patriarch Aleksii, accompanied by Metropolitan Nikolai of Krutitsy and Protopresbyter N. F. Kolchitsky, executive director of the Patriarchate, on the other. (Moscow Patriarchate, *Patriarkh Sergii i ego dukhovnoe nasledstvo* [Moscow, 1947], 376).
9. It is significant that sometime in late May or June 1945, Leonid Ilich Brezhnev, hitherto the political commissar of the Eighteenth Army, was sent to Western Ukraine as chief of Political Administration of Subcarpathian Military District and re-

mained in this post until after the liquidation of the Uniate Church. All arrested bishops and clergy who refused to "convert" to Orthodoxy, as well as captured UPA and OUN members, were tried before military tribunals of this district.

10. Arrested along with the Metropolitan were Bishop Nykyta Budka—his Auxiliary and Vicar General—and Nykolai Charnetsky, the Apostolic Visitator for Volyn; simultaneously, the NKGB arrested in Stanislav (today's Ivano-Frankivsk) the Ordinary, Bishop Hryhorii Khomyshyn and his Auxiliary, Bishop Ivan Liatyshevsky. Several priests, according to some reports, were arrested at the same time. The mass arrests of the clergy came at the end of May, to clear the way for the "Action Group" headed by Rev. H. Kostelnyk. The figure of 100 arrested priests was reportedly supplied by Kostelnyk himself, in his letter to the OUN underground, written in the fall of 1946, under a pseudonym, "Father Author." The letter was transmitted to OUN leaders in the Drohobych oblast by "Father Ikona" (possibly, local Orthodox bishop Mykhail Melnyk). A copy of an OUN report on secret meetings with the latter, including a transcript of Kostelnyk's letter, was preserved in the ZP UHVR archives in New York ("Do t.zv. 'vozziednannia' tserkov," file F3–1).

11. Even before it was officially recognized by the Soviet government, the Action Group stated in its public appeal to the Uniate clergy on 28 May 1945 that it was formed "by permission of the state authorities" and that the latter "will recognize only the directives of our Action Group, and will not recognize any other administrative authority within the Greek Catholic Church." (*Diiannia Soboru hreko-katolytskoi tserkvy u Lvovi 8–10 bereznia 1946* [Lviv: Vydannia Prezydii Soboru, 1946], 23). On behalf of the Council of People's Commissars of the Ukr.SSR, the republican Commissioner of the Council for the Affairs of the Russian Orthodox Church, P. Khodchenko, replied on 18 June that the "Action Group for Re-Union of the Greek Catholic Church is being SANCTIONED with your (present) membership as the ONLY provisional organ of church administration, which is authorized to direct all affairs of the existing Greek Catholic parishes in the western *oblasti* of Ukraine and to carry on the task of reunion of the above parishes with the Russian Orthodox Church." Khodchenko ordered the Group to report to him the "lists of all deans, parish priests and superiors of monasteries who refuse to submit to the jurisdiction of the Action Group" (ibid., 19–20; emphasis added).

12. According to a report by Rev. A. Pelvetsky on the opening day of the "Sobor," 986 priests in the four Galician *oblasti* had "joined the Action Group" by 8 March 1945; he claimed that 281 priests refused (implying that they were still at large); the number of "recalcitrants" listed by Pelvetsky obviously omitted those who were imprisoned by the Soviet police (ibid., 61).

13. The NKGB investigation of the arrested bishops was completed some time in February, at the latest, and the announcement by the Procurator of the Ukr. SSR that summarized their indictment was published in the Lviv *Vilna Ukraina* on 1 March 1946.

14. See *Diiannia*, 28–31.

15. *Diiannia*, 32–52. It is no accident that the Moscow Patriarchate's multilingual "documentary" collection, *Lvivskyi Tserkovnyi Sobor. Dokumenty i materialy 1946–1981* (Kiev, 1984), eliminated from the original *Diiannia* most of the embarrassing documents and passages, including the Action Group's appeal to the Soviet government and, most compromising, Khodchenko's letter of 18 June 1945, confirming on behalf of the government the exclusive authority of this NKGB-hand-picked group to usurp the powers of the arrested bishops and to bring about the Greek Catholic Church's incorporation into the Russian Orthodox Church. For more detail, see Ivan Hvat's review of *Lvivskyi Tserkovnyi Sobor* (1984) in *Suchasnist* 25, no. 1 (January 1985): 111–18.

16. "Do t. zv. 'vozziednannia' tserkov," 1, 4, 5. Cf. K.Ie. Dmytruk, *Pid shtandartamy reaktsii i fashyzmu* (Kiev: Naukova dumka, 1976), 287–8.

17. Kostelnyk's assassin was himself shot by someone in the car which was waiting to help him escape, according to interviews with Kostelnyk family members. No Ukrainian nationalist groups ever claimed credit for this act.

18. This is essentially the argument pursued by "Father Author" (Kostelnyk) in his letter to the UPA-OUN leaders, cited in "Do t.zv. 'vozziednannia tserkov,'" file F-3-1.

19. For an assessment of the losses suffered by the Orthodox Church in Ukraine under Khrushchev, see B. R. Bociurkiw, "The Orthodox Church and the Soviet Regime in the Ukraine, 1953–1971," *Canadian Slavonic Papers* 14, no. 2 (Summer 1972): 191–212.

20. See a declaration of deans of the Lviv diocese in October 1957, in *Pravoslavnyi visnyk* 12 (1957): 371–2. The re-emergence of the Greek Catholic Church in Poland after the October 1956 upheavals was another cause of alarm for the Russian Orthodox Church in Galicia.

21. See B.R. Bociurkiw, "The Uniate Church in the Soviet Ukraine: A Case Study in Soviet Church Policy," *Canadian Slavonic Papers* 7 (1965): 109n.

22. The archdiocese of Lviv was subsequently led by secret Bishop Vasylii Velychkovsky (nominated in 1959, ordained by Metropolitan Slipy in early 1963) until his arrest in 1969 (after three years' imprisonment he was allowed to leave the USSR in 1972 and died in Canada that same year); and Bishop Volodymyr Sterniuk, ordained in 1969. The Ivano-Frankivsk diocese was led from 1957 by Bishop Ivan Sleziuk, who died in December 1973; he was succeeded by Bishop Sofron Dmyterko.

23. Bishop Oleksander Khira, who, after his imprisonment from 1949 to 1956, was exiled to Karaganda, Kazakhstan, where he died in May 1983. He was assisted by Fr. Mykola Murany, Administrator of the Mukachiv diocese, who, after his release in 1957, continued to direct the illegal Church in Transcarpathia until his death in January 1957 (A. Pekar, OSBM, *"You Shall Be Witness Unto Me"* [Pittsburgh: Byzantine Seminary Press, 1985], 41–58).

24. Bishop Iosafat Fedoryk, OSBM, ordained by Bishop O. Khira in the early 1960s for the Ukrainian Catholic diaspora in Central Asia; he returned to Lviv in 1968 and died there in late 1979.

25. According to Bishop Velychkovsky's account in Rome, 8 April 1972. The same figure was cited by Cardinal Slipy in 1980.

26. A. Levitin-Krasnov, "V oboroni Ukrainskoi Katolytskoi Tserkvy," *Suchasnist* 15, no. 1 (January 1975): 108.

27. Author's interviews with visiting Ukrainian Greek Catholic priests from Ukraine and émigré visitors to Ukraine. Cf. a *samvydav* account, "Z zhyttia Ukrainskoi Katolytskoi Tserkvy," in Osyp Zinkevych and Taras R. Lonchyna (eds.), *Martyrolohiia Ukrainskykh Tserkov*, vol. 2: *Ukrainska Katolytska Tserkva* (Toronto-Baltimore: Smoloskyp, 1985), 707–25.

28. Alternative designations of the two currents reflecting their respective self-perceptions.

29. The latter tendency has been represented by Iosyf Terelia and *The Chronicle of the Catholic Church in Ukraine* (1984–7).

30. See B. R. Bociurkiw, "Institutional Religion and Nationality in the Soviet Union," in S. Enders Wimbush (ed.), *Soviet Nationalities in Strategic Perspective* (London: Croom Helm, 1985), 195–6, 204n–205n.

31. See Ivan Hvat, "The Ukrainian Catholic Church, the Vatican and the Soviet Union During the Pontificate of Pope John Paul II," *Religion in Communist Lands* XI, no. 3 (Winter 1983): 264–80.

32. *Ouno-uniaty*—a Soviet counterpropaganda label for the Ukrainian Catholics which insinuates a close alliance between the underground Organization of Ukrainian Nationalists (OUN) and the Uniate Church. For an authoritative outline of Soviet strategy against the Ukrainian Catholic Church, see L. M. Kravchuk (head of the Party Central Committee's Propaganda Department in Ukraine), "Ateisticheskoe vospitanie i zadachi kontrpropagandy," in the proceedings of the 1982 Riga conference on the nationalities problem, *Neprimirimost k burzhuaznoi ideologii, perezhitkam natsionalizma* (Moscow, 1982), 35–50.

33. *Shematyzm dukhovenstva Ukrainskoi Katolytskoi Tserkvy v Nimechchyni* (Munich: Zahrava, 1947).

34. Author's estimate based on the comparison of the pre-war and 1947 *shematyzmy* with the lists of the clergy in Canada published in the postwar *Svitlo* calendars.

35. Ukrainian immigration from overseas figure for 1945–54 was derived from William Darcovich and Paul Yuzyk (eds.), *A Statistical Compendium on the Ukrainians in Canada, 1891–1976* (Ottawa: University of Ottawa Press, 1980), 500.

36. See, e.g., editorial "Nasha vidpovidalnist pered lytsem istorii," *Ukrainski Visti* (Edmonton), 11 June 1946.

37. Archbishop Ivan Buchko, *Ukraintsi v 50-richchia isnuvannia i diialnosty Sviashchennoi Kongregatsii dlia Skhidnikh Tserkov* (Munich: Khrystiianskyi holos, 1970), 35.

38. *Persha Ukrainska Katolytska Mytropoliia v Kanadi* (Winnipeg: Mytropolychyi odrynariiat, 1957), 52.

39. Ibid., 77–8.

40. See Mykola Chubaty's commentary on this event in *Ameryka* (Philadelphia), 2 March 1957.

41. Hansjakob Stehle, *Eastern Politics of the Vatican, 1917–1979* (Athens, Ohio: Ohio University Press, 1981), 305–9.

42. For samples of the English-language smear campaign against the Ukrainian Catholics, see Klym Dmytruk (pseud.), *Swastikas on Soutanes* (1981), and O. S. Onyshchenko (ed.), *Uniate Church: Forcible Establishment, Natural Failure* (1983), both published by "Politvidav Ukraini" (*sic*) in Kiev.

43. The Vatican's only public criticism of the 1971 Sobor's action came in the course of an interview "On Relations between the Catholic Church and the Russian Orthodox Church," offered by Cardinal Willebrands to *L'Avvenire* some time after his return from the USSR, and published on 4 July 1971: "I must however mention one point: the Council [Sobor] noted the annulment of the Unions of Brest and Uzhgorod, which took place in the 16th and 17th centuries. As is well known, in 1946 and 1949 these two unions were unilaterally declared to be abolished, with the result that these communities were placed under the jurisdiction of the Patriarchate of Moscow. It is quite certain that we cannot share the thesis whereby by the annulment of these acts of union, the ecclesial situation of our Eastern Catholic brethren in the Soviet Union has found its solution. The Catholic Church is certainly glad that in the course of recent years, with God's help, important progress has been made in her relations with the Russian Orthodox Church. However, in this dialogue of charity which is now developing, we continue to be firmly convinced, as we have ever been, that such thorny problems cannot be resolved unilaterally" (cited in the bulletin of the Vatican's Secretariat for Promoting Christian Unity, *Information Service*, no. 15 [August 1971], 9).

Vasyl Markus

The Role of the Patriarchal Movement in the Ukrainian Catholic Church

The 1960s and 1970s were marked by the quest for a patriarchal structure for the Ukrainian Catholic Church. A new era began in the life of Ukrainian Catholics in the diaspora when the late Metropolitan of Halych, Iosyf Slipy, was released from the Soviet Gulag and, after his arrival in the West in February 1963, established his residence in Rome.

The Ukrainian Greek Catholic Church was officially abolished in Ukraine after World War II, but some 1.5 million faithful in the Western world and in Eastern Europe outside the USSR continued to practice their religion and to maintain their church structure. These faithful always referred to the jailed Metropolitan Slipy as their spiritual leader and Primate, while praying for him in Liturgy, even though in reality there was no such central authority in the Ukrainian Catholic Church. Individual eparchies and exarchates were autonomous but dependent on local Roman Church authorities or on the Congregation of Eastern Churches of the Holy See or both. When, in the late 1950s, two Ukrainian church provinces (Canada and USA) were established, there were some ties among the eparchies in the two Metropolias, but there was no unifying authority between them.

The situation changed with the arrival of Metropolitan Slipy in Rome. Surrounded not only by the aura of martyrdom, but also by reverence and honours in the Vatican, physically and mentally competent to lead his flock, the seventy-one year-old Slipy was anxious to achieve those objectives he had been unable to realize in Ukraine during his captivity. He inspired the faithful with a sense of unity and mission. It was natural to regard Slipy as the actual head of the church.

The Holy See also encouraged Slipy to assume leading moral authority in the Ukrainian Greek Catholic Church by recognizing his status as and prerogatives of the Archbishop Major and by conferring upon him the dignity of Cardinal. Slipy did more than was expected from him, however. He arrived in Rome at a time of major reforms in the entire Catholic church. During the first session of Vatican II, fifteen Ukrainian bishops-in-exile issued a statement about the "Great Absentee," Metropolitan Slipy of Lviv. The authors of the declaration protested against the presence, as observers at the Council, of representatives of the Russian Orthodox Church, which absorbed Ukrainian Catholics. Not only did this move embarrass the Vatican, it also helped those trying to secure Slipy's release from Siberia.

When Slipy appeared in St. Peter's Basilica at the second session on 10 October 1963, the assembled conciliar fathers welcomed him enthusiastically as the spokesman of the Church of Silence. In his speech next day, he proposed elevating the Ukrainian Greek Catholic Church to the status of a Patriarchate.[1] Although the Council did not address this question specifically, the initiative was of historic significance: a patriarchal idea was born among Ukrainians in modern times, and the patriarchal movement had begun.

The Ukrainian Patriarchate

The Ukrainian Church, united with Rome since 1596, with 5.5 million faithful, including those forcibly converted to the Russian Orthodox Church in Ukraine, is the largest Oriental Catholic Church body. Yet it lacks ecclesiastical autonomy and the patriarchal status enjoyed by some minor Oriental churches in the Middle East and by the Orthodox churches in Eastern Europe. A Patriarchal system means an autonomous church government, synodal rule, and unity of all territorially dispersed church entities. It implies less control by the Vatican. For Ukrainians such a structure would help to preserve their rite and its uniformity, and would strengthen their spiritual ties with their church in Ukraine. Politically, a Ukrainian Patriarchate would stress the national identity of all Ukrainian people (in the homeland and in diaspora) and might enhance the status of the Ukrainian national movement.[2] These possibilities inspired members of the Ukrainian Catholic community to embrace wholeheartedly the cause of the Patriarchate. More than twenty years of dedicated effort has been devoted to this cause.

Ideally, Slipy's initiative would have been assigned to a conciliar committee for further study and, after a favourable opinion from the Curia, could have reached the Council's floor for approval. Alternatively, it would have been tabled *ad Calendas graecas* or simply lost among the Council's papers. In both cases, there would not have been a patriarchal movement.

Slipy understood church government. He had a realistic perception of the internal politics of the Roman Church and of its external policies and diplomacy. Therefore he brought the issue of the Ukrainian Patriarchate to the Council without prior consultation with Vatican authorities. He had a tendency to ignore the many suggestions offered to him and to act independently following his personal instincts based on experience with the powerful and on his pessimistic assessment of governing bodies.

Although it seemed probable that the church authorities would bestow on him the patriarchal dignity, Slipy realized that it was not likely to happen spontaneously. Instead, he decided to make the patriarchate a popular cause, worthy of the involvement of the entire religious and national community. It would be a generation-long confrontation between Roman Catholic authorities and the Ukrainian Greek Catholic Church. As a result, the patriarchal movement that emerged shook the very foundation of the Ukrainian church, initiating many changes. An observation first made by this author a decade ago still holds true today:

[The Patriarchate] movement began in the mid-1960s generated partially within the Church itself (among clergy and laity) and supported by some civic quarters, including patriotic organizations. This movement favored the idea of a patriarchal system for the Ukrainian Catholic Church. Having exhausted or achieved some of the previously mentioned religious objectives (defense of rite, church autonomy *vis-à-vis* Rome, unity of all Ukrainian Catholic entities) and, above all, personally committed to the would-be Patriarch Cardinal Slipy, the patriarchal program has acquired (and—I would add now—exceeded) the dynamics and combativeness of many previous lay movements. It has seriously undermined the integrity of the Church establishment by questioning the credibility of its leadership. At the same time, it has revitalized many dormant energies and aroused new religious activism among the laity.[3]

Ukrainian Hierarchy and the Issue of Patriarchate

Cardinal Slipy's proposal at the Council to have the Ukrainian Greek Catholic Church declared a Patriarchate both stunned and delighted the Ukrainian bishops.[4] There was some doubt about it because the bishops were not well acquainted with the concept and nature of the Patriarchate, and the likely eventual consequences for the Ukrainian church. When they recognized the usefulness of the idea, they were willing to pursue it.[5]

At their separate conferences during the Council, Ukrainian bishops acted collegially. They passed decisions on matters important for the entire church. One important outcome was a petition to the Pontiff concerning a Ukrainian

159

Patriarchate. All the bishops signed, except the late Metropolitan of Philadelphia, Ambrose Senyshyn. Later there were others who deviated from the common position. The attitude of Senyshyn to the Patriarchate and to Slipy personally requires a separate assessment. Suffice it to say that he became an ardent opponent of Slipy and the concept of Patriarchate. Senyshyn was not willing to subordinate to a higher Ukrainian church authority. Thus, he played into the hands of those questioning the idea of Ukrainian church autonomy. Nevertheless, some progress was made toward a Ukrainian Patriarchate. Four episcopal conferences took place during the Council, three of them under the chairmanship of Slipy. The fourth conference, in the spirit of other Oriental Churches, was declared a synodal meeting.

In Rome, Slipy, now a primate (*Pervoiierarkh*), started a periodical called *Blahovisnyk*, which contained conciliar and papal decrees, synodal decisions, pastoral letters, and other official materials. He established a chancery to be a central administration of the Ukrainian church. Also he established St. Clement's Ukrainian Catholic University (a centre for Ukrainian religious studies), returned the ownership of the Ukrainian church of St. Sergio and Bacchus, set up a Ukrainian museum, and restored the monastic order of Studites, providing them with a monastery near Rome.

Some bishops collaborated closely with Slipy; some were neutral and oscillated in their loyalty between their own Protohierarch and the Oriental Congregation of the Roman Curia. The latter was staunchly opposed to the patriarchal designs of Cardinal Slipy. Pope Paul VI, although favourably disposed to the Ukrainian churchman, nevertheless followed the advice of the Curia officials and declined several requests for a Ukrainian patriarchate.[6] Some bishops opposed Slipy's claims to higher authority over the Ukrainian church in exile and joined forces with those in the Vatican who opposed the movement.

Despite the many odds against him, Slipy was an astute church politician and more than once succeeded in outmanoeuvring the Curia bureaucrats, even surprising the Pope. On the occasion of the blessing of the newly built church of St. Sophia in September 1969, attended by Pope Paul VI, another synod was held, demonstrating the will of the Archbishop Major and of the overwhelming majority of bishops to ascertain their synodal authority as a church with its own Patriarch. Again Bishop Senyshyn abstained. Subsequently, he was joined by several other bishops in Western Europe who were financially dependent on the Curia's support.

A major setback for Slipy was the Pope's unilateral appointment in 1970–5 of five new bishops for the Ukrainian church, without prior consultation with Slipy or adherence to the rules established by the various Synods of Ukrainian Catholic bishops. The Curia and Pope thus demonstrated their authority over the Ukrainian church and their disregard for the movement led by Slipy. Once again Cardinal Slipy managed a master stroke in his conflict with the Curia. In November 1971, he convened a new Synod and the bishops responded to his call. That was probably the most dramatic episode in Ukrainian-Vatican relations regarding this movement. Although not recognized by the Vatican as such, the Synod elected a permanent synodal council. It met twice even though not all of its members were sympathetic to Slipy's ideas. The lack of papal approval, however, led to an increasing disaffection with the old Cardinal's tactics. Slipy could not achieve much without the unanimous support of the bishops. At the same time, the Curia admonished individual bishops and "persuaded" them not to disobey established norms and authority.

Twice more, in 1973 and 1975, Slipy convened episcopal meetings in Rome. They were no longer called Synods because their participants were reluctant to provoke the Roman authorities. The November 1973 episcopal conference (to Slipy, the sixth Synod) approved a draft of the constitution of the Ukrainian Catholic Church.[7] The document was never confirmed by the Pope, but some of its provisions were applied by usage (via facti).

In spring 1975, Slipy unexpectedly signed a pastoral letter as a "Patriarch of the Particular Ukrainian Catholic Church."[8] This move gained the active support of some bishops, clergy and lay people. Then, in July of the same year, during a well attended Ukrainian celebration in St. Peter's Basilica, Slipy was solemnly commemorated in the liturgy as the "Patriarch of Kiev-Halych and of all Rus'." The title was used again in a more secular setting during a concert and a banquet in his honour.[9] To Ukrainian pilgrims in Rome and to many others elsewhere, the event signified a "proclamation of the Patriarchate." Others regarded it as a self-proclamation. The bishops became even more divided; a majority was critical of the move and troubled by the Vatican's negative position (although the coup caught the Curia and Pope by surprise).

Followers of Cardinal Slipy, now a proclaimed Ukrainian Patriarch, referred to ancient church practice when certain acts, including the election of hierarchy, were performed by the people of God directly. They realized that the event did not conform with existing Canon law, but argued that the proper authority acted against the spirit of the church's traditional structure and the wishes of the people. Their political action was, as a consequence, appropriate. Sooner or later the supreme authority would have to recognize the *fait accompli*.

A real casualty of this patriarchal coup of 1975 was one of Cardinal Slipy's bishops who led the opposition to the Patriarchate, thus becoming a tool in the hands of the Curia against his Ukrainian superior. Similarly, Bishop Horniak of England alienated 80 per cent of his faithful, who openly rose in opposition against him and set up a parallel church organization. This con-

161

flict between the bishop and the majority of his flock has finally been resolved.[10]

It seemed to many that a rift between the Vatican and Cardinal Slipy was imminent. Neither side, however, pressed for a showdown, because they realized what the consequences might be. Paul VI and his advisors also took into account Cardinal Slipy's advanced age, but in fact Paul VI died six years before Slipy. The new Pope, John Paul II, greeted by many Ukrainians with apprehension, showed more sympathy to Ukrainians and their spiritual leader than his predecessor had. Slipy soon developed a working relationship with John Paul II and with Cardinal Woadysoaw Rubin (responsible for the Oriental Congregation). Slipy persuaded the Pope to convene a Ukrainian synod and both consented to its election of the successor to the Halych Metropolia. Papal confirmation followed the election.

In 1980, Ukrainian synodal rule was recognized in form and the succession to the See of Lviv in Ukraine was firmly established.[11] While the Vatican conceded the *form* of a Synod to the Ukrainians, it insisted that the expressed permission of the Pope was required before convening, and that its agenda must be approved and no decisions promulgated—or announced—without the permission and approval of His Holiness. Two electoral Synods took place that year and another Synod was convened in 1983, still under Slipy's nominal chairmanship. No one seriously challenged the assumed and acclaimed title of Patriarch that was applied to Slipy. John Paul II had shown good will to Slipy, as well as to the Ukrainian Greek Catholic Church in diaspora. He also demonstrated some understanding of the Ukrainian Catholic Church's problems in Ukraine. Ukrainians appreciated this new attitude and so, finally, one could speak of easing the tense relations between the Vatican and Ukrainians.

The passing of Patriarch Slipy in September 1984, painful and distressing as it was, brought about further normalization in Vatican-Ukrainian relations. This is reflected in the Synod of October 1985. At the succession of Archbishop-Metropolitan Lubachivsky to the position held by Cardinal Slipy, the question was whether and how the new prelate, with little episcopal experience, would carry out the late Cardinal's responsibility and patriarchal designs. The transition was smoother than many anticipated. Lubachivsky took charge of the patriarchal institutions in Rome and accepted the offer of co-operation from the late patriarch's close associates. He was also willing to raise the issue of the Ukrainian patriarchate at several forums. He appears to be a staunch defender of the rights of the Ukrainian Catholic Church under the Soviet regime. Also, he is willing to co-operate with his fellow bishops by accepting collegial rule not only in the Synod, but also in the established presidium of the Synod. Lubachivsky does not openly object to being called Patriarch by lay people and clergy or to being commemorated by that title in the liturgy. While he does not use this title for himself, he does refer to the late Iosyf Slipy as Patriarch.

The question now is not so much whether Cardinal Lubachivsky is willing to head the Ukrainian Catholic Church as its Protohierarch, but whether he will have the loyalty and commitment of all his bishops.

The Attitude of Clergy and Monastic Orders

The church's infrastructure could have been as important to the patriarchal movement as the hierarchy of bishops. The clergy and nuns were in a position to influence the faithful to create strong support for the patriarchal cause. This has only partially been achieved, however, because the Patriarchate was promoted as a general idea, relevant primarily to the entire Ukrainian church, not to local eparchies or parish communities. In the eyes of many, it was the "old country's" problem, without much concrete rapport in the diaspora. Further, it was a nationalistic issue, with which many second-and third-generation immigrants were not willing to associate.

Ukrainian Catholic clergy in the Western hemisphere fell into two categories: those who belonged to the old immigrant group and those who came from Ukraine after World War II or were born to post-World War II immigrants. The former, particularly in Canada and the United States, constitute that breed of hyphenated Ukrainians acculturated to the New World in the 1940s and 1950s. Their clerical formation was conducted in the spirit of assimilation with the rest of the Roman Catholic Church. The Patriarchal idea was new, if not alien, to this segment of the clergy. As a movement it was linked to the Ukrainian language, which was no longer their everyday language. In the personal conflict between a Metropolitan who had been identified with America since 1938 and a Metropolitan who had "lost his Metropolia," (Slipy) these priests overwhelmingly sided with the one closer to them and their immediate superior. With few exceptions, the American-born clergy did not support the Patriarchal movement. The idea, as it unfolded with Slipy, was considered alien to the diaspora, and was even tendentiously presented as an un-North American concept.

A similar situation developed in monastic communities. Both Basilian and Redemptorist priests and monks had an even larger number of priests born in diaspora. In the case of the Basilian fathers, their Ukrainian cultural identity was reinforced by their study in Rome. The attitude of the Basilian order toward the Patriarchate was also tainted by the animosity between Slipy and the order's leadership in Rome.[12] The differences in the 1960s between Palazzina dell' Arciprete and Aventino in Rome[13] decisively undermined the prospects of the Patriarchate. Basilian communities in individual countries naturally followed the positions set in Rome. Some Basilian fathers could have contributed to the cause of the Patriarchate. They did not and some even worked against it.

The same could be said of the Redemptorists in Canada. A small branch of Ukrainian Salesians in Rome initially supported Cardinal Slipy and his patriarchal movement but were strongly pressured by the Oriental Congregation to turn against him. The small Studite community, however, was fully behind Slipy.

Eighty per cent of women's monastic orders consisted of members born outside Ukraine. Their formation was very much in the pre-Conciliar spirit and had an assimilationist bent. The idea of the Ukrainian Patriarchate was distant, if not alien, to them. They followed their superiors and local bishops. Slipy was able to establish co-operative relations with Basilian nuns, but not with the Sisters Servants of Mary Immaculate (*Sluzhebnytsi*), who traditionally were under the influence of the Basilian Fathers.

Brazilian female monastic communities were comparatively large and displayed a passive attitude toward the patriarchal movement, with some signs of open hostility. There was also a segment of the clergy, born and educated in Ukraine, which did not want to antagonize the bishop by pro-patriarchal activities if he was lukewarm toward the Patriarchate. Few of the Ukrainian-born priests declared themselves inimical to Slipy, but most of them took an active part in the movement. Some even engaged in open conflict with their bishops over the issue. In the eparchies of Toronto, Edmonton, and Australia, and in parts of France and Germany the movement had considerable support. The three American eparchies were divided. Many clergy were rewarded by Slipy, who bestowed on them Eastern Oriental ranks of *kryloshanyn*, Mytrate priest or Archimandrite. These who supported the Curia received the Latin distinction of Monsignore, Prelate or Chamberlain.

Although there was a hyper-active group of pro-patriarchal priests, eventually many of them were not in a position to advance the cause. Former faculty and most of the graduates from the Lviv Academy stood firmly for the Patriarchate and for Slipy. They belonged to the older generation of priests who in the 1960s and 1970s lacked the necessary dynamism. To this group Slipy entrusted the initiative to restore Lviv's Sacerdotal Society of St. Andrew and the quarterly magazine *Nyva*. Slipy believed they would play an important role in Ukrainian church life but it was not to be. With the exception of some regional branches (West Europe, Australia), the Society soon became inactive.[14] The ranks of the old generation pro-patriarchal priests were strengthened by younger priests who were imbued with the spirit of the Council and acted under the charismatic leadership of Cardinal Slipy. The clergy were in a position to exert influence over their bishops if they entered into the movement as an independent factor, but they did not, and were ineffective in their influence over laity as well.

The Lay Movement and Patriarchal Societies

A dynamic lay movement for the creation of a Ukrainian Catholic Patriarchate has existed since 1964 with the organization of an *ad hoc* committee in New York to collect signatures petitioning Paul VI to establish one with Cardinal Slipy as its head. The Committee collected over 40,000 signatures, mostly in the United States, but it elicited little response from the Vatican. A year later the Patriarchal committee was reorganized as the Society for the Patriarchal System in the Ukrainian Catholic Church. It established branches, including some in Germany, France, Belgium and Argentina. In the late 1960s, an attempt was made to establish a world federation of patriarchal societies. The periodical, *Za Patriiarkhat* (now simply *Patriiarkhat*), was published and it criticized bishops and priests who allegedly were undermining patriarchal aspirations.

Support for patriarchal ideas also came from Catholic lay circles which objected to the policy of Latinization and Americanization of the Ukrainian Catholic Church in the United States and Canada. Concurrent with the patriarchal movement, a grass-roots struggle against a change from the liturgical (Julian) to Gregorian calendar ensued in Rochester, New York and Chicago. Some bishops and clergy believed that such a change would facilitate assimilation. A series of committees in defence of the rite, calendar and language were organized in Chicago, Toronto, Cleveland, Newark, Boston, Philadelphia and other places. These groups set up a central committee and launched publications such as *Za ridnu tserkvu* and *Myrianyn*. From the very beginning the defence movement adopted the patriarchal programme and saw Cardinal Slipy as its protector. The group pleaded with him to intercede with local bishops for their cause, which he did.

The calendar became a symbol in a struggle involving issues which related to the very existence of the Ukrainian Church. It also became a mark of allegiance to Cardinal Slipy and the issue of the Patriarchate. Reverberations from the dispute were felt throughout the Ukrainian diaspora as well as in the Roman Curia. Slipy mediated in favour of the traditionalist camp and helped its sympathizers to establish separate parishes, including four in the United States.

These "patriarchal parishes" were established along the lines of lay congregationalism (*Parafiialni rady*). Their watchword was: "Let us protect our Ukrainian Church" (*Zberezhim ridnu tserkvu*). They also established the Alliance of Ukrainian Catholic Church Brotherhood and Sisterhood organizations. A parish bi-weekly, *Tserkovnyi visnyk*, published since 1968 in Chicago, became a voice for this traditionalist movement.

In 1969, on the occasion of the fourth Synod, some representatives of lay organizations proposed establishing a ten-million-dollar patriarchal fund, but

VASYL MARKUS

it was only in the late 1970s that the St. Sophia Association was founded for
that purpose in Rome with branches in the United States, Canada, the United
Kingdom and Belgium. The Ukrainian Catholic community began to conduct
fund drives and collections. There were priests and bishops whose treasuries
suffered from this activity and they resented the grass-roots patriarchal movement.

More support for Cardinal Slipy and the Patriarchate came from Ukrainian
civic and émigré political organizations. Some of them decided immediately
after the fourth Synod in 1969 to create civic inter-organizational councils for
the promotion of the Patriarchate. This action did not succeed in the United
States, where an active Patriarchal Society already existed. The desire of the
Ukrainian Congress Committee (UCCA) and its components to join the
council strengthened opposition to this "new" pro-patriarchal organization
on the ground that the UCCA in the past had supported anti-patriarchal
bishops and opposed the radical actions of the existing patriarchal societies.
In Canada this organizational model did survive due to the support of one
bishop. The Patriarchal Society was based on individual membership. The
Council, however, was composed of representatives of various organizations
whose commitment was divided between the interests of the patriarchal
movement and those of their own organizations.

Great Britain followed a similar organizational pattern in the Central Committee for Ukrainian Patriarchate, which published a monthly bulletin. This
body gained the strong support of major organizations and became a significant instrument in opposition to the dissident bishop. In Australia, the official eparchial alliance of lay'organizations supported the patriarchal movement from the beginning. Tacit support also emerged from Argentina. In
Brazil, however, the laity did not develop organizational participation in the
movement. Since 1974 the efforts of all these lay organizations have been co-
ordinated by the World Federation of Ukrainian Patriarchal societies.

Secular Ukrainian society displayed considerable interest in the patriarchal
cause, thinking it might advance the cause of Ukraine's liberation. Through
it Ukrainians abroad would gain international recognition and, in turn, would
be in a better position to support the suppressed Ukrainian Greek Catholic
Church in their homeland. Eventually, almost all Ukrainian national and international organizations endorsed the Patriarchate and supported Cardinal
Slipy. Some Ukrainian politicians and their political centres-in-exile were
particularly active. The strongest Ukrainian political grouping, the Organization of Ukrainian Nationalists (OUN), became active in the Patriarchal
movement when it was clear that if Slipy's authority grew significantly in international esteem, he could contribute to the émigrés' anti-Soviet struggle.
This support added to the patriarchal movement a political and even partisan
connotation which some saw as an "unholy alliance" between the Ukrainian

166

church and political radicals. More exaggerated criticism was advanced by Soviet propagandists and spokesmen of the Russian Orthodox Church, all of whom were anxious to degrade the movement and the Ukrainian cause.

Two major organizations supported the Patriarchate. The Ukrainian Congress Committee of America (UCCA) initially flirted with Metropolitan Senyshyn. When OUN sided with Slipy, the UCCA, under its influence, favoured the Patriarchate. The Ukrainian international umbrella organization, the World Congress of Free Ukrainians (SKVU), favoured the idea from the outset, however, difficulties emerged with the representatives of the Orthodox churches. The Canadian Orthodox bishops strongly advocated SKVU's non-commitment on the patriarchal issue, since it was controversial and might hurt Orthodox sensibilities. Twice resolutions favouring the Patriarchate were defeated by Orthodox representatives. The Ukrainian secular press in general endorsed the Patriarchate. The Catholic religious press was divided.[15]

The patriarchal movement in the United States and the United Kingdom had open demonstrations and public challenge to the hierarchy and to Vatican spokesmen. There was open opposition to Cardinal Furstenberg, head of the Oriental Congregation, who went to Philadelphia in December 1969 to help celebrate the tenth anniversary of Senyshyn's Metropolia. Another vocal demonstration took place at the Apostolic Delegation in Washington, D.C. in June 1970, when the Curia prevented Cardinal Slipy's visit to his flock in North America.[16] Ukrainians called Slipy the Vatican's prisoner. On 25 May 1971 4,000 Ukrainian Catholics demonstrated at the cathedral in Philadelphia, arguing that the appointment by Rome of two auxiliary bishops violated the rights of the Ukrainian church and did not properly regard the authority of Cardinal Slipy. That dismayed the Vatican and its supporters and solidified Ukrainian laity in the controversy. Similar demonstrations took place later against Bishop Horniak in England on the ground of his non-compliance with the July 1975 *de facto* patriarchal system in the Ukrainian church.

There were also numerous religious occasions in Rome when thousands of Ukrainians gathered from all over the world in support of the Patriarchate and of Cardinal Slipy. The most important gatherings were for the benediction of the cathedral of Saint Sophia, the Anno Sancto pilgrimage in 1975, the fortieth anniversary of the episcopal ordination of Slipy, and his ninetieth birthday in 1982. Similarly, the Cardinal's visitations in Western Europe, Australia, South America and North America presented an opportunity to mobilize support for the Patriarchate in the Ukrainian communities. Thirty thousand participants in Toronto in June 1968 made that visit a triumph for the Patriarchate and Slipy.

Conclusions

This survey of the Ukrainian patriarchal movement suggests a few general observations.

1. In contrast to previous attempts at establishing a Ukrainian Patriarchate, the current movement gained public attention and became both a national and international issue. The Vatican, the Soviet government and the Russian Patriarchate became concerned parties, along with the Latin-rite hierarchy of the countries of the Ukrainian diaspora.

2. The Ukrainian church as a whole was involved in this effort, using theological, canonical and historical-political arguments on the issue. Opponents in the Curia resorted to existing canon law based on territoriality (a Patriarchate requires a politically autonomous land) and on political considerations (a Ukrainian Patriarchate would endanger relations with Moscow).

3. The Ukrainian Catholic community took an active part in setting up separate organizations, initiating activities, and publishing popular and scholarly literature. No other issue in the post-World War II period had so intensely mobilized Ukrainian opinion. It also produced a new type of activist—lay people (*myriany*)—and patriarchal activists (*patriialkhalnyky*).

4. The religious consciousness of the people had deepened and awareness of the Ukrainian church and its national identity became more acute. It encouraged those on the way to assimilation into Roman Catholicism to search for their patrimony. The patriarchal ideology, by focusing on the relationship between nationalism and religion, attempted to synthesize Ukrainian historical experience. Many saw in it a ground for their ethnic-national survival outside Ukraine.

5. A traditional and formalistic attitude toward religion gave way, for some activists, to a serious individual commitment and personally motivated religious stance. Church communities were able to recruit activists not only from the patriarchal movement, but also from other segments of civil life. People also emerged from the ranks of the intelligentsia, which had traditionally been secular in its orientation.

6. The patriarchal movement deepened the sense of unity between the church communities in the diaspora and the church in Ukraine. Its fate as a persecuted and outlawed community has become a concern for many Ukrainian Catholics who otherwise were likely to lose contact with their homeland. The struggle of Ukrainian Catholics for survival in their homeland and the

response from abroad is becoming more purposeful through the patriarchal concept.

7. The Ukrainian Catholic community is coming to accept its Oriental nature. It seeks to rid itself of Latin ritual forms, to hold Eastern Christian tradition in high regard, and to infuse in the church institutions and rituals Eastern Christian features. It is a blend of modernization and a return to the sources of the Christian faith.

8. At first, the movement was largely political. However, many have come to see the way religious and political concepts and issues are intertwined.

9. The person of Cardinal Slipy, Patriarch Iosyf, became central to the entire movement. His charismatic, virtually cultic personality has been viewed by some as a weakness because the movement focused more on his personality than on the issues at hand. What they fail to realize is that he generated a human response, not only to his person, but also to him as a living symbol of the suffering Ukrainian church and the vision of its revival. No one else in the past forty years has been in a position to catalyze such energy and commitment.

10. Elsewhere I have argued that the first fifteen years of the patriarchal movement can be divided into several phases. I have called the years 1963–6 the lost years (lost opportunities); the phase between 1969 and 1975 the stormy years, and 1975–80, the challenging years. The article heralded the subsequent phase as the "creative years." For them to be "creative," the lessons of the past had to be learned. The process of *Sturm und Drang* has passed. The church lost nothing of substance, but has achieved many things. The experience of the entire Ukrainian Catholic Church has been substantially enriched by the last twenty-five years.

NOTES

1. Andrii Sapelak Preosv. *Ukrainska Tserkva na II Vatykanskomu Sobori* (Rome-Buenos Aires, 1967), 158.
2. Literature on the Ukrainian Patriarchate is scarce. Here are a few titles: U. M. Schuver, "Een Oikraiens Patriarchaat?" *Het Christlike Osten* 18 (1965–6); E. Piddubcheshen, *And Bless Thine Inheritance* (New York, 1970); V. J. Pospishil and H. M. Luzhnycky, *The Quest for an Ukrainian Catholic Patriarchate* (Philadelphia, 1971); J. Madey, *Le Patriarchat Ukrainien. Vers la Perfection de l'Etat juridique actuel* (Rome, 1971); Th. Bird and E. Piddubcheshen (editors), *Archepiscopal and*

tuel (Rome, 1971); Th. Bird and E. Piddubcheshen (editors), *Archepiscopal and Patriarchal Autonomy. A Symposium, held on July 15, 1972* (New York, 1972); I. Nahaievsky, *Patriiarkhaty, ikh pochatok i znachennia v Tserkvi ta Ukrainskyi Patriiarkhat* (New York, Munich, Toronto, 1973).

3. V. Markus, "A Century of Ukrainian Religious Experience in the United States," in *The Ukrainian Experience in the United States*, ed. Paul R. Magosci (Cambridge: Harvard Ukrainian Research Institute, 1978), 121.
4. In the first speech at the Vatican Synod after his release from the Soviet Union, Metropolitan Slipy raised the issue of the Ukrainian Patriarchate while speaking of the persecuted church in Ukraine. Since the speech was warmly received, Slipy himself and Ukrainians in general interpreted the Synod's response as an endorsement of this proposal.
5. Bishop Isidore Borecky of Toronto Eparchy informally talked about this in his sermon in Rome, 23 September 1979.
6. Paul VI in a letter to Cardinal Slipy of 7 July 1971 denied Ukrainian patriarchal aspirations on two counts: the lack of territorial integrity of the Ukrainian nation and political considerations as reflected in the Vatican's *Ostpolitik*. See *Visti z Rymu*, 21 October 1971.
7. *Patriiarshyi Ustav Pomisnoi Ukrainskoi (Ruskoi) Katolytskoi Tserkvy* (Castel Gandolfo, 1974). See also my commentary, *Konstytutsiia-Ustav Pomisnoi Ukrainskoi Tserkvy* (Chicago, 1975). The proposed "Constitution" was flatly rejected by the Pope. See R. Hyde, "Rejection of Proposed Constitution for the Ukrainian Catholic Church," *Eastern Churches*, 6 (1974): 64.
8. See *Visti z Rymu*, nos. 5–7, 26 March 1975. Easter pastoral letter was published in most Ukrainian papers, which enthusiastically endorsed Slipy's new title.
9. Cf. an address by Bishop Ivan Prashko of Australia published in I. Nahaievsky, *Patriiarkhaty ta Ukrainskyi Patriarkhat* (London, 1976): 181–5. Ulisse A. Floridi referred to *de facto* Ukrainian patriarchal system as *patriarcato per acclamazione*. *Giornale d'Italia*, 23 June 1973.
10. In early 1988, Bishop Horniak was persuaded by Rome to resign and Bishop Michael Hrynchyshyn of Paris was charged with the temporary administration of the Exarchate of Great Britain.
11. Important papal statements regarding legalized Ukrainian synods are in R. P. Moroziuk, *Politics of a Church Union* (Montreal, 1983), 92–7.
12. This was the most unfortunate episode in the patriarchal movement, with adverse consequences for both.
13. Palazzina dell'Arciprete was the seat of Cardinal Slipy in the Vatican. The Basilian General Curia is located on the Aventino Hill in Rome.
14. Regular general meetings of the St. Andrew's Society are not held; only four issues of *Nyva*, launched as a quarterly journal in 1976, appeared.
15. Newspapers affiliated with eparchies whose bishops supported the Patriarchate promoted the cause, for example, *Nasha meta* (Toronto), the Ukrainian section of *Postup* (Winnipeg), *Ukrainski visti* (Edmonton) and *Tserkva i zhyttia* (Melbourne, Australia). *Pratsia* (Curitiba, Brazil), *Khrystyianskyi holos* (Munich), *Progress* (Winnipeg) and *America* (Philadelphia) were largely neutral. *Svitlo* (Toronto), *Nova zoria* (Chicago) and *Shliakh* (Philadelphia) were critical and, at times, hostile. The Orthodox press did not support the idea of a Ukrainian Catholic Patriarchate.
16. Cardinal Furstenberg, Head of the Oriental Congregation, conveyed to the Ukrainian Cardinal the Pontiff's "advice" not to make the trip. Slipy wanted to hold the fifth Synod of Ukrainian Bishops in Canada. See Ulisse A. Floridi, *Mosca et il Vaticano* (Milan, 1976), 314.

Oleh Wolowyna

Linguistic-Cultural Assimilation and Changes in Religious Denominations of Ukrainian Canadians

Since the very beginning, religion has always been an integral part of the Ukrainian people, its culture and identity. Two major denominations are identified with Ukrainian culture: the Ukrainian Greek Catholic Church and the Ukrainian Orthodox Church. More recently several Protestant sects have taken hold, but numerically their adherents were rather insignificant within the total population of Ukraine.

As part of the assimilation process in Canada and other countries, Ukrainians began to adapt their religious life to the forms of the locally prevalent Roman Catholic or Protestant denominations. While little is known about this process in quantitative terms, the purpose of this paper is to describe the religious composition and characteristics of Ukrainians in Canada, using data from the 1981 Canadian census of housing and population. Five major religions or groups of religions which are significant among Ukrainians in Canada have been selected for analysis: Ukrainian Catholic; Ukrainian Orthodox; Roman Catholic; Protestant (Anglican, Baptist, Lutheran, Presbyterian and United Church); and Fundamentalist (Mennonite/Hutterite, Pentecostal and other minor fundamental sects).

After a brief description of the data set used and selection of the sample, there is a general description of each of the five religions/groups. This is followed by a comparative description of the five religions/groups. Finally, some aspects of the relationship between linguistic and religious assimilation are examined.

Data Used and Selection of Sample

As published tabulations on religion for Ukrainians are rather scarce, the analysis was done using the 2 per cent Public Use Sample Tape, Individual File. This is a representative sample of full census records of a 1/50 part of the total Canadian population in 1981, which allows the researcher to produce tabulations, limited only by the aggregation of some of the variables due to confidentiality considerations, and by the number of cases in each cell. Although the numbers produced will differ from published results due to sampling error, this error is small if the disaggregation is not too detailed.

The sample of Ukrainians was elicited using the following criteria: Ukrainian ethnicity or Ukrainian mother tongue or Ukrainian language spoken at home or Other Catholic (practically equivalent to Ukrainian Catholic). These inclusive criteria were chosen to partially compensate for the low estimate of Ukrainians due to classification procedures used in the 1981 Census: multiple answers were allowed on the ethnicity question and all persons who responded with Ukrainian and British or Ukrainian and French were classified as British or French, respectively. This enhanced sample gave an estimated total of 580,800 Ukrainians, significantly larger than the 1981 Census estimate of 529,615. The difference of about 51,200 persons between the two estimates is mainly a result of the misclassification of persons with dual ethnicity who were captured with the mother tongue, language at home or Ukrainian Catholic criteria. There are also persons of non-Ukrainian ancestry but with Ukrainian mother tongue or language, those who are Ukrainian Catholic due to intermarriage and persons who adopted the Ukrainian Catholic religion for a variety of reasons. There are about 24,000 Ukrainian Catholics who are not of Ukrainian ancestry, do not have Ukrainian as their mother tongue, and do not speak the language. There are also about 3,000 persons who speak Ukrainian, but do not satisfy either the ethnicity or the mother tongue criteria.

Some Characteristics of Ukrainians in Canada, 1981

Ukrainians were a fairly old group, with a median age of thirty-seven years. Only about 14 per cent were under fifteen years of age, and the group sixty-five years or older represented 14 per cent of the total (Table 3). Almost 84 per cent were Canadian-born. Among the immigrants, about half came before World War II, while 11 per cent arrived in Canada after 1960 (Table 4). The largest concentration was found in the prairie provinces (60 per cent), 27.5 per cent lived in Ontario and Quebec (mostly in Ontario), and 12 per cent lived in British Columbia; very few Ukrainians lived in the other parts of Canada (Table 5). Edmonton had the largest number of Ukrainians with

172

70,900, followed by Toronto with 68,300 (Table 6). Ukrainians were highly urbanized, with 60 per cent living in Census Metropolitan Areas (CMA, i.e., cities with 100,000 or more inhabitants) (Table 7).

Their mean number of years of schooling was almost eight. There were about 7 per cent functional illiterates (fewer than five years of schooling), although about 9 per cent had a bachelor's degree or higher (Table 8). Among men almost half had blue-collar occupations, while 13 per cent were engaged in farm and other primary occupations. The high white-collar occupation category (managerial-administrative, sciences, social sciences, teaching, medicine and health, art, literature, and recreation) comprised 22 per cent of the male labour force. Almost half of the females were in sales and clerical occupations, 23 per cent in the high white-collar category, and only 5 per cent in primary occupations (Table 9). The median income for males was $16,262, and for females, $5,063; the median household income was $25,140 (Table 10).

About 89 per cent of the whole group were of Ukrainian ethnic origin, almost half of them had Ukrainian as their mother tongue, and 15.5 per cent spoke Ukrainian at home (Table 11). If only persons of Ukrainian ancestry are considered, the percentage speaking Ukrainian increases to 16.0. Among the persons of non-Ukrainian ancestry, most were of British (single or multiple) and Polish ethnicity (Table 12).

Table 1 presents the number of Ukrainians by religious denominations, from 1931 to 1981. (It should be noted that the 1981 data are not quite comparable to the 1971 data, as in the 1981 sample table 'no religion' and 'other religions' were put into one category; this explains the large size of the 'other' category compared to 1971. Also the 1981 data may not coincide with the published data for two reasons: (1)we are using a sample, and (2)the population used for analysis contains a non-trivial component of persons with non-Ukrainian ethnicity.) The number of Ukrainian Orthodox began to decline in 1961, and if we subtract from the 191,300 Ukrainian Catholics in 1981 the 24,000 who did not satisfy any of the Ukrainian criteria (ancestry, mother tongue or languages), we note a slight decline between 1971 and 1981. With the exception of Roman Catholic and Pentecostals, there was a slight decline in the other denominations between 1971 and 1981, but the general trend has been a steady increase for most of non-traditional denominations. This growth is especially noticeable in the United Church (Table 2). This denomination has by far the largest number of Ukrainians among the Protestant denominations, and among the traditionally new Ukrainian denominations is surpassed in numbers only by the Roman Catholic Church which, with over 100,000 members, rivals the Ukrainian Orthodox membership.

Ukrainian Catholics

There were about 191,300 Ukrainian Catholics in Canada in 1981, with 24,000 of them of non-Ukrainian ethnicity (Table 1). This number constitutes about one-third of all Ukrainians in Canada (Table 2). There were slightly fewer females than males (49 per cent), and half of them were thirty-eight years of age or older. Almost 16 per cent were under fifteen years of age and about the same percentage were sixty-five years or older (Table 3). Slightly under 79 per cent were born in Canada, and of the non-natives, the majority came after World War II. Thirteen per cent of all immigrants arrived in Canada after 1960 (Table 4).

The great majority of Ukrainian Catholics lived in the prairie provinces (62 per cent), with the highest concentration in Manitoba (48,100). About 30 per cent lived in Ontario and Quebec, and only about 7 per cent lived in British Columbia. The number of Ukrainian Catholics living in other parts of Canada was insignificant (Table 5). More than half lived in a CMA but this percentage showed a great regional variation. The percentage in a CMA was 75 per cent for Quebec-Ontario, in the 44–52 per cent range for the prairies and British Columbia, and only 8 per cent for the Atlantic region (Table 7). (The percentage for the Other region is always zero, as it does not contain cities with 100,000 or more inhabitants.) The regional variation in this percentage is strongly affected by the distribution in each region of cities with 100,000 or more inhabitants. The largest number of Ukrainian Catholics was in Winnipeg with 28,350, followed by Toronto with 23,600 and Edmonton with 19,550 (Table 6).

Socio-economic characteristics of Ukrainian Catholics are presented in Tables 8, 9 and 10. Their mean number of years of schooling was 7.5. At the other extreme, more than 7 per cent of all Ukrainian Catholics had a bachelor's degree or higher (Table 8). Almost half of all males in the labour force had blue-collar occupations, while nearly 22 per cent were in the high white-collar category; there were still a considerable number, 14 per cent, working in primary occupations. Most of the females worked in sales and clerical occupations (low white-collar category). Their percentage in the top category was higher than for males (23 per cent), but fewer than 7 per cent worked in agriculture (Table 9). The median income for males was $13,761/year, while for females it was $4,934. The median household income was $24,815. Among Ukrainian Catholics, 82.5 per cent owned the house they lived in.

Ukrainian Orthodox

There were about 103,700 Ukrainian Orthodox in Canada in 1981, which constituted about 18 per cent of all Ukrainians. With a median age of forty-seven years, they are a very old group. Only 10.5 percent of them were under fifteen, and 22.4 per cent were sixty-five or older (Table 3). About 77 per cent were born in Canada, and the majority of immigrants, 57 per cent, came to Canada before World War II. Only 37 per cent of all immigrants were Displaced Persons, and fewer than 6 per cent arrived after 1960 (Table 4). About 65 per cent of them lived in the prairie provinces, and two-thirds of those lived in Alberta (70,000). Nearly 26 per cent lived in Quebec-Ontario and about 8 per cent in British Columbia (Table 5). Almost half lived in a CMA; the percentage for Quebec-Ontario was 68, about 45 each for the prairies and British Columbia, and 25 per cent for the Atlantic region (Table 7).

Edmonton had the largest number of Ukrainian Orthodox in Canada: 17,250. Winnipeg and Toronto had about 9,000 each, while the other major cities had less than half that number (Table 6). While the number of functional illiterates among Ukrainian Orthodox was very high, the percentage with at least a bachelor's was also high. About 48 per cent of males in the labour force worked in blue-collar occupations, nearly 23 per cent were in the high white-collar category and almost 18 per cent worked in agriculture. Among females, 22 percent had occupations in the high white-collar category and only 5.6 per cent had primary occupations (Table 9). Median income for males was almost $12,000, and 5,257 for females. Median household income was $22,230 (Table 10). Almost 84 per cent of Ukrainian Orthodox in Canada were homeowners.

Roman Catholics

Roman Catholics constitute the third largest group in 1981 with 100,600 members, although this includes about 24,000 who were not of Ukrainian ethnicity. This translates into 17.5 per cent of the whole group (Tables 1 and 2). Roman Catholics were a relatively young group with a median age of thirty-six years, and only 12 per cent aged sixty-five or more (Table 3). Fewer than 10 per cent of them were immigrants and most of them, 57 per cent, came before World War II, while 15 per cent of the migrants arrived in Canada after 1960 (Table 4).

Slightly over half of them lived in the prairie provinces, with the highest concentration in Alberta (48,000). Almost 11 percent of them lived in British Columbia (Table 5). About 48.6 percent lived in a CMA with regional percentages of 55 per cent in Quebec-Ontario, 44–46 per cent in the prairie provinces and British Columbia, and nearly 32 per cent in the Atlantic region (Table 7). Winnipeg had the largest concentration with 12,000, followed by Edmonton with almost 10,000 and Toronto with more than 8,000. The number of Roman Catholics in other major cities ranged between 1,950 and 4,800 (Table 6).

Roman Catholics had an average of 7.9 years of schooling and the percentages with fewer than five years of schooling and with bachelor's degrees or higher were each 6.1 per cent (Table 8). More than half of the males had blue-collar occupations, 22.5 were in the high white-collar category and only 10 percent worked in rural activities (Table 9). The percentage in the high white-collar category was slightly higher for females, and only 5 per cent of females worked in agriculture. The median income was $15,893 for males and $4,941 for females. The median household income was $25,770.

Main Protestant Religions

There were 110,800 Ukrainians in the major Protestant denominations (United Church, Anglican, Presbyterian, Lutheran, Baptist) in 1981, with 62 per cent of them belonging to the United Church. Anglicans had about 18 per cent, and Presbyterians, Lutherans and Baptists had about 7 per cent each (Table 1). At 19 per cent, they were the second largest religious group among Ukrainians in Canada. Their median age was thirty-four years, and persons sixty-five years or older made up 7.3 per cent of the total (Table 3). Almost 95 per cent were born in Canada, and 71 per cent of the immigrants came before World War II. Only 21 per cent of them arrived between 1946 and 1960, and 8 per cent arrived after 1960 (Table 4).

About 56 per cent lived in the prairie provinces, with two-thirds of these in Alberta (32,300). About 26 per cent lived in Quebec-Ontario, 16 percent in British Columbia and 1 per cent in the Atlantic region (Table 5). Across the country 47.8 per cent lived in a CMA while the respective regional percentages were 53 per cent for Quebec-Ontario, 49 per cent for British Columbia, 46 per cent for the prairies and 17 per cent for the Atlantic provinces (Table 7). Edmonton had the largest contingent with 13,800, followed by Winnipeg with 10,650, Vancouver with 8,900, Toronto with 7,100, and Calgary with 5,150 (Table 6). With only 2.8 per cent with fewer than five years of schooling, the mean years of schooling was quite high at 8.3. Over 6.5 per cent had a bachelor's or higher (Table 8). Just under 49 per cent of males worked in blue-collar occupations, while 23 per cent were in the high white-collar category, and 9.6 per cent worked in agricultural occupations. Significantly more females, 26.5 per cent, had high white-collar occupations, and only 3 per cent worked in primary occupations (Table 9). Males had a median income of $17,761, females of $5,529 and the median household income was $28,000. Fewer than 79 per cent of them lived in their own home.

Fundamentalist Denominations

This group is formed of Ukrainians who belonged to Mennonite, Hutterite, Pentecostal and other minor fundamentalist groups. In 1981 they numbered 25,200 or 4.6 per cent of the whole group. The largest denomination was

176

Pentecostal, with 8,400 members (Table 1). Although the absolute numbers in these denominations are small, their relative growth with time is significant (Table 2). The group was quite young, with a median age of thirty-three. Although 11.5 per cent were sixty-five or older, this was counterbalanced with the high percentage under fifteen, 18.0 per cent, which is a consequence of their relatively high fertility (Table 3). Eighty-nine per cent of them were born in Canada and most of the immigrants, 67 per cent, arrived before World War II. A relatively large number of the immigrants, 22 per cent, arrived in Canada after 1960 (Table 4).

Most of them lived in the prairies, 61 per cent, but almost 20 per cent did live in Quebec-Ontario and 18.7 per cent lived in British Columbia (Table 5). About 7,000 lived in Alberta, 4,000 in Manitoba and Saskatchewan, and hardly any in Quebec. Only 40 per cent lived in a CMA. The respective regional percentages were Quebec-Ontario 52.5 per cent, prairies 37.7 per cent and British Columbia 36.2 per cent (Table 7). The largest concentration was found in Edmonton with 2,950, followed by Winnipeg and Vancouver with close to 2,000 each (Table 6).

Their mean years of schooling was 7.5; 7.3 per cent had fewer than five years of schooling and only 5.6 per cent had a bachelor's or higher (Table 8). About 13 per cent of males worked in agriculture, 50 per cent in blue-collar occupations, and only 17 per cent had occupations in the high white-collar category. Females had a high of 21 percent in the white-collar category, while 29 per cent worked in the blue-collar sector and only 2.9 per cent worked in agriculture (Table 9). The median income for males was $14,227, and $4,568 for females; the median household income was $22,568 (Table 10). Only 73 per cent of them lived in their own house.

Comparative Analysis of Religious Groups in Canada

Ukrainian Catholics constitute the largest group with 33 per cent, followed by the major Protestant group with 19 per cent, Orthodox with 18 per cent, Roman Catholic with 17 per cent and Fundamentalists with 4.5 per cent. In terms of age structure, the youngest group was the fundamentalist, followed by the major Protestant group. Orthodox were by far the oldest group, with 22 per cent of their population over sixty-five. This demographic fact implies a rapid decrease in their numbers in the not too distant future. Slightly fewer than 25 per cent of each of the two traditional Ukrainian religions were immigrants, while for the other three religious groups, only about 10 per cent were born outside Canada, and most of the immigrants came before World War II. A significant difference between Ukrainian Catholic and Orthodox immigrants was that for the former the majority of immigrants came after World War II (Table 4).

For all five groups the great majority continued to live in the prairie provinces, with slight variations: Ukrainian Catholic and Orthodox had the highest percentages while Roman Catholic had the lowest. The highest percentages for British Columbia belonged to the major Protestants and the fundamentalists (Table 5). Ukrainian Catholics had the highest degree of urbanization (defined as places with 100,000 or more inhabitants), while the fundamentalists had the lowest level. The level of urbanization in the prairies was fairly uniform for all the groups except the fundamentalist, for which it was lower. The three non-traditional religious groups had the lowest level of urbanization in Quebec-Ontario, Roman Catholics had the highest percentage in the Atlantic provinces, and Ukrainian Catholics had the highest percentage in British Columbia.

The largest concentration of Ukrainian Catholics was in Winnipeg, while Edmonton was the stronghold of Orthodox. Ukrainian Catholics had an absolute majority in Winnipeg, Toronto, Edmonton, Montreal and Hamilton, while the major Protestants dominated in Vancouver and Calgary. In the largest cities, both Roman Catholics and the major Protestants constituted roughly between one-third and one-half of the number of Ukrainian Catholics, and their numbers were of the same order of magnitude as the Orthodox in Winnipeg and Toronto. The major Protestants had by far the highest mean years of schooling and the Orthodox the lowest. The Orthodox had the highest percentage with less than five years of schooling but also, together with Ukrainian Catholics, the highest percentage with a bachelor's degree or higher. It is clear that the religiously unassimilated Ukrainians are taking full advantage of the educational opportunities in Canada, and have surpassed the more traditional segment of society in terms of higher education. There is no clear distinction between Ukrainian Catholics and Orthodox and the other religious groups in terms of occupation, with the exception of the percentage in agricultural occupations. Here Orthodox males and females have the highest percentage, Ukrainian Catholics and fundamentalists are in the middle and the major Protestants and Roman Catholics have the lowest percentages. In most cases females had a higher percentage in high white-collar occupations than did males. Major Protestants had by far the highest average income both for males and females, as well as for the household. Ukrainian Catholics had low individual incomes but relatively high household income, which would indicate multiple incomes. Orthodox males had the lowest average income, while Orthodox females had the second highest income. Orthodox and Ukrainian Catholics had the highest percentages of home ownership.

The general pattern is that the two traditional Ukrainian religious groups tended to be older, more urbanized, with higher percentages in agricultural occupations, and with lower socioeconomic status, especially in terms of income (with the exception of Orthodox women). Although the two traditional Ukrainian churches had large percentages of functional illiterates, significant progress has been made at the higher educational level by successive generations. Ukrainian Catholics still constitute a clear majority; however, both Roman Catholics and Protestants provide significant competition to these churches in cities with the largest Ukrainian communities.

Religious and Linguistic Assimilation

Table 11 illustrates the relationship between linguistic and religious assimilation. Here religious assimilation is taken as the transition from one of the two traditional Ukrainian religions to Roman Catholicism or to one of the Protestant denominations. Linguistic assimilation is measured in terms of loss of the Ukrainian language.

Among the whole group, about 11 per cent were of non-Ukrainian ethnic origin (Table 12). If we disregard the category 'other sing.,' which means other single-answer ethnicities, the largest group of these non-Ukrainians was the British, single or jointly with other ethnicity, probably with Ukrainian in most cases, followed by Polish. The highest percentage of non-Ukrainians (by the ethnicity criterion) was found among Ukrainian Catholics and Roman Catholics. In the latter case, the majority of them were Poles, while in the Ukrainian Catholic case, the majority were of British ancestry.

The degree of language retention is highest for Ukrainian Orthodox and Ukrainian Catholic with 28.1 per cent for the former and 25.5 per cent for the latter. The major Protestant group had the lowest percentage, 3.6 per cent, followed by Roman Catholics with 6.9 per cent and fundamentalists with 9.3 per cent (Table 11). Table 13 presents the odds of speaking Ukrainian if a person is Ukrainian Catholic or Orthodox, versus the other denominations. For example, on average, a Ukrainian Catholic is seven times more likely to speak Ukrainian than is a member of one of the major Protestant denominations. The highest odds are for the major Protestants, with an order of magnitude of seven or eight to one, about four to one for Roman Catholics and three to one for fundamentalists. The odds are better for Orthodox than for Ukrainian Catholics. This is probably because the Orthodox are older, less urbanized, and of lower socioeconomic status, all characteristics associated with higher language retention.

Table 14 addresses the question of the effect of language assimilation on religious assimilation. Three subgroups were created, which can be considered as points on an ordinal scale of language assimilation. 'Ethonly' is the category of persons who were of Ukrainian ethnicity, but neither their mother tongue nor the language spoken at home was Ukrainian; this is the most assimilated category. 'Eth + m.tongue' is formed of persons whose ethnicity and mother tongue were Ukrainian, but who did not speak Ukrainian at home; this is the intermediate category. For them, the language assimilation process occurred in their generation. Finally 'eth + m.t. + lang' are those who spoke the language at home and whose ethnicity and mother tongue were Ukrainian; these are the unassimilated ones.

It can be observed in Table 14 that there is a strong relationship between speaking Ukrainian and belonging to one of the two traditional Ukrainian religions. More than half of Ukrainian Catholics belonged to the unassimilated group, while for the Orthodox it was about 32 per cent. For the other religious groups, the percentage of unassimilated was very small. In order to evaluate the odds of a person speaking Ukrainian belonging to any of the five denominations, it is necessary to standardize for the size of each religious group. The results are presented in Table 15. For a person belonging to the linguistically unassimilated group (ethnicity, mother tongue, and language spoken at home are Ukrainian), the odds of being Ukrainian Catholic are seventeen to ten and of being Orthodox are nineteen to ten. The odds of belonging to a fundamentalist religion, on the other hand, are low for Roman Catholics and the most disadvantageous for the major Protestant denominations.

Discussion

It has been clearly established that linguistic and religious assimilation go hand-in-hand. Chances are very slim that a person who speaks Ukrainian belongs to a Protestant denomination or is Roman Catholic and, vice-versa, if a person belongs to any of these denominations odds are small that the person speaks Ukrainian on a regular basis. As Ukrainian speakers are heavily concentrated among immigrants and older persons, the small percentage of immigrants and the relatively old age structure of Ukrainian Catholics and Orthodox are likely to contribute to an acceleration of the religious assimilation process. Perhaps the transition to one of the major Protestant denominations is partially motivated by social mobility aspirations and will be more difficult to influence, but the socio-economic differences between Roman Catholics and Ukrainian Catholics and Orthodox are less marked, and here the politics of the two Catholic churches can be an important policy factor in the struggle to slow down the assimilation process.

TABLE 1 Number of Ukrainians by Religious Denomination, 1931–1981

	Uk. Cat.	Orthodox	R. Cath.	United	Anglican	Presb.	Lutheran	Baptist	Pentec.	Mennon.	Other	Total
1981	191,300	103,700	100,600	68,800	20,000	6,300	7,800	7,900	8,400	500	60,400	575,700
1971	186,460	116,700	88,835	80,790	26,950	7,725	10,175	8,250	5,545	1,195	48,035	580,660
1961	157,559	119,219	79,638	59,825	19,140	5,483	6,590	6,113	3,372	711	15,687	473,337
1951	164,765	111,045	56,650	28,190	10,082	4,521	3,435	3,723	0	465	12,167	395,043
1941	152,907	88,874	37,577	9,241	3,131	2,919	1,686	2,439	1,241	657	5,257	305,929
1931	130,534	55,386	25,781	3,667	755	1,823	1,180	1,262	105	385	4,235	225,113

TABLE 2 Per cent Distribution of Ukrainians by Religion for 1931–1981

	Uk. Cat.	Orthodox	R. Cath.	United	Anglican	Presb.	Lutheran	Baptist	Pentec.	Mennon.	Other	Total
1981	33.1	18.0	17.4	11.9	3.5	1.1	1.4	1.4	1.5	0.1	10.5	99.9
1971	32.1	20.1	15.3	13.9	4.6	1.3	1.8	1.4	1.0	0.2	8.3	100.0
1961	33.3	25.2	16.8	12.6	4.0	1.2	1.4	1.3	0.7	0.2	3.3	100.0
1951	41.7	28.1	14.3	7.1	2.6	1.1	0.9	0.9	0.0	0.1	3.1	99.9
1941	50.0	29.1	12.3	3.0	1.0	1.0	0.6	0.8	0.4	0.2	1.7	100.1
1931	58.0	24.6	11.5	1.6	0.3	0.8	0.5	0.6	0.1	0.2	1.9	100.1

* Some columns do not add up to 100 owing to rounding error.

TABLE 3 Age Distribution of Ukrainians by Selected Religions, 1981 Census

Age	Ukrainian Catholic	Orthodox	Roman Catholic	Major Protestant	Funda- mentalist	Total
0–14	15.7	10.5	13.1	14.0	18.1	13.9
15–39	35.9	32.4	41.0	43.8	41.7	38.6
40–64	32.8	34.8	34.0	34.9	28.8	33.1
65 +	15.7	22.4	11.9	7.3	11.5	14.3
Median	38.0	47.0	36.0	34.0	33.0	37.0

TABLE 4 Percentage of Canadian–Born and Immigrants by Period, by Selected Religions, 1981 Census

Category	Ukrainian Catholic	Orthodox	Roman Catholic	Major Protestant	Funda- mentalist	Total
Canadian–born	78.5	77.1	90.5	94.5	89.1	83.9
Immigrants	21.5	22.9	9.5	5.5	10.9	16.1
Total	100.0	100.0	100.0	100.0	100.0	100.0
Immigrants						
WW II	39.7	56.9	57.3	71.2	67.3	50.1
1946–60	47.4	37.4	27.6	20.8	10.9	38.5
1961–81	12.9	5.6	15.1	8.0	21.8	11.4
*Total	100.0	99.9	100.0	100.0	100.0	100.0

* One column does not add up to 100 owing to rounding error.

182

TABLE 5 Percentage of Ukrainians in Regions by Selected Religions, 1981 Census

Region	Ukrainian Catholic	Orthodox	Roman Catholic	Major Protestant	Fundamentalist	Total
Atlantic	0.3	0.2	1.1	1.0	0.2	0.7
Quebec–Ontario	30.4	25.9	32.4	26.3	19.6	27.5
Prairies	62.3	65.4	55.5	56.6	61.1	59.8
British Columbia	6.8	8.2	10.7	15.9	18.7	11.9
Other	0.1	0.2	0.2	0.1	0.4	0.1
*Total	99.9	99.9	99.9	99.9	100.0	100.0

*Some columns do not add up to 100 owing to rounding error.

183

TABLE 6 Number of Ukrainians in Selected CMAs, by Selected Religions, 1981 Census

CMA's	Ukrainian Catholic	Orthodox	Roman Catholic	Major Protestant	Funda-mentalist	Undeclared	Total
Winnipeg	28,350	8,850	12,000	10,650	1,850	6,600	68,300
Toronto	23,600	9,300	8,100	7,100	1,000	2,700	51,800
Edmonton	19,550	17,250	9,950	13,800	2,950	7,400	70,900
Montreal	8,150	2,800	2,450	1,250	100	1,150	15,900
Vancouver	6,700	3,850	4,800	8,900	1,700	8,050	34,000
Calgary	4,600	3,450	3,700	5,150	1,000	900	18,800
Hamilton	4,600	3,000	1,950	2,100	550	1,900	14,100

TABLE 7 Percentage in CMAs by Regions and Selected Religions, 1981 Census

Region	Ukrainian Catholic	Orthodox	Roman Catholic	Major Protestant	Funda-mentalist	Total
Atlantic	8.3	25.0	31.8	17.4	0.0	23.7
Que.–Ontario	75.4	68.5	55.4	52.7	52.5	64.3
Prairies	44.8	43.2	46.0	45.9	37.7	45.5
B. Columbia	52.1	44.8	44.4	49.0	36.2	49.3
Other	0.0	0.0	0.0	0.0	0.0	0.0
Canada	54.4	49.7	48.6	47.8	40.1	59.0

TABLE 8 Level of Education Indicators for Ukrainians by Selected Religions in Percentages, 1981 Census

Years of Education	Ukrainian Catholic	Orthodox	Roman Catholic	Major Protestant	Funda-mentalist	All Ukrainians
Less than 5	9.2	12.5	6.1	2.8	7.3	6.8
Bachelor's degree or higher	7.3	7.4	6.1	6.7	5.6	7.5
Mean years of schooling	7.5	7.3	7.9	8.3	7.5	7.8

**TABLE 9 Percentage of Ukrainians in Major Occupation Categories,
by Religion and Sex, 1981 Census**

Occupation Categories	Ukrainian Catholic	Orthodox	Roman Catholic	Major Protestant	Funda- mentalist	All Ukrainians
Males:						
High W. Collar	21.9	22.7	22.5	23.2	17.1	22.2
Low W. Collar	15.1	11.2	15.5	18.3	19.6	16.1
Primary	13.8	17.8	10.0	9.6	13.3	12.6
Blue Collar	49.2	48.4	52.0	48.8	50.0	49.1
Females:						
High W. Collar	23.3	22.1	22.8	26.5	21.0	23.0
Low W. Collar	43.8	43.6	48.5	49.7	47.1	47.2
Primary	6.6	5.6	4.9	3.3	2.9	5.2
Blue Collar	26.3	28.7	23.8	20.6	29.0	24.6

**TABLE 10 Income Indicators for Ukrainians by Selected Religions,
1981 Census**

Income	Ukrainian Catholic	Orthodox	Roman Catholic	Major Protestant	Funda- mentalist	All Ukrainians
Median male income	13,761	11,949	15,893	17,761	14,227	16,262
Median female income	4,934	5,257	4,941	5,529	4,568	5,063
Median household income	24,815	22,230	25,770	28,000	22,568	25,140

TABLE 11 Linguistic Assimilation Indicators by Selected Religions, 1981 Census

Percent Ukrainian	Ukrainian Catholic	Orthodox	Roman Catholic	Major Protestant	Funda-mentalist	All Ukrainians
Ethnic origin	83.2	96.5	86.1	94.9	93.7	88.9
Mother tongue	59.2	68.3	39.8	33.0	40.1	49.6
Home language	25.5	28.1	6.9	3.6	9.3	15.5

TABLE 12 Selected Ethnic Origins of Persons of Non-Ukrainian Ethnicity by Selected Religions, 1981 Census

Ethnic Origin	Ukrainian Catholic	Orthodox	Roman Catholic	Major Protestant	Funda-mentalist	Total*
Oth. sing.	28.5	45.7	27.1	29.4	34.9	25.2
Brit. other	17.3	11.4	3.8	13.7	3.2	12.6
British	23.2	11.4	6.8	27.5	12.7	17.1
Polish	11.9	22.9	58.6	21.6	31.7	22.5
French	4.2	0.0	2.3	0.0	6.3	3.6

* Includes all non-Ukrainians in Canada claiming knowledge of Ukrainian language, 1981.

TABLE 13 Odds of Speaking Ukrainian if Ukr. Catholic or Orthodox vs. Each of the Other Religions, 1981 Census

	Roman Catholic	Major Protestant	Fundamentalist
Ukr. Cath.	3.7	7.1	2.7
Orthodox	4.1	7.8	3.0

TABLE 14 Percentage Distribution Within Categories of Linguistic Assimilation for Selected Religions, 1981 Census

Category	Ukrainian Catholic	Orthodox	Roman Catholic	Major Protestant	Funda- mentalist	All Other	Total
Ethonly	19.6	12.6	22.3	28.8	6.0	10.7	100.0
Eth + m.tongue	36.8	23.4	14.6	15.1	4.2	5.9	100.0
Eth + m.t. + lang.	56.0	32.2	4.0	3.4	1.9	2.5	100.0

TABLE 15 Odds that a Person Belonging to Eth + M.T. + Lang Belongs to Each of the Following Religions, 1981 Census

	Ukrainian	Orthodox	Roman Catholic	Major Protestant	Funda- mentalist
Odds	1.7	1.9	1/4.3	1/5.6	1/2.4

Religion, Ethnicity and
Jurisdiction:
Case Studies

Vivian Olender

Symbolic Manipulation in the Proselytizing of Ukrainians: An Attempt to Create a Protestant Uniate Church

The Presbyterian Church at the turn of the century was the largest Protestant church on the prairies and the second largest in Canada. As the prairies were opened for settlement, Presbyterian leaders advocated establishing a new and righteous society in the West.[1] The Presbyterian Church must be involved in all aspects of life, setting and guarding the standards of the community, and fostering good citizenship. By the last decade of the nineteenth century the dominating influence of the Scottish or Ulster Presbyterian was making its mark in the West:

> The population is largely from Scottish and North of Ireland stock and Presbyterian in belief. And as in every land the influence of the Presbyterian element is not to be determined by numbers. Three of the Superior Court Judges in Winnipeg were reared in Presbyterian homes, two are sons of the manse. Four of the Five Ministers of the Crown are Presbyterians, and about half the Legislature. The same is true of the Legislature of the Territories. In the management of the great commercial enterprises, in things educational, social, and professional, Presbyterians hold the leading place. The Boss in the lumber camp, the foreman in a construction gang, the captain in a mine, ten chances in one has in him blood from Scotland or the north of Ireland. These people are going to make the West. The Church has to say what they shall make of it.[2]

Presbyterians believed that the prairies should be developed on British foundations with white Anglo-Celtic ideals and traditions. Because British civilization was held to be the highest interpretation and expression of Christian culture, their vision for Canada was a homogeneous Anglo-Celtic country. The Dominion of Canada would be "His Dominion" and Presbyterians would build their share of the Kingdom of God.[3] Many Canadian Protestants believed that God had preordained a special destiny for Canada in the twentieth century. The Rev. R. G. MacBeth, a prominent Presbyterian clergyman and historian, echoed the prevalent view in his messianic portrayal of Canada's future:

> If, it be true, as history seems to say, that the star of the Empire has, from the beginning, been wending its way westward, then because on our Pacific shore the Orient and the Occident face each other, the star will hover over Canada and under it some great messianic achievement for the good of the world may be born. This Dominion, if we are faithful, seems destined to become in the hands of God a chosen instrument for turning the rest of the world unto Him, and if we fail in our duty we shall lose the peerless opportunity of the world's history and the nations of mankind beyond will suffer.[4]

In general, Anglo-Canadians reacted negatively toward the influx of Ukrainian immigrants. Because of popular belief in the Northern myth and Social Darwinism, Ukrainians were considered to be members of an inferior "race." As a result, a stereotype of Ukrainians which emphasized their presumed inferior cultural and behavioural characteristics was sanctioned by the Presbyterian Church. Such Continental European immigrants were perceived as a threat to the messianic dream of establishing the Presbyterian version of the kingdom of God in Canada.[5] Rather than setting an example of tolerance and brotherhood, Presbyterian leaders, like most Anglo-Canadians, advocated a policy of assimilation for all Continental European immigrants. Moreover, they wanted their church to be "foremost among the assimilating forces."[6] It was vital that the Presbyterian Church make them good Christians and good Canadians.

Of all the ethnic groups in the west, Ukrainians were considered to be the most serious obstacle to Anglo-Canadian hegemony on the prairies. Ukrainians immigrated in larger numbers than other ethnic groups, settled in isolated block colonies that hindered assimilation, and had larger families than the average Anglo-Canadian family.[7] Ukrainians might eventually outnumber the Anglo-Celtic settlers.[8] Some Presbyterians even suggested it was ultimately a question of whether Ukrainians would assimilate Presbyterians or the Presbyterians the Ukrainians.[9]

Presbyterians also did not approve of the two traditional Ukrainian churches, the Ukrainian Greek Orthodox Church and the Ukrainian Catholic Church. Allegedly the Ukrainian churches did not provide their laity with a proper moral foundation on which to build good Christian citizenship.[10] Presbyterians thought Ukrainian Catholics were the hapless victims of priestcraft. Because Presbyterians thought the Eastern-rite liturgy was only an elaborate superstitious ceremony, they failed to appreciate or understand the significance of the symbolism.[11]

The Rev. Dr. A. J. Hunter, a medical missionary to Ukrainians in the Teulon, Manitoba, area for over forty years, saw the Eastern-rite liturgy as the supreme form of ritualistic worship; Rome "pales before it" and Anglicanism "becomes almost invisible."[12] Ritual and the "display of gorgeous colours" were used to induce the lay person to turn off his powers of reason and intelligence. The appeal was to the emotions and senses rather than to the spiritual as in the Protestant worship service. As a result, Hunter concluded, the concept of religion as a force to improve society was not to be found in the Ukrainian churches.[13]

Hunter also believed that both his people and his church were more progressive than the Eastern-rite church and the Ukrainian people. He was certain that, given the opportunity and freedom to choose their church, the more progressive Ukrainians would turn to Protestantism.[14] Hunter and other Protestant missionaries tried to convince Ukrainians that because they readily adopted the technological improvements of the Anglo-Celtic people, they should logically also accept the more advanced and progressive form of Christianity.[15]

Presbyterians were faced with the serious problem of how to approach the Ukrainians. They tried to hire Ukrainian Protestants to work among their own people, but the Rev. Dr. Robertson, Superintendent of missions for the prairies, reported to the General Assembly that it was "almost impossible"[16] to secure native Ukrainian workers with "evangelical views and Christian character."[17] One solution advocated was to provide education and training for Ukrainian converts at Manitoba College, the Presbyterian seminary in Winnipeg. The first contact between Presbyterian leaders and Ukrainians was Cyril (Karol) Genik, who worked for the Department of Immigration in Winnipeg as an interpreter. The Presbyterians approached Genik to recommend young Ukrainians to be trained as teachers and missionaries.[18] In 1898 John (Ivan) Bodrug and John (Ivan) Negrich visited Genik and learned of the offers of free education.[19]

According to Bodrug's memoirs he and Negrich decided to visit a church of each Protestant denomination before they made their decision. The Anglican service did not appeal to them because of its similarity to Roman Catholic ritual.[20] A Methodist worship service they found "devoid of ritual," but the conduct of the congregation was judged to be uncultured and even fanatical.[21] At Knox Presbyterian Church they were favourably impressed with the simplicity and regulation of the service.[22] The two young men were greeted by the minister, who promised to intercede on their behalf with Dr.

King, the principal of Manitoba College. The next day they went to the college and were accepted as students for a brief period.

The similarity between Bodrug's method of choosing a church and the way Volodymyr the Great chose an official religion for Ukraine in 988 is striking. Possibly Bodrug believed that he was a new Volodymyr ushering in a new national religion and a new golden age of culture and progress for the Ukrainian people in Canada. Bodrug, however, was attracted to the Presbyterian Church because of its simplicity, decorum and emphasis on sermons or appeal to the intellect. In contrast, Volodymyr's envoys favoured the Eastern rite because the beauty of the ritual and ceremony convinced them that "God dwells there among men."[23] The beauty of the Eastern-rite church is not mere decoration, but expresses the joy of man's union with Christ. The sanctuary itself symbolizes the Kingdom of Heaven and the Liturgy begins with the doxology, "Blessed is the kingdom of the Father, and of the Son, and of the Holy Spirit, now and ever, and unto ages of ages." Symbolically the Divine Liturgy is a re-enactment of the life of Christ from His nativity to His ascension to heaven. Eastern-rite Christians receive Christ by their participation in the Liturgy, a participation that involves the whole body and appeals to all of the five senses. The culmination of the Liturgy is the Eucharist. While the Eastern-rite Liturgy invites the faithful to " . . . taste and see that the Lord is good" (Ps. 34:8), the Presbyterian minister proclaims that " . . . Faith cometh by hearing, and hearing by the Word of God." (Rom. 10:17).

Bodrug worked for the Presbyterians as a teacher and school organizer until the spring of 1903 when an "independent" Russian Orthodox Bishop named Seraphim arrived in Winnipeg.[24] Seraphim, or Stefan Ustvolsky, was a former Russian Orthodox priest who had been excommunicated by the Holy Synod in St. Petersburg. He had travelled through the Middle East before his arrival in North America and claimed consecration by three Eastern Orthodox hierarchs. How Seraphim came to Canada is uncertain. Bodrug is silent on this matter. However, a memoir written by the Rev. A. E. Eustace (or Eustafiewicz) claimed that Nicholas Zaitseff, a Russian living in Winnipeg, read about Seraphim in a Russian American newspaper and invited him to come to Canada.[25]

Seraphim set up a chapel in the immigration building and began to celebrate Divine Liturgy with his assistant, a monk named Makarii Marchenko. He also offered to ordain Ukrainian Catholic cantors as priests for a fee of $25.00. Bodrug, Negrich and Genik decided to join forces with Seraphim, gain control over his budding church movement, and direct it toward Protestantism.[26] By maintaining formal ties with Seraphim, they hoped to escape the charge of self-ordination without apostolic succession.[27]

After Bodrug and Negrich were ordained they turned to the Presbyterian Church for help. With the assistance of the Principal and professors of Manitoba College a ten-part constitution was devised.[28] The original name Bodrug and Negrich chose for their new church was the Ruthenian Independent Greek Church of Canada. However, their Presbyterian advisors asserted that they should not use a "nationalist" name such as Ruthenian because in Canada only the Church of England followed this practice. They suggested that the church should be called simply the Independent Greek Church. This constitution was prepared without the knowledge or approval of Seraphim or, most likely, the rest of his priests.

In August an organizational meeting to form a parish was held in Winnipeg with 200 people present.[29] Seraphim was out of the city. Bodrug, the main speaker, talked for an hour and a half on the need to establish a Ukrainian independent church which should be free from the tyranny of both Rome and St. Petersburg, evangelical in theology, and governed by the people rather than the hierarchy. Negrich then read an "abbreviated" version of the prepared constitution. According to Bodrug's memoirs it was accepted unanimously. A "Church committee" and trustees were then elected. Three hundred dollars in cash were collected and twenty-seven families became members of the new church. In the fall a hall was constructed on one lot at the Pritchard and MacGregor Streets and used for worship services until the church was completed on a neighbouring lot two years later. The architecture of the church followed the traditional Orthodox tradition with one large cupola in the centre and four smaller ones.[30]

After the hall was constructed Bodrug began a missionary journey to the major Ukrainian areas of settlement. At Fish Creek, Saskatchewan, he was met at the church by parishioners brandishing rifles, axes and even pitch forks. The new church movement had not escaped the notice of the Roman Catholic Church. The French Roman Catholic priest from the neighbouring Indian Reserve convinced the Ukrainian settlers not to allow Bodrug to use their church building. Fearlessly Bodrug advanced with his cross in one hand, his Bible in the other, and armed with his two strongest weapons, his golden voice and his charismatic personality. Standing on a pile of rocks by the church, he read from the Epistles and preached a forceful sermon. The whole parish fell to their knees, weeping and praying. Later, in the church itself, Bodrug celebrated Matins and Divine Liturgy.[31] Bodrug was not the only priest to encounter opposition. In Stuartburn, the local Independent priest was denied access to the Ukrainian Catholic Church and later Seraphim and Bodrug himself were refused admission.[32] Another priest was seized and thrown out of a Ukrainian Catholic Church near Gimli while he was celebrating Matins.[33]

In the fall of 1903 Seraphim announced that he planned to return to St. Petersburg to obtain financial aid and also ecclesiastical recognition and sanction for his movement.[34] While he was absent, a church assembly (*Sobor*) was convened in Winnipeg in January 1904 with all the priests in attendance as well as delegates from each congregation.[35] Bodrug, the main speaker, stated that the purpose of the assembly was to create and legally incorporate an Independent Greek Church. The constitution for the Independent Greek Church, which had been translated into Ukrainian, was accepted by the assembly.

The following day the topic of discussion was the reform of Orthodox dogma and the pace at which the reforms should be introduced. Changes were "to be cautious" and "not demolish the old house, before the new one has been built,"[36] because emphasis was to be placed on teaching the younger generation while the older generation would be permitted to retain their traditional forms of worship and spirituality. Bible teaching was to be stressed and the laity encouraged to read the Scriptures. A Protestant form of communion was to be introduced eventually. Apostolic succession was rejected and in the future, ordination was to be performed by the consistory rather than by a bishop. Funds were also collected to establish a newspaper, *Ranok*. The first consistory was elected by the assembly. Alexander Bachinsky was elected head, John Danylchuk secretary, Basil Novak treasurer, and Bodrug superintendent, missionary organizer and editor of *Ranok*. The assembly closed on the fourth day with the celebration of the Divine liturgy, which included a general confession.

Seraphim, who returned to Winnipeg in the fall of 1904, was astounded at what had happened during his absence. He immediately excommunicated Bodrug, Bachinsky and Negrich. On 8 September 1904 the *Winnipeg Telegram* published a letter from Bodrug and his confederates in which they rejected the excommunication and announced that they were under the jurisdiction of the consistory of the Independent Greek Church. Seraphim thus became a bishop without a church.[37]

From the very beginning of Bodrug's religious activity he had sought the financial assistance and approval of the Presbyterian Church. He established a close working relationship with the Rev. Dr. J. A. Carmichael, the Superintendent of Home Missions for Manitoba and the North-West Territories. The Home Mission Committee, Western Section, reported to the General Assembly of the Presbyterian Church in 1904 that the priests of the Independent Greek Church had appealed to them "for counsel and assistance" in setting up their new church.[38] Financial aid was also given to seven of the Independent priests who were employed as colporteurs by the Presbyterians.[39]

The Presbyterians also provided Bodrug with a Protestant catechism for use by the followers of the Independent movement. *The Christian Catechism For the Use of Schoolchildren and Young People Together With Psalms and Hymns For the Worship of God* was issued by the authority of the Independent Greek Church and printed by the North-West Press in Winnipeg in 1904. It was the first Ukrainian book published in Canada.[40] The catechism was written by Dr. J. Oswald Dykes for use by the Non-Conformist Churches in Britain and translated into Ukrainian by Bodrug.[41] It was also used as a textbook in a one-month course for the priests at Manitoba College in October 1904.[42]

While its origins are well documented, it is impossible to determine the number of Ukrainians who supported the Independent movement. Because of the scarcity of both Orthodox and Ukrainian Catholic priests, in the early years Ukrainian settlers were willing to accept the services of any Ukrainian priest who travelled through their area. However, this did not always mean that they were willing to formally join the new church movement. Ukrainian Catholics, with a stronger tradition of anti-clericalism, were more willing to accept Independent priests than were Orthodox Ukrainians from Bukovyna. In 1906 Carmichael reported that 25,000 Ukrainians had "identified" themselves with the movement while another 30,000 were "studying it" and attending services.[43] He did not indicate how these figures were reached. Because of the language barrier the Presbyterians relied solely on Bodrug for information. In order to sustain the flow of funds there might have been a tendency to exaggerate the extent of the movement.

The year 1907 marks a turning point in the relationship between the Presbyterians and the Independent movement. During the early years, the Presbyterians had been content to offer financial assistance and theological advice and training at Manitoba College. By 1907 the Presbyterians played a greater role in the government of the Independent Church: "This consistory takes no important step without the knowledge and approval of the Executive of the Synodical Home Mission Committee in Winnipeg."[44] The following year Carmichael wrote of even stronger control:

> The Home Mission Committee has no more important and delicate work under its care than the guiding and controlling of this Independent Greek Movement, in the highest interests of the religious well-being of the Ruthenians, in the best interests of the Christian citizenship, colored and shaped by Canadian sentiments and aspirations.[45]

Since the church was left without a bishop, priests were now ordained by the consistory. At first the candidates were ordained "in a kind of secret way, for fear that the people would not accept them as ministers."[46] Later new candidates were ordained publicly by the laying on of hands jointly by Independent leaders and Presbyterians.[47] The procedure by 1910 was for the candidate to submit his application to the consistory of the Independent Greek Church.[48] The applications were then forwarded to the Synodical Executive Committee of the Home Missions Committee, Western Section, of the Presbyterian Church.

Another major change came in 1910 with the introduction of a new reformed liturgy[49] and the publication of *Service Book and Collection of Church Songs* (*Sluzhebnyk i zbirnyk tserkovnykh pisnyi*).[50]

The most significant theological and symbolic change in the new reformed liturgy was the sermon replacing the eucharist as the highpoint of the service. In most Canadian Presbyterian congregations at this time communion was served approximately four times a year in a separate service. In the Orthodox Church the eucharist is celebrated every Sunday. The symbol of the Christian minister also changed from priest as the celebrant of the sacraments to pastor as the teacher of the Word.

During the early years of the Independent movement the Presbyterians assumed that once Ukrainians were confronted with the more excellent way they would rush to become real Presbyterians and voluntarily abandon the useless externals of the Eastern-rite liturgy. Thus, the Independent Greek Church was to be simply a transitional body. With the new servicebook, Protestant traditions of worship were introduced to the congregations. The Winnipeg congregation celebrated the new Protestant form of communion for the first time in July 1910.[51] Approximately 125 of the 400 people present received communion. These reforms were met with stiff opposition and an exodus of parishioners.[52] The reforms continued, however, and early in 1911 Carmichael wrote that the Winnipeg Independent Pastor Michael Bachinsky had eliminated all "distinctive" Orthodox and Catholic usages from his worship services.[53]

Gradually other congregations began to introduce Protestant reforms. Sometimes crude methods were used to persuade the congregation. Orthodox rituals and traditions were ridiculed both from the pulpit and outside the church. Incense, one priest claimed, was wasted in the church and could be put to better use in the stable or the outhouse.[54] Bells were said to be only for children not adults. Orthodox and Uniate priests used bells to relieve boredom and keep their parishioners awake during their sacred performances. Vestments were also derided. The *epitrachelion* was said to be a yoke and therefore more suitable for horses than men. Priests would underline this message by going outside the church building and placing their *epitrachelion* around a horse's neck.

By 1910–11 the Independent movement began to show signs of decline. A number of men with little education or even spiritual inclination had been ordained. Accusations of immorality and adultery brought discredit to the whole movement.[55] The Ukrainian press, especially the *Ukrainian Voice*, openly criticized the relationship between the Presbyterians and the Independent movement, attacking the Independent Church as a vehicle of assimilation.[56] Ukrainians were not willing to give up the beauty and symbolic harmony of their liturgy for a worship service which emphasized the sermon. Another factor influencing the decline of the Independent Greek Church was the arrival of Ukrainian Catholic priests and nuns from Galicia and finally, in 1912, the creation of a separate Ukrainian Catholic eparchy under Bishop Nykyta Budka. By 1910 the Russian Orthodox Church was also well-established with many parishes in Manitoba and Alberta.

The Independent movement had its own martyr. Joseph Cherniawsky served a parish near Goodeve, Saskatchewan, which had been settled primarily by Ukrainian Catholics from Galicia. Cherniavsky was supposedly murdered on the road in 1912. In an attempt to make his death look like an accident the body was taken to the railway tracks, where it was crushed by a train. A suspect was arrested, but released after the trial for lack of evidence. Bodrug and M. Glowa presided over the funeral service, which lasted three days and attracted a large number of people.[57]

In spite of the serious opposition the Independent priests faced over the Protestant reforms, by 1912 the Presbyterians demanded a faster rate of transition. They asserted that the time had come to put an end to the Independent Greek as a separate church body.[58] The Board of Home Missions also expressed reluctance to invest more money in a venture that they did not directly control.[59] They also had doubts about the soundness of doctrine preached from Independent pulpits.[60]

A special committee was appointed to examine the future relationship of the Presbyterian Church with the Independent Movement. In August 1912 the decision was made to withdraw all financial support from the Independent Greek Church and instead establish Presbyterian congregations in Ukrainian settlements.[61] These mission congregations and workers would be directly under the control of the local Presbyteries. The Independent priests were given the option of submitting applications for acceptance as ministers or missionaries of the Presbyterian Church. In autumn the special committee met again in Winnipeg to examine each applicant on his theological beliefs. Nineteen of the former priests were accepted but Bodrug refused to apply for admission.[62]

Most of the congregations refused to follow their pastors into the new fold. With a small number of their followers, the ministers attempted to continue their work as an openly Protestant religious movement:

> On [sic] the beginning of my work here, I called a meeting on 21st of January last year and in the subject "The Presbyterian and Independent Greek Church" I had [to] explain to the people what is [sic] Independent Greek Church, who supports her and what [sic] future of this church must be. Then I introduced the people with [sic] dogma and doctrine of the Presbyterian Church and after [sic] while they understood that the Independent Church is just a bridge to the Presbyterian and of course it is no use to continue any longer to be *Independent*, but we must be real Presbyterians. . . .[63]

In some areas congregations were forced to go to court to have the ministers removed and to gain control of their church building.

A variety of forms of worship was used by the Ukrainian ministers. The

199

Rev. William Simmons, Superintendent of Home Missions for Northern Alberta, reported in 1915 that there were still some congregations which used Bodrug's reformed liturgy, because the older generation demanded it.[64] The Rev. Theodore Bay, a Ukrainian minister stationed in Rossburn, Manitoba, served two congregations which had lost the majority of their parishioners. The Rossburn congregation still used the reformed liturgy "interspersed with Presbyterian hymns and extemporaneous prayers" in an attempt to win back those who left in 1913. The congregation in Sandy Lake met in a private home and used only the Presbyterian worship service.[65]

Eventually the reformed liturgy fell out of use everywhere. In 1922 a new Ukrainian hymn book, the *Ukrainian Book of Praise*, was issued jointly by the home mission boards of the Presbyterian and Methodist Churches.[66] Because of the mass exodus of most of their parishioners after the demise of the Independent Greek Church, opposition from remaining laymen against reforms, and problems with their Anglo-Celtic superiors, the Ukrainian clergymen began to leave the ministry. By 1925, when the Presbyterian Church joined with the Methodist and Congregational Churches to form the United Church of Canada, there were only five ministers left serving rural Ukrainian parishes on the prairies.

A small number of Independent priests refused to join the Presbyterian Church. Some joined the Russian Orthodox Church while others remained outside of any jurisdiction until the Ukrainian Orthodox Church of Canada was formed. St. Stephan's Orthodox Church in Pleasant Home, Manitoba, with Fr. Dmytro Drohomyretsky as parish priest, continued to function as an Independent Church until 1964, when the congregation agreed to accept the services of a priest of the Ukrainian Orthodox Church of Canada.

The Independent Greek Church was a unique ecclesiastical structure; it is possible even to call it a Protestant Uniate Church.[67] The Presbyterian missions failed to make an impact on the Ukrainian community between 1900 and 1925. Many of the Ukrainian ministers believed this was due to the abandonment of the Eastern-rite liturgical form of worship.[68] The Rev. Paul Crath (Krat) stressed that "Ukrainians do not feel sacredness when they are in our prayer gatherings."[69] Peter Svarich, a prominent Ukrainian businessman in Vegreville, expressed similar views. He was attracted to the Presbyterian work in the early years and was even a main speaker at the "First Ruthenian Presbyterian Convention" held on 6–7 July 1915.[70] Like many Ukrainians from Galicia he was anti-clerical, but he did not want to join a church that was out of harmony with Ukrainian cultural traditions:

During this short time of my activity among the Protestants I became convinced that the Ukrainian soul would never be satisfied and be filled with the grace which the Protestant religion gives its faithful. Our character is more natural, poetical, profound, loves ritual, singing, ceremonies, the

200

splendor of church decorations and religious mysticism, but that is not available among the Protestants. Everything there is dry, abstract, empty. Therefore, it is no wonder that the Presbyterian mission among the Ukrainians was not a success.[71]

Svarich later became a member of the "National Committee" which established the Ukrainian Greek Orthodox Church of Canada and was also elected to the church's first consistory.[72] Many others of the initial supporters of the Independent Greek Church later helped to create the Ukrainian Greek Orthodox Church in 1918. Their connection with the Independent movement had made them realize it was necessary to create a religious body totally independent of Rome or any other church, and completely controlled by Ukrainians.

Thus, we can conclude that although the Independent Greek Church failed as a religious movement, it did influence the development of an alternative religious body to the Ukrainian Catholic Church and the Russian Orthodox Mission. The Ukrainian settlers chose to abandon the Independent Greek Church when it adopted a Presbyterian form of worship. The Presbyterians failed to perceive that the ritual and rich symbolism of the Eastern rite did meet the spiritual needs of the Ukrainian people. Ukrainians had the freedom to choose in Canada; they also had the opportunity to experience Protestant worship and were exposed to the sermons and teachings of a "more progressive" religion and resolutely made the decision to keep their traditional faith.

NOTES

1. Rev. E. D. McLaren, "The National Aspect of Home Mission Work," *Presbyterian Record*, January 1907, 10.
2. "Mr. Gordon's Report," *The Acts and Proceedings of the General Assembly of the Presbyterian Church in Canada*, 1897. Appendices, 18. Hereafter cited as *Acts*.
3. Rev. William T. Gunn, *His Dominion* (Canada: Canadian Council of the Missionary Education Movement, 1917). Gunn was a Congregational minister, but the theme of Canada as "His Dominion" dominated the contemporary literature of the Presbyterian and Methodist Churches as well.
4. Rev. R. G. MacBeth, *Our Task in Canada* (Toronto: Westminster, 1912), 22.
5. N. K. Clifford, "His Dominion: A Vision in Crisis," *Studies in Religion/Sciences Religieuses*, 2 (1972–1973): 315–25. See also his "The Religion of WASPs," *Christian Outlook*, 7 (April 1964): 3–7.
6. Mrs. Joseph M. West, "Our Church and the Stranger," *Presbyterian Record*, February 1915, 199. This view was generally held by the main-line Protestant denominations including the Social Gospel Faction. See Marilyn Barber, "Nationalism,

Nativism and the Social Gospel," in *The Social Gospel in Canada*, ed. Richard Allen (Ottawa: National Museums of Canada, 1975), 186–226. National Museum of Man Mercury Series. History Division Paper No. 9.

7. "Uncontaminated with views, and innocent of practices that check the growth of population elsewhere, their rate of increase will be much higher than that of ordinary Canadians, hence the necessity in the interests of sincere patriotism, good government, public morality and true religion that they should be evangelized and assimilated as speedily as may be." Rev. Dr. Robertson, "Review of Last Year's Work: North-Western Canada," *Acts*, 1899. Appendices, 17. On the issue of block colonies see Rev. E. H. McLaren, "The Perils of Immigration," *Presbyterian Record*, January 1906, 11.

8. "If the foreigners are not educated and made loyal, they are sure to prove a menace to the free play of popular government. If not evangelized and brought up to our moral level, they are sure to drag us down to theirs." "Rev. Dr. Robertson's Last Appeal on Behalf of North-West Mission," *Presbyterian Record*, March 1902, 100.

9. "Annual Meeting," *Missionary Messenger*, May 1920, 154.

10. "Manitoba Provincial Society Annual Meeting," *Missionary Messenger*, May 1915, 155.

11. John A. Cormie, "Galician missions," *Presbyterian Record*, January 1901, 13. See also Dr. A. G. Hunter, "Christmas Among Our N. W. Galicians," *Presbyterian Record*, January 1907, 4–5. "Of course when there is so much ceremony there is sure to be a great deal of superstition, but the free air of Canada is gradually producing a change. In time there will be less ceremony and a more intelligent faith, fewer forms and more effort after a nobler life."

12. A. J. Hunter, *A Friendly Adventure, The Story of the United Church Mission Among New Canadians at Teulon, Manitoba* (Toronto: Board of Home Missions at the United Church of Canada, 1929), 43.

13. Ibid., 50.

14. Ibid., 33.

15. "It is not easy for them [Ukrainians] to get away from the idea, that they ought to be loyal to their ancestor's form of religion. Evangelical missionaries have met this argument in the following way. They have pointed out that the English-speaking people have invented binders, threshing machines and various useful things which the Ukrainians have adopted as being far superior to the old sickles and flails. Then they point out the great strength both of individual and national character that has been given by the Protestant religion to the Northern peoples and ask why the Ukrainians should not accept improvements in religion as well as improvements in machinery." Ibid., 52–3.

16. "Report of Rev. Dr. Robertson, Superintendent of Missions for Manitoba, the North-West Territories and British Columbia," *Acts*, 1901, Appendices, 10.

17. Rev. Dr. Robertson, "Review of Last Year's Work: North-Western Canada," *Acts*, 1900, Appendices, 10.

18. John Bodrug, *Independent Orthodox Church Memoirs Pertaining to the History of a Ukrainian Canadian Church in the Year 1903 to 1913* (Toronto: Ukrainian Canadian Research Foundation, 1982), 8–9. These three were all from the village of Bereziv in the Kolomyia region of Galicia. Bodrug and Negrich had completed the lower gymnasium and graduated from the teacher's seminary in Stanyslaviv.

19. Ibid., 9.

20. Ibid.

21. Ibid., 10.

22. Ibid.

23. When Volodymyr decided to choose a new religion to unite the people of his realm he sent out envoys to investigate the faith of the Muslims, the Khazars who practised Judaism, the Roman Catholic Germans, and the Greek Christians. After his envoys praised the beauty of the service in St. Sophia in Constantinople, Eastern Christianity was chosen. Samuel H. Cross (trans.), *The Russian Primary Chronicle* (Cambridge, Mass.: Medieval Academy of America, 1953), 111.

24. Bodrug, *Independent Church Memoirs*, 36. P. Bozhyk, *Tserkov ukraintsiv v Kanadi* (Winnipeg: Ukrainian-Canadian, 1927), 25–7. Achille Delaere, *Mémoire sur les tentatives de schisme et d'hérésie au milieu des Ruthènes de l'Ouest canadien* (Quebec: L'Action Sociale, 1908). *Propamiatna knyha z nahody zolotoho iuvileiu poselennia ukrainskoho narodu v Kanadi* (Yorkton: Redeemer's Voice, 1941), 60–2.

25. A. E. Eustace (Eustafiewicz), "The Beginnings of Religious Movements Among the Ukrainian People of Manitoba," 1940. Typescript located in the Canadian Institute of Ukrainian Studies, University of Alberta, Edmonton, Alberta.

26. Bodrug, *Independent Church Memoirs*, 37.

27. Oleksander Dombrovsky, *Narys istorii Ukrainskoho ievanhelsko-reformovanoho rukhu* (New York and Toronto: Ukrainian Evangelical Alliance of North America, 1979), 134.

28. Bodrug, *Independent Church Memoirs*, 41–5. The head of the church was Jesus Christ and the Bible the rule of faith and practice. The sacraments were reduced to the two instituted by Christ, Baptism and Communion, and the five mysteries proclaimed by the Apostles: Chrismation, Confession, Holy Orders, Matrimony and Unction. Private confession was no longer compulsory, but was available on request. The practice of general confession as the norm was to be gradually introduced. The Liturgy of St. John Chrysostom was to be shortened to an hour and a half and all mention of the Mother of God, the saints and prayers for the dead deleted. (The Presbyterians had wanted a Presbyterian worship service to be introduced immediately, but Bodrug wanted gradual reform in order not to alienate Ukrainians.) Church membership was to be open to anyone who believed in Jesus Christ. Church government was by a consistory made up of all the priests and one delegate from each parish. The consistory was to meet every three years or once a year if necessary. The executive of the consistory was composed of an elected head, a secretary-treasurer, an organizer, and the superintendent (called a bishop in the Ukrainian version). All the priests were to be equal and the church itself democratic in form as the Presbyterian Church.

29. Bodrug, *Independent Church Memoirs*, 51–4.

30. The church building still stands, minus its cupolas. It is now the Winnipeg Central Seventh Day Adventist Church. The hall next door belongs to the Bethlehem Chapel to Indians and Metis.

31. Bodrug, *Independent Church Memoirs*, 58–64.

32. Peter Humeniuk, *Hardships and Progress of Ukrainian Pioneers Memoirs: From Stuartburn Colony and Other Points* (Winnipeg: Author, 1977), 70–1.

33. Bodrug, *Independent Church Memoirs*, 74.

34. "Letter to the Editor," *Winnipeg Telegram*, 8 September 1904. The letter is signed by Bodrug and three other Independent priests. In his memoirs written in 1949 Bodrug mistakenly claimed that Seraphim went to Russia in the spring of 1904. Bodrug, *Independent Church Memoirs*, 75.

35. Ibid., 76–80.

36. Ibid., 80.

37. He existed on the periphery of Ukrainian religious life until he returned to Russia in 1908. His assistant Makarii Marchenko renamed himself Arch-Patriarch, Arch-Pope,

Arch-Tsar, Arch-Hetman and Arch-Prince. He also issued decrees excommunicating both the Pope in Rome and the Holy Synod in St. Petersburg. Bozhyk, *Tserkov ukraintsiv*, 46, 49–50, 330–2.

38. "Report of the Home Mission Committee, Western Section, 1903–4," *Acts*, 1904, Appendices, 7.
39. The colporteurs distributed copies of the New Testament and submitted monthly reports to Dr. Carmichael. J. A. Carmichael, "Report of the Superintendent of Home Missions in the Synod of Manitoba and the North-West Territories," *Acts*, 1904, Appendices, 13.
40. Five thousand copies were printed. Rev. J. A. Carmichael, "Work Among the Ruthenians," *Presbyterian Record*, September 1911, 396.
41. J. A. Carmichael, "Report of the Superintendent of Home Missions in Manitoba and Saskatchewan Synod," *Acts*, 1907, Appendices, 12. The catechism itself consists of fifty-one questions and answers printed on pages one to sixteen with parallel columns of Ukrainian on the left and English on the right. Question twenty-seven outlines the Ten Commandments in Church Slavonic followed by explanations in modern Ukrainian. Question thirty-two includes the "Lord's Prayer" in Church Slavonic with a six-part explanation in modern Ukrainian. Since most Ukrainians knew both the Ten Commandments and Lord's Prayer in Church Slavonic, the liturgical language of both Ukrainian churches, Bodrug probably thought it wise to retain the traditional versions rather than introduce modern Ukrainian translation. Questions thirty-three to thirty-eight give a Reformed Protestant view of the church and its ministers, while question forty, dealing with the sacraments, states that the Orthodox Church recognizes seven sacraments. However, the following question asserts that the principal sacraments are Baptism and the Lord's Supper or the Eucharist. Questions forty-five to forty-seven give a Reformed Protestant explanation of Communion as a memorial, thus denying the Real Presence in the Eucharist. In addition to the catechism there are translations of ten Psalms from the Presbyterian *Book of Praise* and twelve Protestant hymns. The hymns include awkward and crude phrases and images alien to Ukrainian spirituality. In the hymn "Onward Christian Soldiers" the title of "Christ the Royal Master" is translated as "Our Heavenly Hetman" (*Nash nebesnyi Hetman*).
42. Wm. Patrick, "Report of the Senate of Manitoba College," *Acts*, 1907, Appendices, 220.
43. Rev. J.A. Carmichael, "Report of the Superintendent of Home Missions in the Synod of Manitoba and the North-West Territories," *Acts*, 1906, Appendices, 14.
44. "Report of the Home Mission Committee, Western Section, 1906–1907," *Acts*, 1907, Appendices, 7. The 1907 report also stated there were twelve priests receiving financial aid in Manitoba and five in Saskatchewan. These priests reported that a total of 2,484 families were identified with the movement and an additional 628 families were believed to be sympathetic to it. The priests were not paid equal salaries. Bodrug was paid the highest salary at $630 per annum in 1907 while M. Hutney received the lowest amount at $45 a year. The records do not indicate the means used to determine the salaries. "Annual Statistical Report, Galician Work. Manitoba," Acts, 1907, Appendices, 16–17.
   John Bodrug and Alexander Machinsky were in Winnipeg, G. Tymchuk was responsible for the Overstone and Steinbach charges; Onufry Charambura for Pleasant Home and Chalfield; John Danylczuk for Rossburn and Ranchvale; M. Miroff for Stuartburn; A. Wilchynski for Brandon and Portage La Pairie; Julian Bohonko for Ethelbert, Garland and Pine River; B. Pynianski for Sifton, Fishing River, Velaw, Riding Mountain and Valley River; Michael Bachinsky for Brokenhead, Poplar Park,

Whitemouth, and East Selkirk; Maxim Berezynski for Gimli; and J. Radiszewski for Gimli as well as Beausejour and Gonar. In Saskatchewan Joseph Cherniawsky was assigned to Canora, Tetlock, Menofield, Kamsack and Mullock; W. Penykowski to Buchanan and the area north of Lanora; Nicholas Zaitseff to Beaver Hills, Pleasant Forks, Yorkton and Range 8; Alexander Maximchuk for Dana, Vonda, Wakaw and Bonne Madonne; and Nicholas Sekora for Radison, New Ottawa and Great Deer. *Acts*, 1906, 14.

45. J.A. Carmichael, "Report of the Superintendent of Missions for the Synods of Manitoba and Saskatchewan," *Acts*, 1908, Appendices, 12.

46. Rev. J.A. Carmichael, "Report of the Superintendent of Home Missions in Manitoba, Saskatchewan Synods," *Acts*, 1907, Appendices, 15.

47. "Correspondent's Page," *Home Mission Pioneer*, October 1910, 112. He witnessed the ordination of two Ukrainians by Independent Greek leaders, Dr. J. A. Carmichael, Dr. J. F. Farquharson and Dr. G. B. Wilson.

48. M. P. Berezynski to Rev. Dr. J. Farquharson, 28 February 1910, *Presbyterian Church in Canada. Board of Home Missions*, Box 2, File 14 located in the United Church Archives, Toronto, Ont. Hereinafter cited as B.H.M.

49. J. A. Carmichael, "Report of the Superintendent of Missions for the Synods of Manitoba and Saskatchewan," *Acts*, 1909, Appendices, 12.

50. *Sluzhebnyk i zbirnyk tserkovnykh pisnyi* (New York: Soiuz, 1910). Soiuz was the press of the Ukrainian-American Presbyterians. John Bodrug was the editor and translator. It is 176 pages in length with a preface by John Bodrug. In format it is similar to an Orthodox prayerbook. The first part, called *Molytvy* (Prayers), contains traditional prayers in Church Slavonic. The Nicene Creed has the *filioque* added in brackets. Also included is a modern Ukrainian version of the Apostles' Creed, which is not used by the Eastern Church. Noticeably absent are prayers to the Mother of God, Guardian Angel, and the prayers recited before and after communion.

The next part, "Concerning the Truths of the Reformed Church," is in small print. The first half of this section outlines statements of Christian dogma common to all denominations. The second half provides an evangelical Protestant interpretation of salvation by faith alone, the supreme authority of Scriptures and the nature of the Church.

The next part includes the liturgical services of Matins, the Divine Liturgy and Vespers. All these services are shortened by the deletion of all prayers mentioning the Mother of God and the saints. The most drastic changes are in the service of the Divine Liturgy, which is reduced to only ten pages. The Divine Liturgy begins with the Great Litany (*Iekteniia Velyka*). The Little Litany (*Mala Iekteniia*) is omitted except for the priest's concluding prayer. The antiphons are replaced by Protestant hymns chosen from the last part of the book. The Trisigion is retained, followed by a Psalm or Old Testament reading by a layman instead of the Epistle reading. Next is the Gospel reading by the minister, another Litany and the Creed. In place of communion is the sermon followed by the final hymn and doxology. Bodrug and his followers no longer celebrated communion every Sunday, as in the Orthodox Church, but adopted the Presbyterian practice of a separate communion service.

Following the Divine Liturgy is the Lord's Supper service, an original work composed mainly of Presbyterian elements interspersed with Orthodox litanies. The last part of the liturgical section contains the Easter Matins and the Baptism service without Chrismation. The final part of the book holds ninety-two hymns, the majority translated Protestant hymns and nine traditional Ukrainian Christmas carols. There is also a modern Ukrainian translation of the Reformed Protestant marriage service, funeral service, ordination and prayers for the dedication of a church. I would like to thank the late Fr. Michael Yurkiwsky for allowing me to use his copy of this rare book.

51. Rev. J. A. Carmichael, "Work Among the Ruthenians," *Presbyterian Record*, September 1911, 396.

52. "We have had a good many disappointments in our work among these people and perhaps the worse [sic] of all in Winnipeg. Last year the congregation broke up and quite a number left. . . to some extent because they thought he was pushing reform." Dr. J. Farquharson to A. S. Grant, 18 August 1911, *B.H.M.*, Box 2, File 14.

53. Rev. A. J. Carmichael, "Ruthenian Ministers in the West," *Presbyterian Record*, February 1911, 58.

54. Edward Bodrug, "John Bodrug: Ukrainian Pioneer Preacher, Educator, Editor in the Canadian West, 1897–1913," 1975, typescript located in the United Church Archives, Toronto, Ontario, 13.

55. John Bodrug, *Independent Church Memoirs*, 102; Edward Bodrug, U.C. Archives typescript, 69.

56. "Vsiachyna visty z Vinnipegu," *Ukrainian Voice*, Wednesday, 25 January 1911. "Novyny," *Ukrainian Voice*, Wednesday, 1 March 1911.

57. J. Farquharson to Rev. J. H. Edmison, 14 June 1912, *B.H.M.*, Box 2, File 13.

58. "In Alberta there seems to be a very general feeling that the work should be taken over by our church as a distinctly Presbyterian work, and churches should be organized along Presbyterian lines. Hitherto we have been helping them to develop their own type of religion, but it would seem as if the time has come to change our plans. . . . " Rev. W. D. Reid, "Home Missions in Alberta," *Presbyterian Record*, May 1912, 248–9.

59. "Report of the Board of Home Missions, (Western Section), 1912–1913," *Acts*, 1913, Appendices, 7.

60. "Owing to the fact that there are few interpreters between the nationalities, suspicions arose. Some of our Presbyterians began to ask why we were paying good Presbyterian dollars to help the service of another church, a very ritualistic church at that. Then, too owing to the absence of interpreters doubt arose as to the sort of doctrine these men were teaching. Who should tell us? We had only the word of one or two of them who could speak English." A. J. Hunter, *The Story of Ruthenians* (Board of Home Missions, Presbyterian Church in Canada; n.p., n.d.), no pagination.

61. "Memo Re Ruthenian Work," *B.H.M.*, Box 2, File 13. See also "Minutes of the Home Mission Committee of the General Assembly of the Presbyterian Church in Canada, which Met in Knox Church School Room, on Twenty-Ninth May Nineteen Hundred and Twelve, A. D.," *B.H.M.*, Box 2, File 13, and also "Special Meeting of Committee of Board of Home Missions Held at Winnipeg in the Office of Mr. Edward Brown on the 20th Day of August, 1912," *B.H.M.*, File 13.

62. "Minutes of Sub-Committee Dealing with Reception of Ministers of Independent Greek Church into the Presbyterian Church, Winnipeg, Oct. 14th, 1912," *B.H.M.*, Box 2, File 13.

63. Maxim Zalizniak to Rev. Dr. James Farquharson, 29 May 1912, *B.H.M.*, Box 3, File 26. Zalizniak's congregation in Edmonton began as a Ukrainian Presbyterian Church rather than as an Independent Church. This parish was supposed to be a model for the rest of the Ukrainian Independent congregations.

64. Rev. Wm. Simmons, "Ruthenians in Northern-Alberta," *Presbyterian Record*, November 1915, 486.

65. Theodore Bay, "The Historical Sketch of the Background and the Beginning of the

Protestant Movement Among the Ukrainian People in Canada," 1964. *Theodore Bay Papers*, 922.8, B 356. Located in the Glenbow Alberta Institute, Calgary, Alberta.

66. *Ukrainian Book of Praise, Knyha khvaly, skarbnytsia pisen dlia ykrninskoho (sic) naroda* (Toronto: Home Mission Boards of the Presbyterian and Methodist Churches in Canada, 1922). The book contains 200 hymns, of which only 29 (14.5 percent) are of Ukrainian origin, mostly Christmas and Easter carols.

67. The term uniate usually refers to an Oriental or Eastern Church which is united with the Roman See. However, I have used the term Protestant Uniate to describe an Eastern Church under the jurisdiction or influence of a Protestant Church but retaining the Eastern rite for liturgical celebration. While Catholic Eastern-rite churches made some modifications to their theology and liturgy to conform to Roman Catholicism, a Protestant Uniate church would also make similar adaptations to Protestantism. One example of a Protestant Uniate church which fits this definition is the Mar Thoma Church of Kerala, South India. This church has its origins in the ancient Jacobite Syrian Orthodox Church which uses the Eastern-rite Liturgy of St. James. Under the influence of Anglican missionaries a group broke off from the mother church in the last century and underwent a reformation. When the Church of South India was formed in 1947 by an amalgamation of Protestant denominations, the Mar Thoma Church refused to join this body. Today it continues to use ā skeleton version of the Eastern Liturgy of St. James, purged of any mention of Mary and the Saints, but remains under the jurisdiction of its own metropolitan and hierarchy. However, the church remains on very friendly terms with the Anglican Church and continues to be under its influence. See Metropolitan Juhanon Mar Thoma, *Christianity in India and a Brief History of the Mar Thoma Syrian Church* (Madras: K.M. Cherian, 1968).

68. Rev. P. C. Crath, "A Statement of the Ukrainian Mission Work of the United Church of Canada," n.d., 3. *Cormie Papers*. Typescript located in the United Church Archives, Winnipeg, Manitoba. See also Bay, "The Historical Sketch," 6.

69. Crath, "A Statement," 5.

70. Rev. W. G. Brown, "The First Ruthenian Presbyterian Convention," *Presbyterian Record*, September 1915, 392.

71. Petro Zvarych [Svarich], *Spomyny 1877–1904* (Winnipeg: Trident Press, 1976), 237.

72. *The Ukrainian Pioneers in Alberta*, ed. Joseph M. Lazarenko (Edmonton: Ukrainian Canadian Pioneer Association, 1970), 345–6.

Evan Lowig

The Historical Development of Ukrainians within the Orthodox Church in America: A Comparative Study

In terms of broadly defined membership, the Orthodox Church in America (OCA) has a constituency of over 1 million people. Of this number, a plurality, if not an absolute majority, is, to use contemporary ethnographic language, Ukrainian. Western Ukrainians and their descendants in North America who belong to OCA are of particular interest. Magocsi notes that there are 225,000 Carpatho-Rusyns from the old Hungarian Kingdom and their descendants, together with Galician Lemkos in OCA. Clearly, there is a need to make some sort of sociological and spiritual assessment of the phenomenon of large numbers of Ukrainians belonging to a church which, until 1970, was called the Russian Orthodox Greek Catholic Church.

At least in the United States, perhaps the key words are Greek Catholic. Between 1891 and 1916, the Russian Orthodox Church grew by leaps and bounds, as thousands of Austro-Hungarian Uniates left their ancestral hybrid religion to join the "old" Eastern Orthodox Church, which had existed in their homelands before it was suppressed by the Union of Brest-Litovsk (1596) and the Union of Uzhhorod (1646). Archbishop Platon received seventy-two largely Carpatho-Rusyn Uniate parishes into his fold between 1907 and 1914. During Archbishop Evdokim's administration (1914–17), thirty Uniate parishes and thirty-five new parishes, in many cases former Uniates, were added.[1] The Orthodox movement among Greek Catholics, resulting in loyalty to specifically Russian Orthodoxy (at least jurisdictionally, if not in terms of total identity), was never as large in Canada as in the United States. Here, most of the parishes, which were founded as part of the Russian Mission between 1896 and 1914, some of which are OCA today, were made up of Bukovynians who had always been Orthodox.

Every Orthodox parish made up of ex-Uniates underwent the experience of defining what it is to be Orthodox, beginning with St. Mary's in Minneapolis.[2] The return of Uniates also brought increasingly bitter opposition from the Vatican. The entire situation was loaded with political as well as ethnic overtones, with "Ukrainization" versus "Russification" becoming a central issue. Archbishop Platon and his staff devoted much of their energy to these East Slavic problems. They were constantly visiting the new parishes, organizing open public meetings, and taking part in heated discussions and polemics. Religious concerns could be easily obscured by Russian patriotism and loyalty to the tsar.

Indeed, the environment and ideology in the Russian Mission which grew to be the Metropolia (the popular name of what was the Russian Orthodox Greek Catholic Church of America between 1924 and 1970), tended to be very Russophile. As a result, some elements in the Russian church throughout North America showed fierce, indeed, at times pathological opposition to the Ukrainian national movement and the resulting distinct Ukrainian identity. Their attitude exacerbated tensions between the Russian church and leaders of the Ukrainian Orthodox Brotherhood in Canada, which made a complete break with Russian Orthodoxy in 1919, both "nationally" and jurisdictionally. This break has yet to be resolved, much to OCA's shame. It would be less than honest to claim that these elements have completely disappeared in OCA. Nevertheless, despite the name "Russian Orthodox," the Metropolia experience of Western Ukrainians certainly was and is not the same as typically Russian, that is Muscovite. Due to the relatively independent nature of the Metropolia, there was little or no pressure to Russify in the largest and most pronounced "Carpatho-Russian" diocese of OCA, the Diocese of Pittsburgh, which covered all western Pennsylvania and contained fifty-three parishes. The character of the parishes came from the people who comprised them.

It should be borne in mind that Orthodoxy proclaims itself to be the Christian church which transcends all accidents of culture and history. Using western Pennsylvania as our model, we see that parishes made up of ex-Uniates thus faced struggles both for survival and for growth in orthodoxy. The latter meant that the church as such could not accept all forms of popular religion as ipso facto orthodoxy. Furthermore, OCA today does not accept the point of view that religion and nationality walk hand in hand, paving the way for new and exciting possibilities, such as being Ukrainian and Orthodox while belonging to the multi-ethnic OCA rather than to an ethnic jurisdiction.

The reasons for this phenomenon were, in part, almost purely sociological and ethnographic. In the early years of this century, Ukrainian identity among Galicians in western Pennsylvania was not very common; among Carpatho-Rusyns, it was virtually non-existent. With the arrival of Uniate

Bishop Soter Ortynsky in America, the situation changed. Suddenly, to uphold things Orthodox was to be Russian, to uphold things Uniate was to be Ukrainian/Ruthenian.

The creation of the Diocese of Pittsburgh was part of a largely successful plan to minister specifically to Carpatho-Russians who had just left the Uniate Church and for whom being Russian Orthodox was a clear choice of faith and religious identity. This explains the steady efforts in the Diocese since 1916 to become more orthodox. This also applies to the Metropolia as a whole, and accounts for certain features of OCA's psychological make-up.

In the Diocese of Western Pennsylvania and throughout OCA as a whole, there is now a definitely orthodox faith, spirituality, ethos and liturgy. The Metropolia/OCA liturgical tradition is a composite of the Moscow, Kiev and Warsaw traditions.[3] This amalgam can work well in Galician and Carpatho-Rusyn parishes because it is flexible and also because it is a composite: no one group can claim it purely as "our own."

How the standard OCA ordo, or for that matter any ordo, is applied is a matter of pastoral common sense and education. In the context of the eucharistic celebration, one "Holy Trinity" (*Troitsiu Sviatuiu*) does not ruin a liturgy. After the phrase, "Let us love one another that with one mind we may confess... ," Carpatho-Rusyn and Galician service books give the response "Father, Son and Holy Spirit, the Holy Trinity: One in essence and Undivided." Other Byzantine Rite service books, including those of the Russian church, omit the word "Holy" before Trinity.

On the whole, historians, ethnographers, and liturgists today agree that the whole experience of being Rusyn and Orthodox is very good, but that it does not have the same organic self-contained nature as being (to give an obvious example) Greek and Orthodox. The Uniate experience makes it difficult to evaluate the Rusyn tradition and then use it in contemporary OCA parishes.

The late Father Alexander Schmemann had a deep appreciation and love for Galician and Carpatho-Rusyn usages in orthodoxy, yet was probably not far from the mark when he said that they must die to their Uniate incarnation before they can truly live in an Orthodox environment.[4] This process of death and resurrection is complex and often painful. The pastoral problems are great because something new is virtually being invented, since we cannot get into a time machine and find out what orthodoxy was like in Western Ukraine before the Unia. The situation is further complicated by the occasionally gross Latin distortions within Eastern-rite Catholicism and, of course, modern secularization, which attempts to reduce worship to the maintenance of a few randomly selected external ceremonies.

The question of particular usages having Uniate implications is a complex one and has often been coloured by very subjective considerations. Among better-educated OCA clergy who have some feel for the specifically Carpatho-Rusyn tradition (keeping in mind that a fair number are rather recent converts from the Byzantine Catholic Archdiocese of Pittsburgh), there exists a rule of thumb that applies to various secondary liturgical customs. No one has been able to explain adequately certain Rusyn liturgical usages, and these are not ones that are specifically Latin borrowings; rather, they are simply strange and not required by any major ordo. The rule that "unless we know what we're doing, we don't do it" reminds us that the church exists for worship in spirit and truth, not to perpetuate folk customs.

We have established that when the major Uniate return to Orthodoxy in the United States occurred, there was little or no Rusyn and/or Ukrainian Orthodox witness. Thus, very quickly, Rusyns who were Orthodox were advised to adopt Russian forms; this they did, adapting them to their own context. The turn to things Russian within orthodoxy began to have an impact on Rusyn-American culture. Here, liturgical life walked hand in hand with secular culture. By default, parishes made up of recent converts from the Unia in western Pennsylvania and other places throughout North America had to draw from the Russian Orthodox experience. Consequently, Russian folk customs were also adopted. This did not necessarily imply full-blown Russophilism, but rather a certain degree of cultural widening, albeit according to a Russian mode.

This ambiguity surrounding the formation of a concrete ethno-cultural identity among Ukrainians within the Orthodox Church in America is by no means only an Orthodox problem. It applies to the development of Carpatho-Rusyns in the Byzantine Catholic Church, as well. The problem appears rooted in the fact that, of all the eastern Slavs, Rusyns had the least critical consciousness with which to appreciate their own culture, which led to their failure to appreciate their own liturgical usages. Nevertheless, specifically in the area of liturgics, it would be wrong to think that all "corrections" were Russian impositions.

On a cultural level, "our people" in OCA parishes today sometimes feel that the faith is being changed. This feeling is not necessarily a bad thing if it actually refers to the replacement of Uniate usages with authentic Orthodox practice. Consider, for example, immersion instead of sprinkling in baptism, or infant communion followed by a first confession at age seven, instead of first confession and communion at age seven, as is still practiced in certain very Greek Catholic Orthodox parishes. This last practice has, to the best of my knowledge, totally disappeared in OCA. Where the custom still exists it deserves from the Orthodox standpoint condemnation as an arbitrary deviation from orthodoxy and, therefore, it is heretical. Father Thomas Hopko, professor of Dogmatics at St. Vladimir's Seminary, points out that denying communion to infants scandalizes the faithful who belong to parishes and dioceses where the norm is upheld and practiced, and creates the impression (unfortunately, valid in this case), that the differences between the various Orthodox jurisdictions are not only cultural, but that real differences of faith exist, as well.[5]

From a pastoral standpoint, the question of liturgical revision in OCA has been coloured by the simple reality that "our people" are not only narrow and provincial but rather lethargic. Positive evolution has also been hampered by the lack of indigenous leadership among the founders of Russian Orthodox parishes, and also by the social character of Rusyn immigrants. This is why on the surface it often appears as if Galician and Carpatho-Rusyn usages have completely vanished or been stamped out in OCA. On closer examination, however, we see that this is not the case. Sympathetic priests point out that in many OCA parishes, Rusyn piety is generally very positive, when it is kept on track. What is particularly good is the Carpatho-Rusyn Plain Chant (*Prostopiniie*), where it has remained vibrant.

The Metropolia was wracked by huge internal struggles between 1924 and 1946. As a result, about 10 per cent of its 1930s membership ended up in the Moscow Patriarchate. There are between forty and fifty patriarchal parishes in the United States and Canada. The people are almost all of Western Ukrainian origin, and call themselves Russian-Ukrainians and Carpatho-Russians. In the patriarchal parishes, one sees remnants of Rusyn/Ukrainian usages together with contemporary Russian usages. To a degree, Rusyn/Ukrainian survival in the Patriarchal parishes is strengthened by the fact that these parishes exist in the ethnic ghetto mentality, and also because their leadership consciously fosters loyalty to the "Mother Church" and, therefore, to a very broadly defined "Russian" identity. In Canada, perhaps, this is better described as a small "u" Ukrainian identity.

After 1938, a number of Metropolia adherents joined the new American Carpatho-Russian Orthodox Greek Catholic Diocese.[6] They did so to affirm their unique Carpatho-Rusyn ("Russian") identity and customs, which they felt were threatened by the homogenizing tendencies in the Metropolia. The Johnstown Pennsylvania Diocese has been accused, with good reason, of being the dogmatist twin of the Unia as it existed between 1930 and 1935.

After the Metropolia's Cleveland Sobor of 1946, and again after the 1970 autocephaly, some people left the Metropolia/OCA to join the Russian Church in Exile. Most of them were ethnic Russians, and some were strongly Russophile Ukrainians. Throughout the parishes of the Russian Church in Exile, both in Canada and the United States, there are several people who could be identified as Ukrainians. However, for reasons which become obvious, once one is familiar with the Russian Church in Exile, Ukrainian customs tend to be virtually non-existent in these parishes. The members of Ukrainian background would almost all call themselves Russian with the most superficial level of Ukrainian ethnicity; for example, they may partake of the appropriate ethnic foods on special occasions. In terms of any serious ethnic traits, they are of no particular value to this study.

Examining specifically Rusyn ethnic identity in America, we find that perhaps there are reasonable parallels between Hispanics in America and Rusyns in Hungary. In any case, ethnic self-consciousness seems to have coincided with their arrival in the New World. This would appear to hold true for the first immigration of Ukrainians to Canada, as well. In the American context, and specifically with "Russian Orthodox" parishes, it did not take long for Galicians and Transcarpathian Rusyns to realize they were, in some ways, quite different.

It would be unfair to say that when they came to America, Transcarpathian Rusyns were merely ethnographic raw material, yet their identity had, and still has, sufficient vagueness to allow a diversity of appellations. In the Metropolia, various organizations sustained, rather than promoted, a specific Carpatho-Rusyn identity. In the early 1950s, a special administration within the Russian Orthodox Metropolia was formed to accommodate Carpatho-Rusyns. It was made up of a number of parishes which broke from the Johnstown Diocese, which never recognized the *Administratsiia* as legitimately Carpatho-Rusyn. The creation of the *Administratsiia* caused deep hostility between the Metropolia/OCA and the Johnstown Diocese, which is only being overcome today. The *Administratsiia* was dissolved in 1963, with the majority of its parishes returning to the Johnstown Diocese, and the few remaining churches becoming parts of local dioceses of the Orthodox Church in America.

Fragmentation of the American Carpatho-Rusyn community is exacerbated by purist elements, which refuse to recognize other sectors of the same ethnic group as Carpatho-Rusyn. Often, this question of non-recognition was tied to whatever name different groups of Carpatho-Rusyns used to describe themselves. What people call themselves, or are called, often shows how they are perceived or perceive themselves.

In the United States today, most of the Ukrainians in OCA are fourth-or even fifth-generation Americans, who retain little sense of their European national identity. Their loyalty to OCA is purely spiritual. Some variant of Ukrainian and/or Carpatho-Rusyn is spoken by only a small minority. Language schools, for example so-called Russian schools attached to Metropolia parishes, for the most part ceased to exist after World War II. These schools were widespread among both Galician and Transcarpathian Rusyn parishes of OCA, and usually the "instructors" made attempts to teach a literary Rusyn language, although in a few cases the language taught was actually Russian.

Present demographic trends in the United States from the snowbelt to the sunbelt engender pessimism about Rusyn survival in OCA. Given the dynamics of the present situation, it is doubtful whether the Rusyn/Ukrainian ethnic heritage of OCA will survive as anything other than "shadows of forgotten ancestors" beyond the year 2000. Moreover, OCA itself has been joined by thousands of Orthodox Christians who are not Russian in any sense of the word. (For that matter, neither are the twenty to twenty-five thousand Alaskan Orthodox who belong to a local church founded in 1794.) OCA has hundreds of converts in its ranks, and the number of converts among the clergy is fast approaching 51 per cent. In short, the missionary mentality is making OCA both more diverse and more American.

Still, there are younger people in established OCA parishes who are interested in their ethnic background and see no contradiction between their unfaltering loyalty to their Carpatho-Rusyn roots and the ideals and inspiration of Rusyn Orthodoxy, and their commitment to a great, permanent, and truly universal Orthodox Church in America. A concrete example is John Righetti (half Italian, half Carpatho-Rusyn), who is an active member of St. John the Divine Church in Monessen, Pennsylvania, leader of a fairly well-known dance ensemble, "The Carpathians," and a steady participant in the endeavours of The Carpatho-Rusyn Research Centre.

This study would not be complete without a look at specific OCA parishes of Western Ukrainian background. There is no question of ethnic identity among parishioners of St. Michael Church in Portage, Pennsylvania. They are "Carpatho-Russians," but generally refer to themselves as Russians or Slovaks. More specifically, their parents and grandparents came from Uzhhorod and from the neighbourhood of Michalovce. These people are not Russophile, though they do show some admiration for things Hungarian.

Owing to the missionary endeavours of Father Basil Repella, St. Michael Church has always been Orthodox. The present rector, Father David Anderson (a convert from Rome with some Carpatho-Rusyn/Slovak background), says that the piety at St. Michael Church has a decidedly Catholic flavour. Nevertheless, it is quite different from either Greek Catholic or "Johnstown" parishes. Plain Chant is the norm, which says a great deal. The epitome of Carpatho-Rusyn piety and liturgical life is Plain Chant (*Prostopiniie*). To deprive the Carpatho-Rusyn Church of *Prostopiniie* is to seal the fate of all its other typical and distinctive features. The oldest element in traditional *Prostopiniie* is the old *znammenyi* chant. The impression made by Carpatho-Rusyn Plain Chant upon the hearer can be described in terms of great nobility, objectivity and dignity, combined with an ability to express and enhance the emotions evoked by the text. This, no doubt, is a major reason why so many people find *Prostopiniie* both movingly beautiful and profoundly peaceful. When sung congregationally, *Prostopiniie* is an explosive manifestation of the transcendent. This is the case at St. Michael Church.

The people at St. Michael are of simple, working-class stock. Their priest describes them as thoroughly Americanized, but they do observe certain traditional customs quite meticulously, for example, the Christmas Eve Holy Supper, *Sviata Vecheria*. The quieter and less theatrical atmosphere makes St. Michael Church very different from so-called Muscovite or Great Russian parishes. Intensity is shown, however, in some pious practices, such as the entire congregation coming for the carrying out of the *Plashchanytsia*-Shroud (in procession around the church) on Good Friday afternoon at Vespers. Furthermore, many services that became truncated in standard Metropolia parishes are done more fully at St. Michael Church. Unfortunately, although the people of St. Michael Church have a good ecclesiastical sense of community, the parish has little growth potential, since Portage itself is dying because of the closure of the coal mines.

In contrast, St. John the Baptist Church in Conemaugh, Pennsylvania, was until 1978 a standard Metropolia parish. Since that time, it has been led by a priest who is vigorously seeking to improve its liturgical/spiritual level. The parishioners at St. John the Baptist Church are of Galician (Lemko) background, descendants of immigrants from the village of Krasna in southeastern Poland. The clear difference between virtually any Galician parishes in the Pittsburgh Diocese of OCA, and the parishes in the same diocese made up mostly of Transcarpathian Rusyns, is that the Galician parishes have virtually lost their distinctive flavour. In the Johnstown-Altoona Deanery, more often than not things in Carpatho-Rusyn style are used, done well, certainly purified of Uniate distortions, and appreciated by many.

The move in Galician parishes to adopt Russian practices wholesale may stem from an inferiority complex among Galician Rusyns/Ukrainians which, in turn, was caused by the sociological setting of Galicia—rigid class structures, generalized poverty, and widespread illiteracy. The people were insecure, defensive and very argumentative (as well as litigious). All of this has played a role in Orthodox Church life in America, and explains why getting anything done at St. John the Baptist Church is a struggle, while St. Michael Church has a dynamic of its own, which makes the priest's job much easier. One would have to conduct more research about the sociological setting of Transcarpathian Rus' at the time of mass immigration to America before attempting to conclude whether it had an impact on Carpatho-Rusyn parishes in OCA, and, if so, what type of impact it was.

The specific difficulties faced by parishes like St. John the Baptist in Conemaugh will not, and cannot, be solved on the level of ethnic or national consciousness. The parishioners would be no closer to salvation if they were active, conscious Ukrainians. This is because the spiritual problems they face have much more to do with the unity of Orthodox Christians in general and with the office of bishop in the church than with ethnicity. This is not to say that the parishioners do not appreciate that which is "their own." For example, the festal hymn "Oh, who loves Nicholas the saintly" (*O khto, khto*), and certain (but in actuality very few) Galician and Carpathian melodies are used in church, as well as a Carpatho-Rusyn sermon on some special occasion which will still be understood by many, even if the language is now spoken only by a few.

It must also be noted that there are those people in OCA parishes of the western Pennsylvania type, both Galicians and Carpatho-Rusyns, who do not praise any effort to revitalize Western Ukrainian usages in an Orthodox environment, because they seem to think that things Carpatho-Rusyn or Galician are inferior, due to the peasant Greek Catholic experience. In their minds, being definitively anti-Uniate is defined in rather anti-Western Ukrainian terms. When one talks to such people about their own ethnic background, they rather innocently manifest the attitude that being Ukrainian is a regional identity, more or less like being Texan, whereas to be Russian is to partake of full-blown nationality, like being American. This can be attributed to the scheme of Russian history taught at most American universities, which is indeed Russophile from a Ukrainian point of view, and also, perhaps more to the point, to the osmotic influence of self-styled Little Russians like Father Peter Kohanik (1880–1969). He was born in Bereh, Transcarpathian Rus', that is, today's Transcarpathian oblast of Ukraine, and spent his entire priestly life in America. He was a prolific writer of popular works and vehemently insisted that "our people," whether Orthodox or Greek Catholic, are Russians.

Ultimately, the ethnicity of most Carpatho-Rusyns and Galicians in OCA exists primarily, if not exclusively, on the level of reminiscences. Only in Canada do we find the not-quite mass phenomenon of people who have a well-defined Ukrainian identity belonging to OCA because they approve of its Pan-Orthodox character and its use of the English language in worship, while at the same time they maintain "their own" language and culture to some extent.

In my personal experience as a priest, most of the OCA parishes in rural Manitoba are so Ukrainian (in some cases Bukovynian would be more accurate) that one is hard-pressed to believe that they ever belonged to a church which called itself Russian Orthodox. Considering the specifically Ukrainian character of much of its Canadian flock, it is high time for OCA to come to grips with the Ukrainian question.

It is a premise of this study that membership in OCA and Ukrainian nationality are compatible. Therefore, solving the Ukrainian question should be a priority for the primate of the Orthodox Church in America, Metropolitan Theodosius (Lazor).[7] Interestingly, Father George Johnson (half Rusyn, half Swedish), a member of the Diocesan Council of the Pittsburgh Diocese, is in favour of virtually unconditional recognition of the Ukrainian Orthodox Church of Canada by OCA. If there were a legitimate reason for OCA not to be in communion with that church in the now distant past, it no longer exists.

In reality, there is no special Ukrainian problem; it is part and parcel of the canonically irregular situation throughout North America of multiple, for the most part, ethnic jurisdictions. Anyone familiar with the Ukrainian Orthodox Church of Canada must appreciate the hard work of the scholarly, eminently ecclesiastical Ukrainian patriot, Metropolitan Ilarion (Ohiienko) to make the church he headed much more orthodox and appropriately faithful to Kievan (not Muscovite) Orthodox tradition. There has been no American equivalent to Metropolitan Ilarion. Therefore, the American situation may very well be more difficult to deal with for OCA because of a lingering Uniate influence. This attitude tends to favour the perpetuation of obscure rubrics or customs only because they are Ukrainian (that is, if it is Ukrainian, it must be accepted as Orthodox), as well as strong anti-OCA prejudices. In Canada, the present OCA policy on ethnicity (in short, anything goes as long as it is Orthodox) could work even better than in the United States, as a result of this country's multicultural character.

In conclusion, while OCA continues to be comprised mostly of Ukrainians, it is not an ethnic church. It has chosen to try to become a local North American church for all Orthodox Christians. It boldly proclaims that ethnic heritage must "die to itself" if the church is to be renewed and to bear fruit. At the same time, it should strive to broaden its horizons, to be much more amenable to Mediterranean (Byzantine) Orthodoxy, and it should once and for all make clear that it recognizes Ukrainian identity, nationality and language.

NOTES

1. *Orthodox America 1794–1976* (Syosset, New York: Orthodox Church in America Department of History and Archives, 1975), 127.
2. This search for self-definition started with Father Alexis Toth, who looked to Russian Orthodoxy for an objective standard of Orthodoxy.
3. Warsaw is used here to cover the territories made up of Ukrainian and Belorussian Orthodox Christians who belonged to the Orthodox Church of Poland between 1918 and 1945.
4. I discussed this with Fr. Alexander Schmemann at St. Vladimir's Seminary in the late 1970s.
5. Thomas Hopko, "Infant Communion in Ecumenical Discussion," *The Orthodox Church,* October 1980.
6. This was almost entirely a return from the Unia, which suffered a major crisis in the 1930s.
7. This priority should be set specifically to mark the Millennium of the Baptism of Rus'.

Sophia Matiasz

Three Parishes: A Study in the Ethnic Use of Religious Symbols

Introduction— Theoretical Perspective

This paper is an investigation of the importance and function of religious markers that are rooted in bonds of shared past and perceived ethnic interests. While not a determination of religiosity or theological debate, this paper does define religion as human behaviour involving belief and ritual concerned with supernatural beings and forces. Its focus is the overlap between religion and ethnicity via the markers employed therein. The boundaries between the two indicate the forces operating in both ethnicity and religion. The dominance of one may change with respect to the other. This change will vary according to the experiences of the group or individual. This in turn reflects another dynamic: the variability of identity of the group and of the individual.

To examine ethnicity in religious communities the following premises are assumed: (a)Whether engaged in the choice of one form of identity over another or merely accepting the identity given, the individual establishes a sense of belonging; (b) Ethnicity involves a subjective sense of belonging in a group which is open to change through time and circumstances; (c) Ethnicity is primarily a consciousness of kind within a group and this consciousness is on occasion contrasted with other identities of excluded groups of individuals. A tentative working definition has been adopted for this exploration: ethnicity is a collective sociocultural entity of those who share a sense of common origin, whether real or imagined. What matters most in this definition is the historical ethnic consciousness which transcends temporal, geographic and even linguistic boundaries, as in the case of Jewish ethnicity.

One of the obvious means for this consciousness to be delineated is by symbolic 'markers' (cultural, biological and/or territorial). My emphasis is on the acceptance or selection of types of expressions of ethnic identity. Therein the use of symbols and cultural markers reinforces the legitimacy of the choice of expression.

Bearing these issues in mind, several questions may be raised about ethnoreligious data (which will be discussed further). Within the total framework of Catholicism what scope is there for Ukrainians to express ethnic subidentities? Investigation of the literature shows that ethnic groups are not static and are not uniform from one period or one situaiton to another. So what is the legitimate range of activity for Ukrainian Catholics? How does this expression vary from one group of Ukrainian Catholics to another? Is there a difference between one generation of Ukrainian Catholics and another? What are the factors that precipitate this potentially temporal, situational and generational variation? How do factors operating in their homeland at the time of departure affect the need of Catholic Ukrainians to express their ethnoreligious identity? What factors allow for Ukrainian identity to be expressed above Catholic identity?

For many of the immigrants to Canada at the turn of the century national identities were meaningless. For example, Bukovynians and Galicians from Ukraine perceived themselves in a regional rather than a Ukrainian national identity. This was further complicated by the fact that for part of the last century Galicia was occupied by Austria, and Ukrainians who migrated during this period carried Austrian passports. Therefore they were classified as Austrians in Canada. Ukrainian immigrants of that era were treated differently from those who subsequently emigrated from Soviet territory. Thus there is no uniform classification of immigrants from this particular group for any historical period. Ethnic dimensions and intra-ethnic differences have been overlooked because of sweeping generalizations with broad ethnic and religious classifications that have ignored social, economic and political factors affecting ethnicity and religion.

Barth and others have examined the negotiation of ethnicity, particularly the determination and maintenance of boundaries by different ethnic groups. The exclusion/inclusion criteria have been seen in intergroup dimensions. Very little work has been focused on intragroup negotiations of similar subgroup boundaries. Where these subgroup delimitations do exist probably they will be less pronounced, more easily negotiable and perhaps even fluid compared to intergroup markings. Within this sphere, the individual is perceived to be able to identify, establish and maintain or alter an ethnic identity according to circumstances. Durkheim maintained that religion is a reflection of society and that it is much more than creed and faith. Its most fundamental and enduring elements, in his view, are the social aspects of rite, ceremony, hierarchy and community. Therefore the societal power of religion is in its transmission of symbols and rituals. Individuals choose the symbols and rituals most consistent with their perception of acceptable ethnoreligious forms and their choice reflects the pervasive ethnic orientation.

It appears then that if religious organizations are a function of personal expressions of ethnoreligious orientations and if ethnic group identity is variable and able to be classified as a range of typologies, and not a complex of traits, then religious organization (and the manipulation of ethnoreligious symbols therein) is a strong function of intra-group identity. This orientation is particularly important as it emphasizes the voluntary and variable nature of ethnic orientations within heterogeneous groups.

Ukrainian Greek Catholics—Edmonton—1950s and Beyond

The arrival of 2,000 Ukrainians in Alberta had profound repercussions upon the Ukrainian Greek Catholic community. The Papal Bull of 1948 had already proclaimed four Ukrainian Greek Catholic eparchies instead of the one originating in Winnipeg. The creation of the Edmonton eparchy meant that the only Ukrainian Greek Catholic parish (St. Josaphat's) was now a Cathedral. Compensation agreements had been made on behalf of the Basilians who manned St. Josaphat's who then ventured south of the Saskatchewan River to establish their new parish—St. Basil the Great. Many from the original St. Josaphat's congregation followed the Basilians southward.

Throughout my research (1980–4), particularly in interviews, individuals have stressed the importance of certain priests in their lives. The virtues of Father A or Father B would often be cited in interviews without the slightest prompting. Others had relatives, brothers, uncles or cousins who had been Basilians and followed their lead through a strong familial affiliation. Still others had encountered Basilians while farming in the Mundare/Vegreville/Two Hills region. These personal encounters with the Basilians became the major criteria for many in their choice of parish. Not only the Basilians were said to have a personal following. The current parish priest of St. George's was often referred to as a "special person" who had worked in the country district immediately outside Edmonton. He had also maintained traditions carried out in Ukraine before World War II. Therefore, it was mainly the post-World War II individuals and families who personalized their relationship with St. George's parish priest. Those who related closely to Basilians had had a family farming history in the earliest Ukrainian settlements of Alberta.

There is some controversy over how St. George's parish came to be established. In interviews, individuals would not speak openly. Whenever the topic was raised or, indeed, arose in discussion, references were, without exception, obscure. However, the disappointment and dissatisfaction with the events leading up to the separation of the St. George's group was strong. Generally, there was agreement that the post-World War II immigrants (still labelled "New Arrivals" in the 1980s) had begun confidently, and with some authority, to question some of the established practices within St. Josaphat's parish. Frustrated with Latinization the post-World War II arrivals questioned the installation of statues, the absence of the iconostasis and the celebration of Christmas on 25 December (in lieu of 7 January according to the liturgical or Julian calendar).

Constant reference was made by interviewees to a meeting of the whole parish of St. Josaphat's, where a vote had been taken on the procedure to be adopted. Following the vote those who preferred the Julian calendar, the iconostasis, the removal of statues, and Ukrainian as the sole language used in Liturgy left to establish another parish. The third parish was located immediately north of St. Josaphat's in a district of Edmonton often referred to as "Mala Bukovyna" or little Bukovyna, an area in which many Ukrainians first settled in Edmonton. So, within ten years of the proclamation of the Papal Bull of 1948, the Ukrainian Greek Catholic Parish of St. Josaphat's was restructured into three parishes: St. Josaphat's Cathedral parish, St. Basil's parish and St. George's parish. In terms of physical structure St. Josaphat's remained much the same. The walls were embellished with scenes depicting the history of salvation in biblical times and for the Ukrainian people. The iconostasis was added later and the statues (a Latin tradition) were relegated to side altars.

Both St. Basil's and St. George's underwent a two-stage process before they reached their present accommodation but the circumstances within each process were markedly different. St. Basil's members moved south of the river into a wooden structure, formerly home to a French-language Catholic parish. The Basilians then purchased a large parcel of land and began the mammoth task of building the large complex which now includes the church, presbytery, recreational hall and senior citizens' accommodation. Current members of St. Basil's parish explain proudly that members took out personal mortgages on their homes to raise the capital required for this building programme. Such statements were often disputed by other interviewees. However, there is definitely a strong sense of "we went away and did this on our own" about the establishment of St. Basil's.

The St. George's group moved into a building formerly used by a Polish-language Catholic parish. This modern structure was razed by arson in late 1979. A community hall functioned as a church until a sixteenth-century Ukrainian-style church built was completed in 1982. In adapting the sixteenth-century architectural style to Canadian twentieth-century conditions, the parish of St. George's was not engaging merely in nostalgia. There was a strong sense of pride. Many interviewees spoke in detail about the time, effort and commitment of the committee that investigated and proposed the project. They tried to be faithful to the symbolic tradition of their Orthodox ancestors. There was a strong community spirit behind both the erection of the building and the fund raising drives to reduce the debt incurred. Following Ukrainian tradition and the Eastern Rite, the interior of the church boasts an elaborate chandelier imported from Greece, complete with small icons. The walls, in the course of time, will be covered with icons. An iconostasis was erected in 1985. Included in the parish complex is a community hall and a house for the parish priest which serves as the presbytery.

St. Basil's provides an interesting architectural contrast with cream-coloured brick, modern design, majestic simplicity, and very high ceilings. It could pass as a middle-class post-Vatican II Catholic parish anywhere in the world except that the priest, as celebrant, still has his back to the people for most of the liturgy. The walls are without icons. Instead, an enormous mosaic of the Resurrection is found behind the altar on the east wall. There is no iconostasis and there are no plans to have one.

The architectural structures within each parish differ dramatically, but each has at least one dome on its roof. There is, however, debate on what is appropriate or Ukrainian about the domes employed. Of importance to our discussion is that each parish and its members are convinced of the "Ukrainianness" of their parish. Who are the people who make up these parishes? The prevailing view, which predates my research, is that St. Basil's contained the more upwardly mobile, professional, third- or fourth-generation Ukrainians who spoke English more than Ukrainian and perceived their ethnic identity as Canadian rather than Ukrainian. St. Josaphat's was thought to be a mixture of all generations who were believed to have a Canadian Ukrainian identity that fluctuated according to circumstance and socio-economic status.

St. George's, then, became a parish of mainly post-World War II immigrant Ukrainians. There was some debate on the number of professionals who attended the parish. This parish was popularly perceived to be the least upwardly mobile, yet people also believed that the post-World War II migration consisted of a large number of intelligentsia from Ukraine. There was no doubt that this parish was predominantly Ukrainian, yet I was told repeatedly that St. George's had members of organizations especially concerned with issues and concerns in Ukraine today: political freedom and nationhood, and the establishment of a patriarchate in the diaspora.

Participant observation and interviews were conducted in all parishes as well as with Ukrainian Greek Catholics outside these parishes and with non-Catholic Ukrainians (who provided an occasional outsider's perspective). Finally I conducted a telephone survey. In the latter part of this survey individuals were asked to give their views on the significance of a variety of symbols relevant to everyday life. The interviews also explored each individual's choice from the Ukrainian Greek Catholic parishes. (The choice could have depended on a variety of factors, both sociological and religious—changing rite, or denomination, however, a few people changed parishes for reasons of geography or marriage.) Those interviewed were in the main still members of the parishes into which they had first moved. The parish had become their spiritual home. The participant observation stage of the research examined many of the stereotypical labels applied to each Ukrainian community parish.

St. Basil's had Liturgy solely in Ukrainian, whereas other Liturgies had English sermons; its parish newsletters were written in English. The cars parked outside were bigger, newer than in the other parishes, and it was difficult (during the winter) to avoid noticing the abundance of fur coats.

St. Josaphat's appeared to have an older congregation dressed in a less flamboyant style. However, a great proportion of both congregations actively participated in communion. Even after several visits, the darker, more traditional interior of St. Josephat's gives the impression that it is smaller than St. Basil's.

St. George's appeared to consist predominantly of older people, though on special occasions (*Paskha,* Christmas) younger members attended in droves. People were dressed in a more subdued manner. A close bond between members was apparent as they greeted one another. St. George's exuded a community spirit. All the liturgies attended were solely in Ukrainian. Church bulletins were written in Ukrainian only, and portions of the homilies dealt with the issues of the Patriarchy, the state of Ukraine, and Ukrainian culture in Canada. More significantly, the parish priest was married. His wife assisted him in parish duties. Here was a pre-World War II social microcosm transferred from Ukraine celebrating in a modern version of a sixteenth-century traditional church.

The hymns sung were most traditional in St. George's. Frequently in these hymns, prayer and praise of God was juxtaposed with messages about the safety and future of Ukraine. The Ukrainian hymns sung at St. Basil's were prayers set to tunes and rarely included such references to Ukraine. Furthermore, traditional tunes had been infused with something akin to country and western style. St. Josaphat's use of hymns followed the more traditional pattern found at St. George's.

The telephone survey yielded 100 members each from St. Josaphat's and St. Basil's parishes. The sample was drawn randomly by selecting names from the parish list supplied by each parish priest. (A random numbers list was pursued in obtaining the sample). St. George's apparently did not have a similar parish register or families/individuals who formally paid (in sealed envelopes) into the church coffers. However, the parish priest of St. George's himself drew up a list of appropriate interviewees. Interestingly, all the people on the list of 139 names were men. Of these, fifty contacts were interviewed by phone. In the two larger parishes, I called the number and asked for the individual on the list or head of household. (When these were not available, there was a brief introduction and a request for an interview. Most often the interviewee himself answered the phone.) In both St. Josaphat's and St. Basil's a sizeable majority (70 per cent and 69 per cent respectively) were also males. At St. George's, twenty-seven out of fifty were men. The whole process of selection appears reflective of the traditional Ukrainian view that women should not participate in significant positions within the church.

Sixty-two per cent of the members of St. Josaphat's and 42 per cent of St. Basil's parish were over fifty-five years of age. Thirty out of fifty of St. George's were in this age bracket. Eighty-four per cent of St. Basil's, 51 per cent of St. Josaphat's and 4 per cent of St. George's were born in Canada. The respective Ukrainian-born were 8 per cent; 42 per cent and 80 per cent. Of the 84 per cent of St. Basil's that were Canadian-born, over 60 per cent were descendants of immigrants from the first wave. Only 28 per cent of interviewees of St. Josaphat's had ancestors who arrived in this first wave. None of St. George's respondents could trace arrival of immediate relatives to this time.

In summary, then, St. Basil's emerged as the most upwardly mobile of the three parties, with a younger, better educated population. St. Basil's had by far the highest number of parishioners born in Canada along with the highest incidence of English spoken with spouses and children. St. George's had the highest number of parishioners born in Ukraine and the highest number using Ukrainian with spouses and children at home. Even though St. George's is without doubt the parish of new arrivals, its congregation appears very stable, with 60 per cent of those interviewed claiming at least twenty years' membership within that parish. The longest established parish, the Cathedral's parishioners, emerged as most stable with 37 per cent having been members for over thirty years. St. Josaphat's also had the largest number of parishioners over the age of 55. In all other aspects—country of origin, use of English, use of Ukrainian—St. Josaphat's fell between St. Basil's and St. George's. Its members had the lowest percentage with more than nine years of formal education.

On the question of symbols in Ukrainian Greek Catholic practice in Edmonton, some interesting results emerged. Eighty-four per cent of St. Basil's, 73 per cent of St. Josaphat's and 84 per cent of St. George's agreed that it was common practice for choirs to be used in the Liturgy. Most people considered choirs to be more traditional than having the congregation singing (83 per cent for St. Basil's, 70 per cent for St. Josaphat's and 80 per cent for St. George's). Most concurred on the use of icons (83 per cent at St. Basil's, 76 per cent at St. Josaphat's and 96 per cent at St. George's). Embroidered vestment use followed with 83 per cent of St. Basil's, 75 per cent of St. Josaphat's, and 92 per cent of St. George's members agreeing. Most also agreed on the Liturgy recited and the use of embellished church walls, on the use of the iconostasis, and on Taras Shevchenko being a Ukrainian national symbol, although only 39 per cent of St. Josephat's interviewees (compared to 65 per cent for St. Basil's and 54 per cent for St. George's) felt the latter to be the case. The use of the Rosary posed some problems in interpretation. Forty-five per cent of St. Basil's respondents thought that the Rosary was not a traditional Ukrainian practice, even though this was the parish in which Rosary evenings were most frequently conducted. At St. Josaphat's, 31 per cent thought it was Ukrainian, 32 per cent thought it was not and 30 per cent were unsure (7 per cent chose not to respond). There was a similar division from St. George's respondents, where 48 per cent thought it was Ukrainian and 44 per cent disagreed. Another area of differences was the Knights of Columbus. Seventy-six per cent of St. Basil's, 39 per cent of St. Josaphat's and 66 per cent of St. George's parishioners thought that the Knights were not of Ukrainian origin.

The three-barred cross was seen as Orthodox by the majority, St. Basil's (58 per cent) and a minority of St. Josaphat's (41 per cent). A large percentage (16 per cent and 24 per cent respectively) did not know. Sixty-eight per cent of St. George's respondents recognized the three-barred cross as Ukrainian. Statues in churches were generally accepted as Ukrainian practice (by 58 per cent at St. Basil's, 38 per cent at St. Josaphat's and 48 per cent at George's). The use of a confessional brought similar results (70 per cent at St. Basil's, 64 per cent at St. Josaphat's and 60 per cent at St. George's). The Ukrainian flag was clearly but not unequivocally a national symbol for all parishes (68 per cent at St. Basil's, 54 per cent at St. Josaphat's and 88 per cent at St. George's); nine per cent, 18 per cent and 2 per cent respectively recognized the national flag as a symbol of faith rather than nationality. Finally, in this section the Trident (often used as an insignia) had national significance for 25 per cent of respondents at St. Basil's, 37 per cent at St. Josaphat's and 0 per cent at St. George's. It represented a symbol of faith for 25 per cent at St. Basil's, 18 per cent at St. Josaphat's and 64 per cent at St. George's.

The significance of the Marian Sodality was one area of apparent disagreement between the parishes. Of the St. Basil's respondents 16 per cent thought it was Ukrainian, 25 per cent that it was not, 45 per cent did not know, and 14 per cent chose not to respond. As for St. Josaphat's respondents: 21 per cent thought it was Ukrainian, 19 per cent that it was not Ukrainian, 56 per cent did not know, and 4 per cent did not respond. This contrasted with the St. George's respondents where 84 per cent recognized the Sodality as Ukrainian, 2 per cent thought it was not Ukrainian, 12 per cent did not know, and one did not respond.

Finally, the interviewees were asked about the significance of the then head of the Ukrainian Rite, Cardinal Slipy. Forty-five per cent of St. Basil's respondents saw him as an important national and religious leader, 51 per cent from St. Josaphat's and 82 per cent from St. George's. Papal representation (a less significant role) was indicated by 15 per cent of St. Basil's respondents, 7 per cent of St. Josaphat's and 12 per cent of St. George's. Seven per cent of St. Basil's respondents, 3 per cent of St. Josaphat's and 0 per cent from St. George's felt Iosyf Cardinal Slipy had no leadership significance for them.

The three parishes appear to have a great deal in common. The use of the Liturgy of the Ukrainian Greek Catholic Rite is universal. The celebrations differ according to the Julian or Gregorian calendar. Whether the Liturgy is recited, sung by the choir or sung by the congregation appears to be immaterial. However, the Marian Sodality, the Knights of Columbus, and the Rosary do not conform to this practice. Symbols chosen because of their apparently obvious relevance (to the researcher)—the Ukrainian flag, the Trident, and the issue of the Patriarchate symbolized in the Ukrainian Cardinal of the time, Cardinal Slipy, elicited different responses from parish to parish.

What does this data say about ethnic identity among Ukrainian Greek Catholics in Edmonton? It appears that after three or four generations they have retained a separate group identity. Ethnic self-assertion has produced movements to revive cultural distinctiveness, which at different times has been in danger of being lost. At St. Basil's, the traditions of the old culture were transported into the new environment and, after an initial period, new cultural practices were adopted. Ethnic identity, within the context of these three Ukrainian Greek Catholic parishes, has a changing cultural and religious content. The work of Isajiw, Uchendu, Skinner and Hecter highlights the need of ethnic groups to renegotiate identities and recreate strategies for self-expression. It has been demonstrated here that there is variation within and among ethnic groups. Therefore, intra-group and individual expression of identity and ethnicity through religion may change according to time and circumstance.

Religion provides a strong initial base for social identity and ethnocentrism, within which the individual can identify, establish, maintain or alter an ethnic identity according to the situation. Therefore, religious organizations are a function of combined personal expressions of ethnoreligious orientations. The ethnic group is variable and can be classified as a range of typologies. Religious organization and the manipulation of ethnoreligious symbols therein are strong functions of intra-group identity.

Conclusion

Ethnicity can be seen as a collective sociocultural entity of those who share a sense of common origin. From this perspective all three parishes, St. Josaphat's, St. Basil's and St. George's subscribe to an identity revolving around the Ukrainian Greek Catholic Rite. All three parishes are seen as legitimate expressions of the Ukrainian Greek Catholic Rite. However, within this orientation each varies slightly from the other.

Clearly the issues involved here are not fully resolved by the participants themselves. Knowledge of the background, history and application of the practices seem highly correlated to age and gender. Older males are considered by others, and indeed consider themselves to be more knowledgeable of such things. Interestingly enough there appeared to be no specific education programme or campaign within which church ritual or tradition was addressed. Obviously the priests of each parish were the most knowledgeable of the theology and cultural practices within the Ukrainian Greek Catholic Rite and especially within their own parishes.

Individuals in each parish indicated that they had been members for varying lengths of time. Individual preferences for parish priests were reflected. Even more important was association based on past individual or family history. Where parish membership changes were made the reasons given were usually to do with geographical location or another type of convenience.

Most significant inter-parish differences were also seen in terms of the individual's association with traditions or rituals performed. The response "we do practice that in our parish so it must be Ukrainian" was quite common in the telephone interview responses. (Furthermore this response was more prevalent among female respondents.) These symbolic markers are signposts, means of reflecting a consciousness of common origin. These markers, religious and cultural, are a reflection of a group phenomenon.

It could be agreed that the parishes have more in common with each other than they have differences. However, each parish member interviewed indicated an awareness of separateness or "otherness" with regard to the other two parishes. The use of symbols and cultural markers reinforces the legitimacy of expression. However the range of legitimate options was narrowed when viewed from outside the Ukrainian Greek Catholic Rite. From inside, the established practices seem to be rarely questioned.

In Durkheim's view the societal power of religion is in its transmission of symbols and rituals. In the case of these parishes of St. Basil's, St. Josaphat's and St. George's, symbols have been re-interpreted through popular usage to become symbols of group identity. This study suggests that much of this is based on the generation of migration and period of migration of the priests leading the parishes. The individual parish use of religious and/or cultural markers represents their lifestyles and their place in the larger Canadian social universe. Their synthesis of religious markers provides a continuum which extends from an internally focussed model concerned with cultural and rationalistic phenomena through to one focussing outward to the wider Canadian context. Location on the continuum is highly correlated to period of arrival of individuals (or ancestors) in Canada. Within that location the legitimacy of *what* in the parish is done is predominantly the province of the parish leaders: the priests. The combination of these factors led to a manipulating and redefining of the symbols reflective of conditions upon their arrival in Canada. In turn these perceptions and the interim history affect current responses within the individual parish group.

Afterword

Jaroslav Pelikan

Eastern Christianity in Modern Culture: Genius and Dilemma

The Slavs understand better than most other Europeans—and Ukrainians better than most other Slavs—the price of living on both sides of a great divide, for they are the only European people for whom conversion to the Christian faith has meant cultural division rather than cultural unification. Indeed, the gospel has been responsible for giving many nations their alphabet, but to the Slavs it has given three—Glagolitic, Cyrillic and Latin. Partly on account of the cultural division and partly through other historical factors, Eastern Christianity has experienced the challenges of modern culture in ways and at times different from those that have marked the Western developments. This two-fold split, which has made Eastern Christianity unique, has been neither an unmixed blessing nor an unmitigated disaster. Thus this essay may appropriately take the form of a review of some of the implications of the two-fold split of Eastern Christianity from much of the rest of Christendom.

In his famous essay "Answer to the Question: What Is Enlightenment?," Immanuel Kant defined the Enlightenment, and thus the spirit of modern culture, as "man's exodus from his self-incurred tutelage," that is, from the authority of tradition. Since the Middle Ages it has been evident to Western observers that Eastern Christianity has affirmed the authority of tradition more unambiguously or, as those observers would have it, more uncritically, than has the West. Repeatedly, therefore, it has been the vocation of Eastern Christendom to come to the rescue of the West by drawing out from the treasure trove of its memory the overlooked resources of the patristic tradition. So it was in the beginnings of the Renaissance in Italy, when the scholars of Constantinople fled to Venice and Florence before the invader, clutching their Greek manuscripts, and taught Western thinkers to read not only Plato and Homer but also the Cappadocian fathers, John Chrysostom, and the Greek New Testament.

So it has been again in the twentieth century. One of the most striking differences between the First and the Second Vatican Councils—a difference that helps to provide an explanation for many of the other differences—is that between 1870 and 1950 the Western church had once more discovered how much it had been ignoring the theology and culture of Eastern Christendom in the liturgy and spirituality. Thus on one point after another in the decrees of Vatican II, from ecclesiology itself to the collegiality of bishops and the centrality of the liturgy, the one-sidedness of Western ways has been counterbalanced and corrected by characteristically Eastern emphases.

Part of the price that the East has paid for this preservation of tradition is a tendency toward the archaic and a corresponding poverty in the area of scholarship, precisely at a time when so much of the "genius" (as well as the "dilemma") of modern culture has been articulated in the area of humanistic thought and research. For even as we measure the contributions that the Eastern tradition of spirituality and patristic theology has made to Western thought, we must recognize that when it comes to making the monuments of Eastern spirituality and patristic theology available in modern critical editions, Western scholars very frequently have taken the lead. Erasmus, with his editions of Chrysostom, Basil of Caesarea, and Origen, the Bonn editions of the Byzantine historians, the Oriental Institute founded by Pope Benedict IV in 1917, and Adolf von Harnack and the great Berlin corpus of the *Griechische christliche Schriftsteller*, represent the scientific methodology and devoted research of Western scholars, both Protestant and Roman Catholic. These scholars have often borne the principal share of the burden for sorting out the genuine from the spurious in the Eastern heritage and for publishing the results of philological and historical research in a form that both Eastern and Western scholars could use.

This is not to ignore the great achievements of Eastern individuals and institutions. One of the many tragic consequences of the Bolshevik Revolution is that it came just as theological and historical scholarship was beginning to blossom in tsarist Russia, and with special richness in Ukraine.[1] The heirs of that scholarly tradition have valiantly striven to carry it on under conditions of repression or exile and have made valuable contributions, but it does seem clear that the shattering interruption of ecclesiastical and religious life by the Revolution has had a profound effect on scholarship. Thus, by one of the ironies that have always marked the history of Eastern Christendom, Western scholarship still has the primary responsibility for making the East understood, perhaps even to itself.

As I have already suggested, a major element in both the genius and the dilemma of Eastern Christianity in modern culture has been the liturgy, as reformers of Western liturgy have repeatedly acknowledged.[2] Nonetheless, the Latin church has sometimes given the impression that the fundamental meaning of the Christian faith is institutional: "*subesse Romano pontifici omni humanae creaturae . . . omnino esse de necessitate salutis* [it is altogether necessary to salvation for every human creature to be subject to the Roman pontiff]," Pope Boniface VIII declared in his bull *Unam sanctam* of 1302. Many of the Protestant churches, especially the Lutheran, have emphasized doctrinal theology as the normative force in the church, in the process producing a corpus of official doctrine whose total length surpasses by a factor of ten or more the entire dogmatic legislation of the seven ecumenical councils of the ancient and undivided church. Eastern Christianity, while not indifferent to such institutional questions as the authority of the episcopate and certainly vigorous in its espousal of dogmatic and creedal orthodoxy (including the creedal integrity of the only true ecumenical creed, the Nicene, which it has defended against the Western addition of the *Filioque*), has nevertheless put worship rather than institution or doctrine at the centre of the definition of the church.[3]

Once again, however, the genius has also served to pose the dilemma. Western churches have frequently been divided over doctrine: justification *sola fide* versus justification by faith *and* works at the Council of Trent, or verbal inspiration of the Bible versus the historical-critical method in the debates of the nineteenth and twentieth centuries. Sometimes they have been divided over systems of polity and church administration. In Anglo-Saxon Protestantism the nomenclature of many of the major denominations— Episcopalian, Presbyterian, Congregational—has been based on how they have claimed that the church should be organized. In the East, as the history of Christianity in Ukraine demonstrates, many of the most bitter conflicts have come over the forms of worship, so that even questions of church administration and doctrine have focused on such issues as the Latinization of the liturgy.[4]

Worship and ritual is, to be sure, a question of more than strictly ecclesiastical concern: cultus and culture are ultimately the same word. This identification between cultus and culture, though universal, has taken markedly different forms in Eastern and Western Christianity, with the Slavic lands—*Velkomoravska risa* in the ninth century, and Rus'-Ukraine in the tenth and in many subsequent centuries—as the crucible. The two missionary methods of the two traditions have been reflected in the two Christian cultures. Wherever Roman missionaries went, they taught the people the Latin Mass, introduced them to the Vulgate, and thus, quite inadvertently, gave them at least the rudiments of access to Cicero and Vergil, but at the high price of at least stunting, and in many cases destroying, the development of the native tongue. Eastern missionaries—Ulfilas, who came to his Goths from Constantinople, and above all SS. Constantine-Cyril and

Methodius—translated the liturgy and the gospel into the language of the people, creating an indigenous Christian literature. In turn, that blessing also exacted a price, that aspect of Eastern Christian genius also created a dilemma. Although the Greek-Christian culture of Byzantium and then of Greece preserved a continuity with the literature and thought of pre-Christian Hellenism and was therefore far richer in its heritage than was the Latin West, the Slavic daughter churches of Byzantium, with their autochthonous liturgical culture, had less access to classical antiquity than did their Western counterparts.

In spite of what I said earlier about the contrast between East and West on the relative importance of church organization, autochthony in culture has had as its corollary the principle of autocephaly in church structure, another expression of the genius of Eastern Christianity. In opposition to the pyramidal system of the Latin West, where a centrality of authority has also meant a uniformity of practice, each church of Eastern Christendom has, at least in theory, been free to evolve many of its own forms of culture and life. Thus they formed a bond with the total life of the people that no Muslim or Marxist or militarist government has succeeded in breaking. There is nothing intrinsic in Western polité or doctrine that requires an equation of unity with uniformity; but in practice (as Eastern Rite Catholics, especially in the Ukrainian tradition, have had ample occasion to learn), such an equation has frequently been the outcome even when it was not the policy. The encyclical *Orientalium dignitas ecclesiarum* promulgated by Pope Leo XIII on 30 November 1894 documents both the genius and the dilemma of this issue.

Both are likewise formulated very well in the title and the subtitle of this book: the genius of "The Ukrainian Religious Experience," but the dilemma of "Tradition and the Canadian Cultural Context." For autocephaly in Eastern Orthodoxy and autochthony in Eastern Rite Catholicism have been able to express the genius of each of the Eastern, and specifically Slavic peoples, but in the New World they have raised anew the dilemma of how the particularity of any single tradition is to be related both to the universality of a church that confesses itself to be *una, sancta, catholica, et apostolica* and to the new reality of the context of a new people of which those who stand in an Eastern Christian tradition also want to be a genuine part. The anguished struggles of Eastern Christians in Canada and the United States over this dilemma, whether in communion with the Holy See or not, suggest that equal measures of scholarship, wisdom and charity may be necessary to recover the genius and resolve the dilemma.

References to such principles as autocephaly, autochthony and autonomy demonstrate that, *volens-nolens* (*chtiac-nechtiac*), these issues have profoundly political implications as well. Eastern churches that do not have communion with the See of Peter have, as a result, sometimes been able to play a part in the political developments of their nations that might have seemed embarrassing or even dangerous to Rome. Conversely, Western churches have often sought a similar power, as they did most articulately in *The Four Gallican Articles* of 1682 or in the German *Kulturkampf* of the nineteenth century. On the other hand, when a benevolent despot has been replaced by a hostile despot—sometimes by one who is less, sometimes by one who is more, despotic, but hostile to Christianity in either case—that very identification of the church with the native culture and with the political order has often meant that there was no Archimedean *pou stō*, no point of leverage beyond the borders, and hence no recourse to an interdict or other supra-national jurisdiction.

If, however, according to hallowed Eastern teaching, the authority of the church resides ultimately in an ecumenical council, which ever since Constantine I at Nicea has been convoked by a Christian emperor, how does the church convoke a council to deal with the crisis of 1453 when the Sultan occupies the throne of Constantine? Or if, between councils, it is the principle of *pentarchia*, the authority of the five apostolic patriarchates, that is to be invoked, what are the implications for that authority when many millions of Christians live beyond at least the geographical borders of any of the patriarchs? Conversely, how is the church in any specific political context to be free to shape its own political strategy if the central administration in the Vatican thinks it has the divine right to dictate or to second-guess that strategy?

All of these facets, both of the genius and the dilemma of Eastern Christianity, have special relevance to the Ukrainian religious experience in the Ukrainian motherland and in the Canadian diaspora. Having spent the past several years on research in his patriarchal archives in Rome,[5] I have found that His Beatitude, Iosyf Cardinal Slipy, Patriarch of Blessed Memory, a remarkable and heroic man, was in many striking ways the embodiment of most of these facets of genius and dilemma, as a scholar, a national leader, a political prisoner, and as a prelate between East and West. Yet, as Cardinal Slipy would have been the first to insist, he was all of this not as an individual, but as the beneficiary of a rich and varied heritage. So it is that I hope the work of scholars charged with the task of cherishing the genius of Eastern Christianity, while also understanding its dilemmas, may lead to the mutual enrichment of the Old World of our parents and the New World of our children.

NOTES

1. One of the most important items is the massive dissertation of Aleksandr Pavlovich Dobroklonsky, *Prepodobnyi Fedor, ispovednik i igumen studiiskii* on the theological and monastic leader, Theodore of Studios, whose *Antirrhetica against the Iconoclasts* must be recognized as a major statement of the Byzantine apologia. Dobroklonsky's monograph was published in Odessa in 1913–14. Those two years were likewise the dates of publication for such works as N. F. Kapterev, *Kharakter otnoshenii Rossii k pravoslavnomu vostoku*, A. Spassky, *Istoriia dogmaticheskikh dvizhenii*, the *Polnyi pravoslavnyi bogoslovskii entsiklopedicheskii slovar*, and the *Trudy Kievskoi dukhovnoi akademii*, which began publication in 1913 and contains some of the most illuminating articles available on many patristic subjects.
2. For example, the monumental *Liturgiarum Orientalium Collectio* (2 vols., Paris, 1716) of the French scholar Eusèbe Renaudot (1648–1720) was a work of painstaking scholarship and great devotion intended to enrich post-Tridentine Western worship by infusing a better knowledge of the Greek and Near Eastern rites.
3. Thus it is illuminating to note that although Roman Catholics and Protestants have both laid claim to the label "orthodox" for the fidelity of their doctrinal formulations to the doctrine of the Trinity as formulated by the First Council of Nicea in 325, the "Sunday of Orthodoxy" observed in the East is a celebration of the Second Council of Nicea, that of 787, and of an "ortho-*doxy*" that is defined as the right way of rendering *doxa*, the praise of God. Slavic languages have preserved this definition in the very term *pravo-slavie*.
4. Consider the statement of Protopop Avvakum, noted in his *Zhitie* during the 1670s, about what was at stake in the *Raskol* (Schism) of the Orthodox Church of Russia in the seventeenth century:

    Before the time of Nikon, the apostate, in our Russia under our pious princes and tsars the faith of *Pravoslavie* was pure and undefiled, and the church was free from turmoil. It was Nikon the wolf, together with the devil, who ordained that men should cross themselves with three fingers, but our first shepherds made the sign of the cross and blessed men with five fingers, according to the tradition of our holy fathers. . . . God will bless you: suffer tortures for the way you place your fingers, do not reason too much!

    Even without seeking to impose on such a statement the rationalism present in many Western theories of the distinction between symbol and reality, between *signum* and *signatum*, we have to acknowledge that it does pose, sharply and yet poignantly, the dilemma of Eastern Christianity in the area of worship and ritual.
5. See Jaroslav Pelikan's forthcoming book, a portrait of His Beatitude, Iosyf Cardinal Slipy, titled *Between East and West*, forthcoming, Eerdmans, Grand Rapids, Michigan.

INDEX

Adam, 25
Alexander I, 71
al-Marwazī, 12
Anna, 13–15
apokatastasis, 26
architecture, church, 33–4, 37–46; churches,
    Canada, 42–6 passim, 73; churches,
    Ukraine, 15, 32–6 passim
Argentina, 166
Athanasius, St., 77
at-Ṭabarī, 12
Australia, 166
Austria, 71, 81–2, 87
azymos, 12

baptism, 33
baptism of the Kievans, 10–12
Baroque, 40, 44
Basil II, 13–14
Basil the Great, 27, 77
Basilian Fathers, 73, 84, 109, 113, 147, 163
Basilian Sisters, 95–9, 164
Benedict XIV, 70
Blahovisnyk, 160
Bodrug, John, 116–18, 193–201 passim
Boiko region, 40–1, 43
Bolshevik Revolution, 135, 234

Boniface VIII, 235
Bozhyk, Panteleimon, 85
Brazil, 97, 166
Brest, Union of, 69, 89, 96, 131, 133–6
    passim, 145, 209
Budka, Nykyta, Bishop, 84–91, 99, 114,
    119, 123–5, 198
Bukovyna, 83, 109–11, 220
Bukovynians, 77, 104, 210
Byzantine empire, 12
Byzantine tradition, 7–10, 39

Calvary (Golgotha), 25, 31
Canadian Association of Slavists, 2
Cappadocian Fathers, 27
Carmichael, J. A., 196–7
Carpatho-Rusyns, 209–18 passim
Carpatho-Ukraine, 40, 82
Catherine II, 71, 131
Catholic Church, Ukrainian, 1–3, 24, 47–54,
    61, 69–78, 81–91, 95–106 passim,
    111–14, 119–41, 143–51, 157–69,
    171–80 passim, 192, 197–9, 209–11,
    219–29; Patriarchal movement, 139,
    148–50, 151, 157–69, 224–9;
    persecution of, 131–41 passim, 143–51;
    Religious Congregations, 95–106

239

Canadian Institute of Ukrainian Studies
Titles in Ukrainian-Canadian Studies

Ian H. Angus, ed.	Ethnicity in a Technological Age
Jars Balan, ed.	Identifications: Ethnicity and the Writer in Canada
Jars Balan and Yuri Klynovy, eds.	Yarmarok: Ukrainian Writing in Canada Since the Second World War
Radomir Bilash and Barbara Wilberg, eds.	Tkanyna: An Exhibit of Ukrainian Weaving
William A. Czumer	Recollections About the Life of the First Ukrainian Settlers in Canada
Manoly R. Lupul, ed.	Continuity and Change: The Cultural Life of Alberta's First Ukrainians
Manoly R. Lupul, ed.	Osvita: Ukrainian Bilingual Education
Manoly R. Lupul, ed.	Ukrainian Canadians, Multi-culturalism, and Separatism: An Assessment
Manoly R. Lupul, ed.	Visible Symbols: Cultural Expression Among Canada's Ukrainians
W. Roman Petryshyn, ed.	Changing Realities: Social Trends Among Ukrainian Canadians
M.L. Podvezko and M.I. Balla, comp.	English-Ukrainian Dictionary
Frances Swyripa	Ukrainian Canadians: A Survey of Their Portrayal in English-Language Works
Frances Swyripa and John Herd Thompson, eds.	Loyalties in Conflict: Ukrainians in Canada During the Great War
Ol'ha Woycenko	Litopys ukrainskoho zhyttia v Kanadi. Tom shostyi, 1950-1959
Ol'ha Woycenko	Litopys ukrainskoho zhyttia v Kanadi. Tom siomyi, 1960-1969